IMAGES
of Rail

The Lehigh Valley Railroad across New Jersey

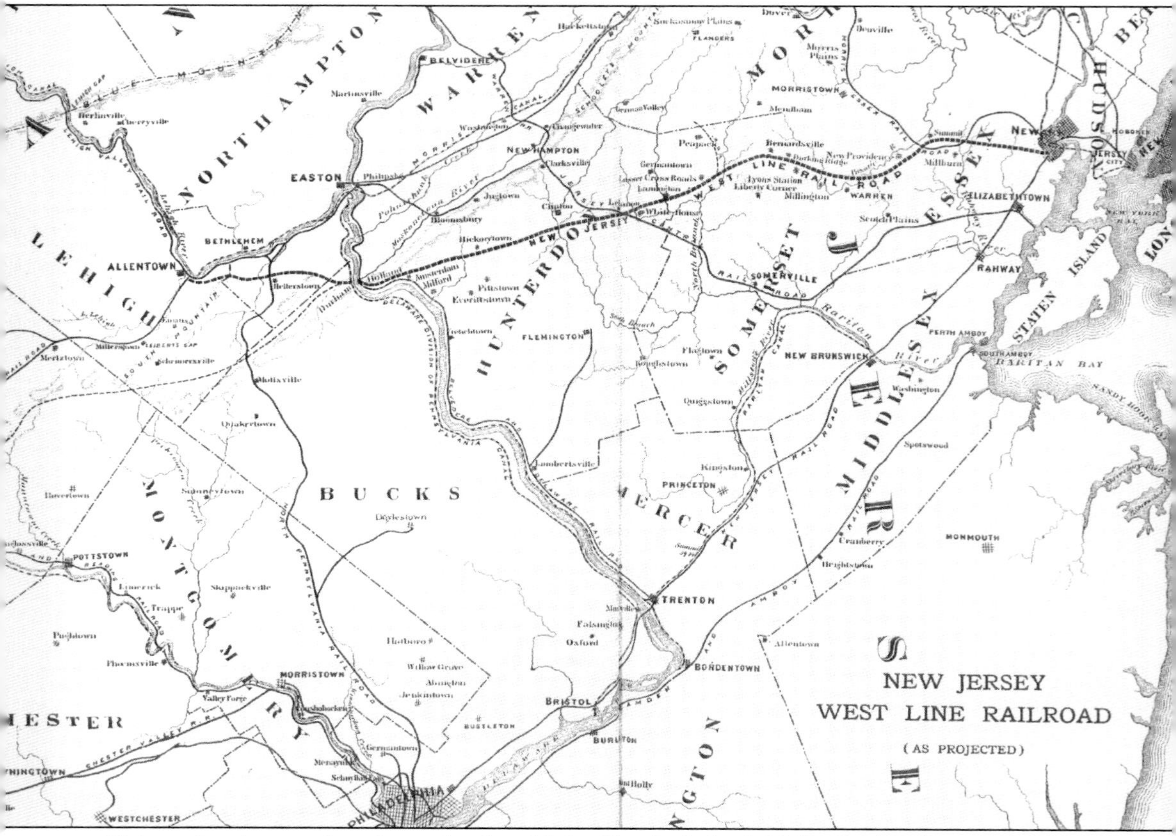

This undated map taken from a book published by the Lehigh Valley Railroad in 1915 shows the projected path of the Lehigh Valley's first attempt to build a railroad line to reach tidewater, the New Jersey West Line Railroad, around 1871. Today the part of the New Jersey West Line to be completed remains in service between Summit and Bernardsville, as the Gladstone branch of New Jersey Transit's extensive commuter rail system, and if one looks closely, a proposed branch can even be seen to reach Peapack, which was eventually built by the Delaware, Lackawanna and Western Railroad after it gained control of the line in the 1870s. (Courtesy of Ralph A. Heiss.)

On the cover: Please see page 69. (Photograph by John Brinckmann, courtesy of Joel Rosenbaum/Tom Gallo.)

IMAGES
of Rail

THE LEHIGH VALLEY RAILROAD ACROSS NEW JERSEY

Ralph A. Heiss

ARCADIA
PUBLISHING

ISBN 978-0-7385-6576-7

Published by Arcadia Publishing
Charleston, South Carolina

Printed in the United States of America

Library of Congress Control Number: 2009920832

For all general information contact Arcadia Publishing at:
Telephone 843-853-2070
Fax 843-853-0044
E-mail sales@arcadiapublishing.com
For customer service and orders:
Toll-Free 1-888-313-2665

Visit us on the Internet at www.arcadiapublishing.com

This book is dedicated to the three most important people in my life, Kathleen McMahon and my parents, Ralph T. and Donna Heiss, for always supporting me and my love of trains, no matter the cost in their own time or money.

Contents

ACKNOWLEDGMENTS

I am forever grateful to the people who offered their photographic collections and gave their spare time by providing historical information and, of course, their moral support.

First, a special thank-you must go to my liaison at Arcadia Publishing, senior acquisitions editor Erin Rocha, for working with me to make this book a reality and for putting me in touch with railroad authors and historians Joel Rosenbaum and Tom Gallo, who very graciously allowed the use of their collection of the late George Votava's and John Brinckmann's photographic works, which were instrumental in beginning the book. A very special thank-you also goes out to my friend Richard Taylor for his generous support and help in proofreading and in supplying photographs at the 11th hour. I would also like to thank, in no particular order, Bob Liljestrand/Bob's Photos, Robert Hall/Railway Negative Exchange, Robert Pennisi/ Railroad Avenue Enterprises, Richard W. Jahn/Anthracite Railroads Historical Society, William Caloroso/Cal's Classics, Gerald Bernett, Richard Chapin, Jack deRosset, Frank T. Reilly, Theodore F. Gleichmann Jr., Gene Collora, the North Jersey Electric Railway Historical Society, Tom McGeehan, M. D. McCarter, Robert J. Lewis, H. G. MacDonald, Craig Zeni, Jim Claflin, William T. Greenberg, Richard T. Steinbrenner, Chuck Yungkurth, David C. Pearce, Robert Mohowski, Tom Kelcek, John McCluskey, Walter A. Appel, David Boone, Michael DelVecchio, Jan Kucsma, C. J. Crawford, R. P. Morris, W. R. Osborne, Don Walworth, William E. Christian, John P. Scharle, G. Lester Whitfield, Lud A. Larzelere, Wayne Brumbaugh, William Nixon, Robert F. Guthlein, O. H. Borsum, Tom Callan, and Tom Fausser, for without their help, this book could not have been possible. To those who may have inevitably been overlooked, please accept my deepest apologies, for your assistance was greatly appreciated and no less important to the success of the book.

My goal with this book was to share the collected memory of the great Lehigh Valley Railroad with future generations, and as with any book, there may be some inaccuracies contained within, however slight, for which I apologize in advance. I hope you enjoy reading this book just as much as I did putting it together. Clear signals ahead . . .

INTRODUCTION

Formed in 1853 under the control of one Asa Packer, the Lehigh Valley Railroad was the culmination of one man's desire to control the movement of what was destined to become the hottest commodity of eastern Pennsylvania, anthracite coal. The story of Packer's railroad has been told many times, but what may not be as well known is the story of its construction across New Jersey to reach New York Harbor.

In 1866, the town of Phillipsburg was a transportation hub—the Lehigh Valley Railroad (LVRR), Central Railroad of New Jersey (CNJ), Belvidere Delaware Railroad (BDRR), Morris and Essex Railroad (M&E), and Morris Canal all met here to exchange freight, and almost all of it coal. For the LVRR, it was content to hand over its coal traffic to one of these other companies that reached Philadelphia or New York. This transfer of traffic worked well for everyone involved until the M&E was leased to the Delaware, Lackawanna and Western Railroad (DL&W) in 1868. Almost immediately the status quo between the railroads that relied upon this traffic was in disarray. Having lost the traffic from the DL&W, the CNJ in 1871 leased the Lehigh and Susquehanna Railroad between Easton and Wilkes-Barre, Pennsylvania, which brought the LVRR and CNJ into direct competition with each other, setting the stage for the LVRR to build a railroad across New Jersey.

On April 1, 1871, the LVRR took its first steps to cross New Jersey by taking out a 99-year lease on the Morris Canal. The goal was to gain possession of valuable waterfront property in Jersey City, owned by the canal for use as a terminal. Around the same time, the LVRR also became involved in developing the New Jersey West Line Railroad (NJWL), which had been built between Summit and Bernardsville, and just as quickly began to expand east from Summit toward a connection with the Pennsylvania Railroad (PRR) at Newark. Unfortunately for Asa Packer, the NJWL never fully fell under his direct control, forcing him to lose control of the project. The CNJ and DL&W found out about the LVRR's involvement in the railroad and also took measures to block control of the railroad by the LVRR. Although stymied in its goal to reach Jersey City, the LVRR continued to look for a route to tidewater. The LVRR did not stand still. By obtaining the dormant charter of the Bound Brook and Perth Amboy Railroad in 1872, and incorporating it into the Easton and Amboy Railroad, the LVRR was able to construct a route of its own in 1875, reaching Perth Amboy. All throughout the 1870s, the LVRR looked for ways to secure its land possessions in Jersey City in order to construct a permanent New York Harbor terminal. Then, beginning in 1887 from South Plainfield, it began construction on its railroad in five distinct parts, finally completing a railroad line to New York Harbor in 1895.

The end of the 1800s brought a close to the formative years of the LVRR in New Jersey, and as it entered the 20th century, it began to expand upon what it had constructed. When first built, the railroad bypassed many major cities on its way across New Jersey, so the railroad constructed a number of branches to reach areas of population and industry. As the 20th century moved forward, large industries like the Johns-Manville Corporation, Bristol Meyers, General Motors, and probably its most famous customer, Lionel Trains, located their factories along the railroad, while most of western New Jersey typically remained a rural area with little on-line industry.

Passenger service on the LVRR was never as heavy as it was on other railroads in the state, although it did provide extremely high-class accommodations in the form of the *Black Diamond*, *John Wilkes*, and *Asa Packer* name trains. Excursion trains were also very popular, and in the late 1880s and early 1900s, the LVRR built its first day park at Packers Island, located just east of Landsdown. This was replaced within a few years with the completion of the much larger Bellewood Park in Pattenburg in 1909. Bellewood Park was located just outside the Musconetcong Tunnel and had its own passenger shelter constructed to receive its patrons. It was an amusement park of its era, complete with carousels, dancing pavilions, and early roller coasters. While the park proved popular initially, by 1916 it was closed by the railroad due to lack of patronage. Commuter traffic was also never very strong on the railroad, which tended to use self-propelled gas-electric cars for local trains. Not having its own dedicated train-to-ferryboat terminal in Jersey City, the LVRR was forced to rely on using the CNJ and PRR terminals to convey its passengers into New York, and throughout the years, the PRR and CNJ would go back and forth hosting the LVRR's passenger trains. The LVRR maintained a dwindling passenger service after World War II and in 1961 ended all passenger service.

Back in the 1920s, the PRR had gained a majority of the LVRR's stock, and from that point forward, it influenced the railroad's operations in subtle, but noticeable ways. With revenue from coal traffic beginning to decline in earnest after the Depression, the LVRR found itself more as a fast freight "bridge line" between the Midwest, Canada, and New England, moving freight from the Buffalo, New York, area, to the New Haven Railroad (NH) via car float at Jersey City. While the LVRR undertook many upgrades in its physical plant in the 1920s and 1930s to the most modern standards, World War II took its toll upon the equipment and physical plant. The year 1956 proved to be the last year the LVRR was able to show a profit, and by 1962, the PRR took steps to finally exercise its stock control over the LVRR, making it little more than a stepchild of the parent railroad. Locomotives and facilities were consolidated and shared, and belt tightening of train operations was the order of the day. As hard as the railroad tried, the entire northeastern railroad industry was quickly falling apart around it, with many other railroads entering bankruptcy and operating on borrowed time. In the wake of the Penn Central Railroad merger in 1970, the LVRR declared bankruptcy and was put into receivership under court-appointed trustees Robert Haldeman and John Nash, who tired their best to run a failing enterprise, by no fault of its own. Even with government loans to purchase new locomotives, the inevitable could not be prevented, and on April 1, 1976, the LVRR was conveyed along with five other Northeast railroads to form the government-run Conrail.

Today the physical plant of the LVRR in New Jersey is mostly intact across the state and used in part by Conrail Shared Assets, the Norfolk Southern Railroad, New Jersey Transit, and CSX. Just as when it was first built, the railroad serves as an important link in the nation's rail network. The LVRR as an independent railroad may be gone, but it will forever live on in its fans and its former employees.

One

PHILLIPSBURG TO MANVILLE

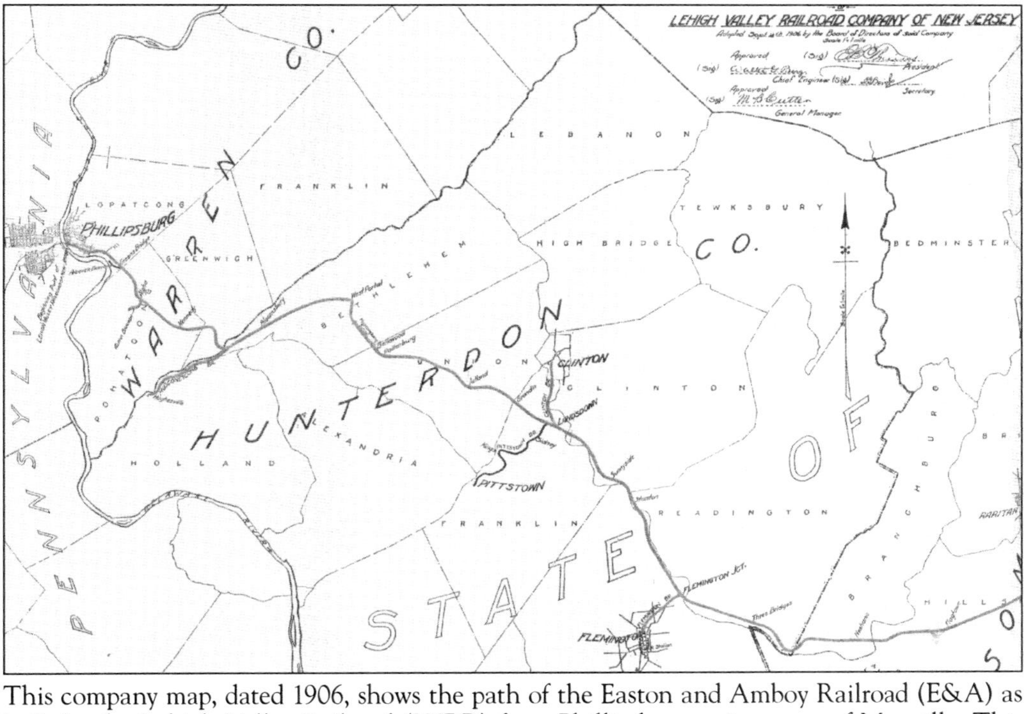

This company map, dated 1906, shows the path of the Easton and Amboy Railroad (E&A) as built by the Lehigh Valley Railroad (LVRR) from Phillipsburg to just west of Manville. This section of the railroad had the most feeder branches built off the main line to serve important towns in the region. The most difficult part of constructing the railroad in this part of New Jersey, however, was encountered at Pattenburg, where the 4,829-foot Musconetcong Tunnel was dug to complete the main line. (Courtesy of Ralph A. Heiss.)

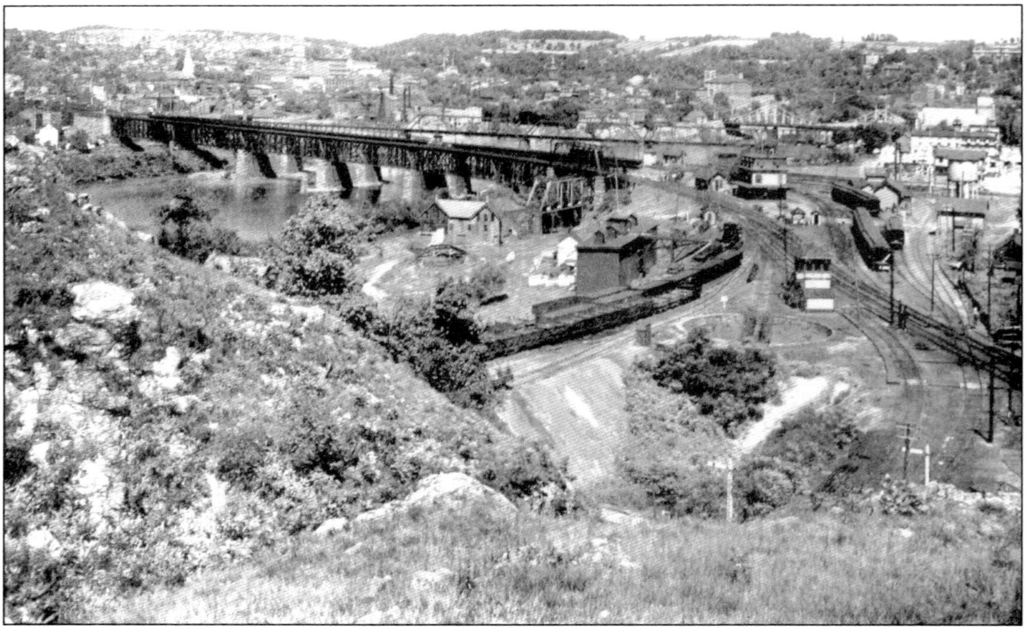

In this view from atop Mount Parnassus in Phillipsburg, one can clearly see why this town was such an important transportation hub. For well over 100 years, Phillipsburg was uniquely situated geographically to provide a meeting point for both railroad and canal alike, and even in this 1895 photograph, one can still see the crossroads of early transportation that today is only a shadow of its former self. (Courtesy of Theodore F. Gleichmann Jr.)

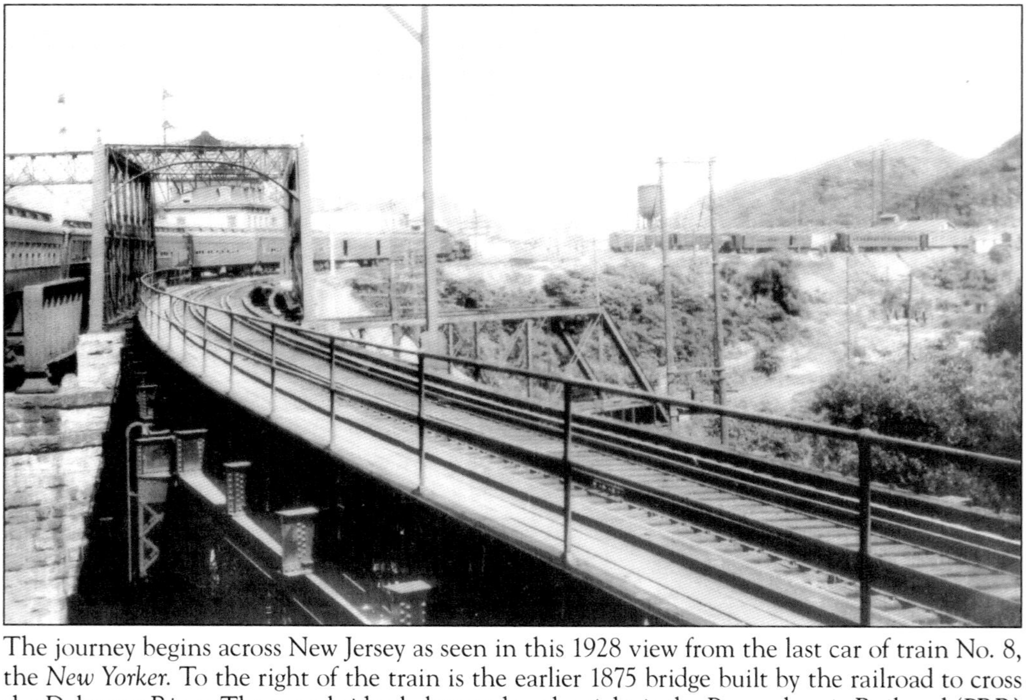

The journey begins across New Jersey as seen in this 1928 view from the last car of train No. 8, the *New Yorker*. To the right of the train is the earlier 1875 bridge built by the railroad to cross the Delaware River. The truss bridge below and to the right is the Pennsylvania Railroad (PRR) bridge crossing over the Morris Canal's abandoned inclined plane No. 11 west. (Photograph by Lud. A. Larzelere, courtesy of Theodore F. Gleichmann Jr.)

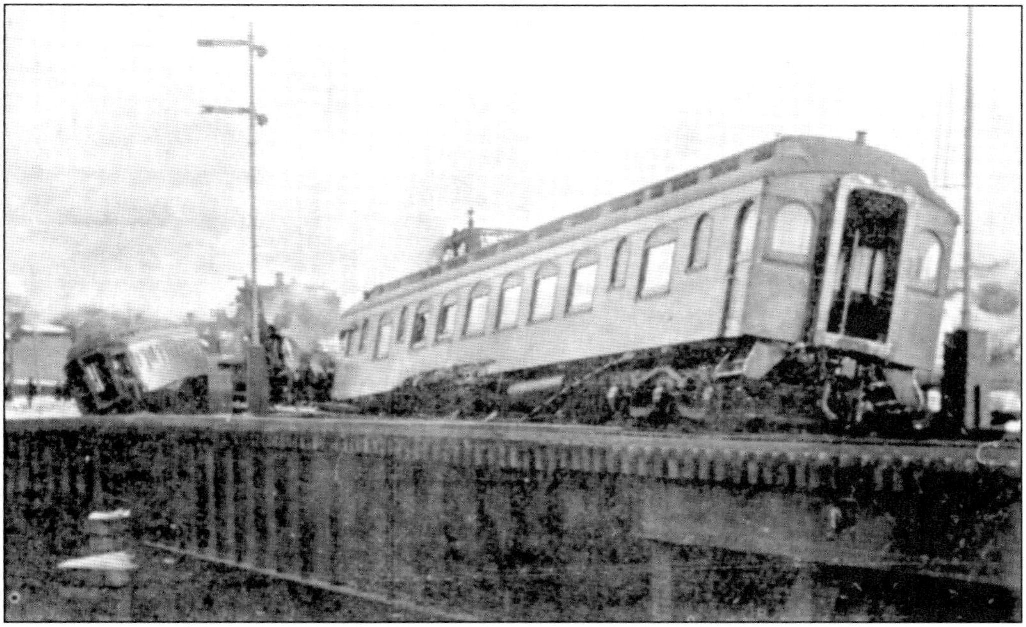

Accidents do happen, as seen in this February 1907 postcard view. The last two cars on the eastbound *Black Diamond* became derailed while crossing the Delaware River bridge that day. The parlor-observation car seen here is precariously resting on an end girder span of the bridge, which was attributed to preventing the car from falling onto the PRR tracks below. Amazingly, only four people were reported injured. (Courtesy of Ralph A. Heiss.)

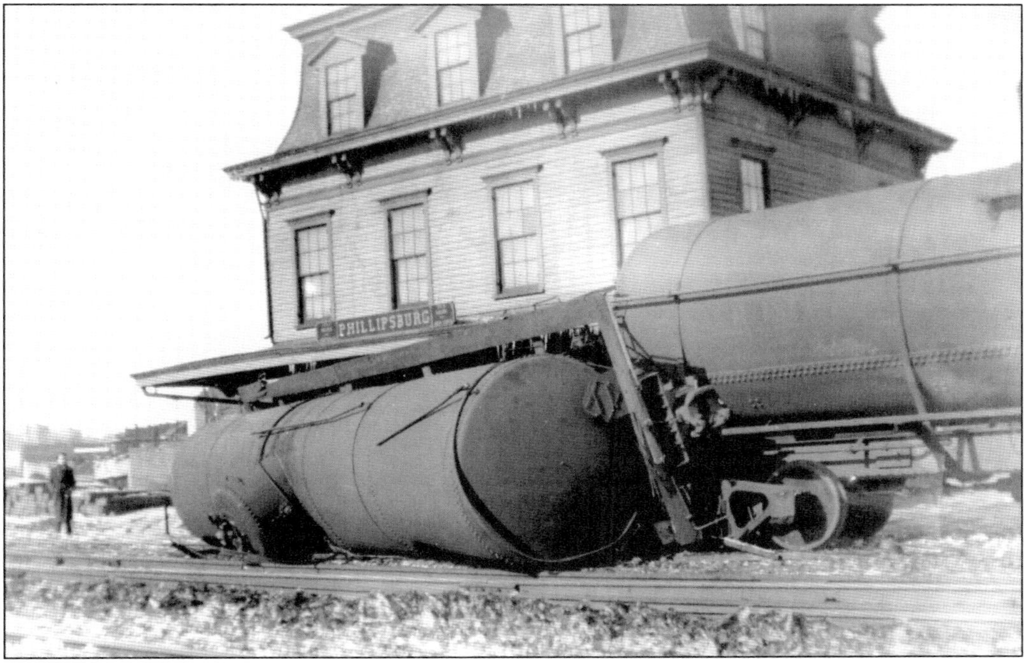

Another accident occurred in front of the Phillipsburg station on a cold February day in 1936. While the unidentified train appears to have avoided inflicting serious damage upon the station, the ground and rail under the tank car appears to be quite torn up, suggesting a more serious mess just out of the photographer's view. (Courtesy of Gene Collora.)

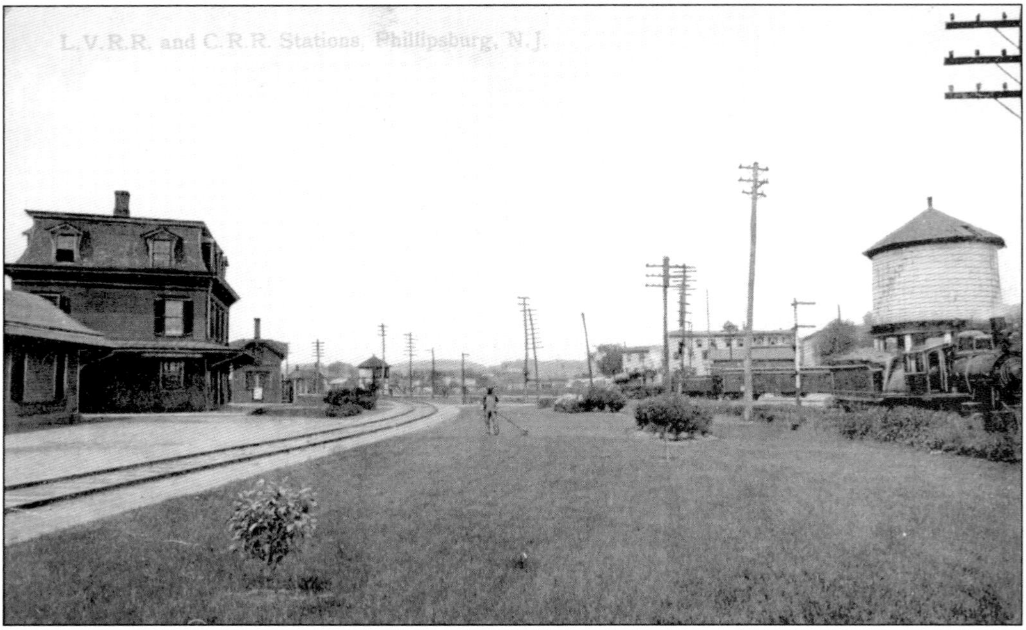

In this undated postcard view, one can see the close proximity of the LVRR and Central Railroad of New Jersey (CNJ) tracks in Phillipsburg. The low building on the extreme left adjacent to the station is the original 1870s station built by the E&A. The utilitarian, if not beautiful, mansard-roofed 1880s vintage station was closed in 1935 and razed in 1938. (Courtesy of Richard Taylor.)

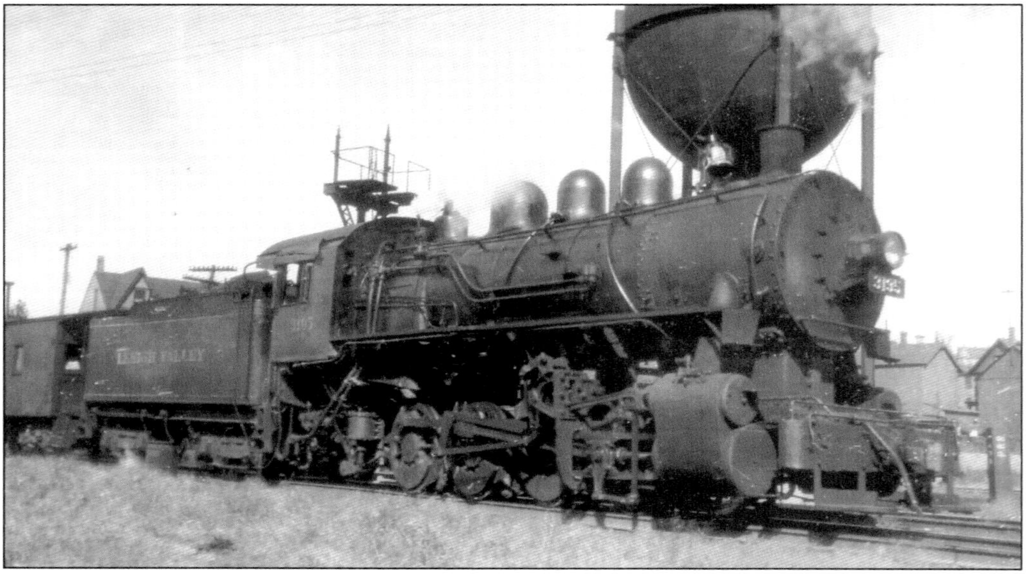

Engine No. 3195, an 0-8-0 of the L-5½ class, is seen switching at the Phillipsburg station area in this 1934 photograph, taken just west of the crossing with the CNJ/PRR interchange track. (Courtesy of Ralph A. Heiss)

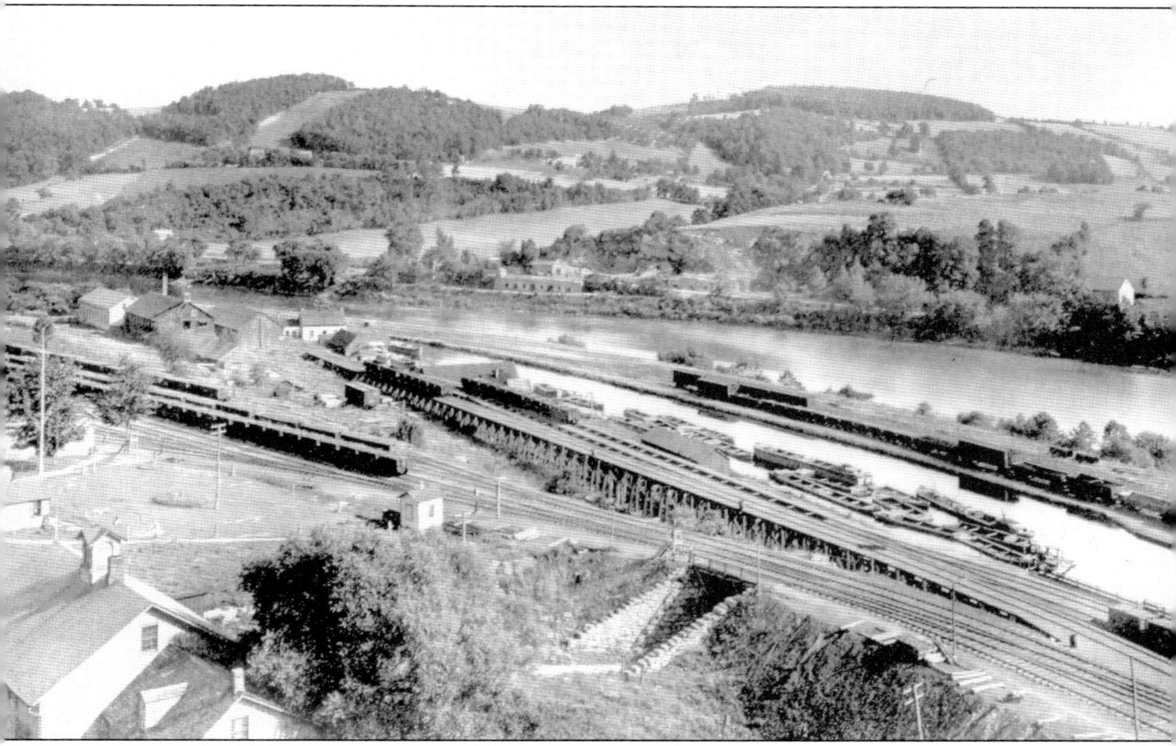

Looking south along the Delaware River off Mount Parnassus, the loading docks of the LVRR can be seen occupying the center of this 1902 view. These coal docks were built by the LVRR when it leased the canal in 1871 to facilitate the transfer of coal. To the right is the main line of the PRR's Belvidere Delaware Railroad branch. The tracks on the left connect the CNJ to the PRR yards. (Courtesy of Theodore F. Gleichmann Jr.)

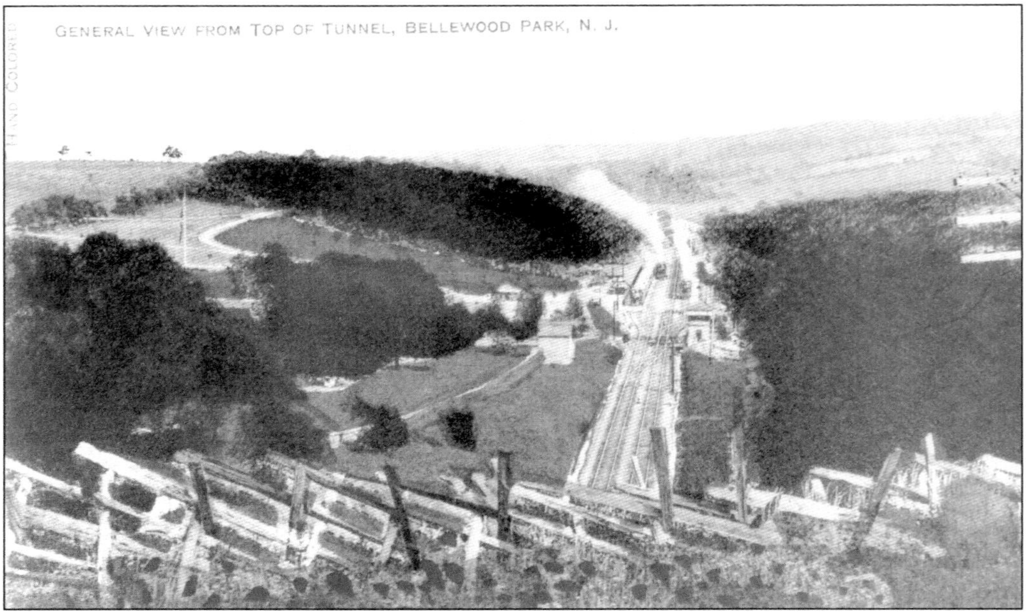

Moving eastward, the Musconetcong Tunnel is encountered, which until completed in 1875 stymied the completion of the E&A. This post-1904 view looks east from atop the ridge, with the interlocking guarding the entrance to the tunnel and the station platform for Bellewood Park, which was on the hill to the extreme left marked by the flagpole. (Courtesy of Theodore F. Gleichmann Jr.)

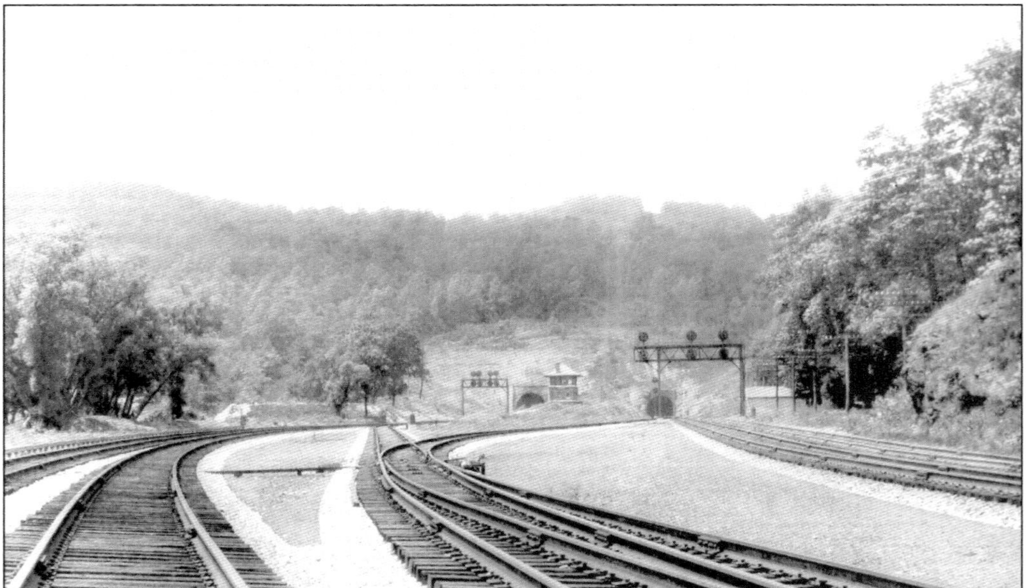

This 1929 photograph highlights the new Bellewood interlocking and double-track tunnel, which opened in November 1928. With the increased traffic of the 20th century, the original 1875 tunnel became a bottleneck to traffic, so the decision was made to dig a larger double-track tunnel through the mountain, and the original tunnel was then single tracked. These improvements allowed a much greater flexibility to move trains over the railroad. (Photograph by Lud. A. Larzelere, courtesy of Theodore F. Gleichmann Jr.)

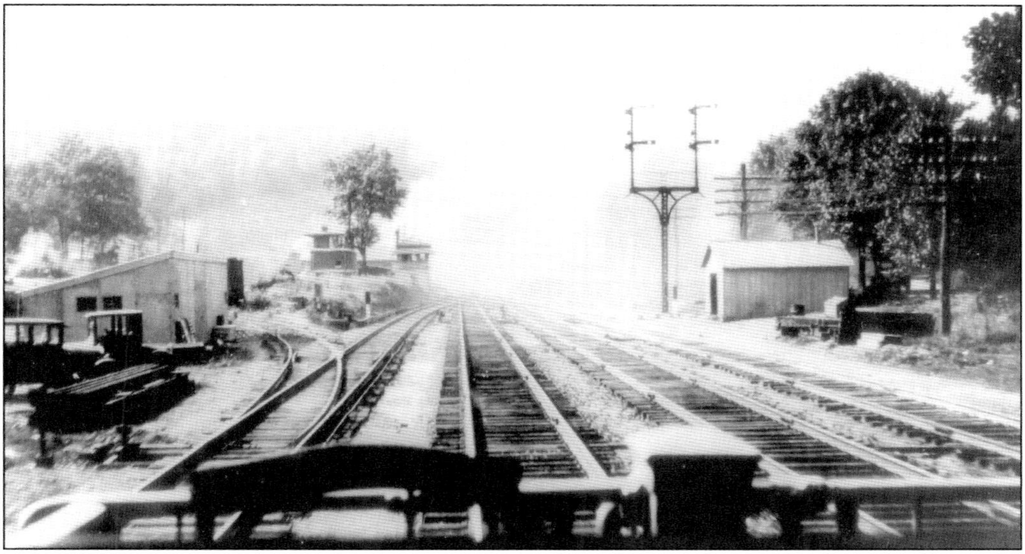

In another 1928 view taken from the rear of the parlor-observation car on train No. 8, the *New Yorker*, the construction work on the new interlocking at Bellewood is progressing, with both the new and old towers side by side. The small building at right marks the location of the Bellewood Park station closed 12 years previous. (Photograph by Lud. A. Larzelere, courtesy of Theodore F. Gleichmann Jr.)

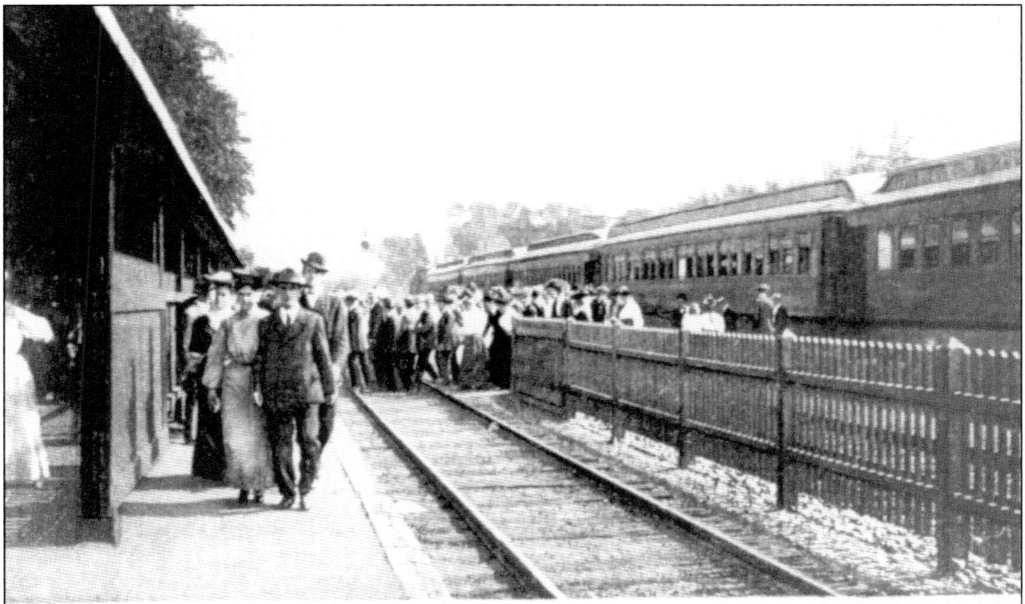

Another trainload of happy, if not staid, Victorian patrons arrives from Pennsylvania for another day of merriment at Bellewood Park in this c. 1910 view looking eastbound. As many as 10 trains a day stopped here during the park's open season, which lasted from Memorial Day to mid-October. (Courtesy of Theodore F. Gleichmann Jr.)

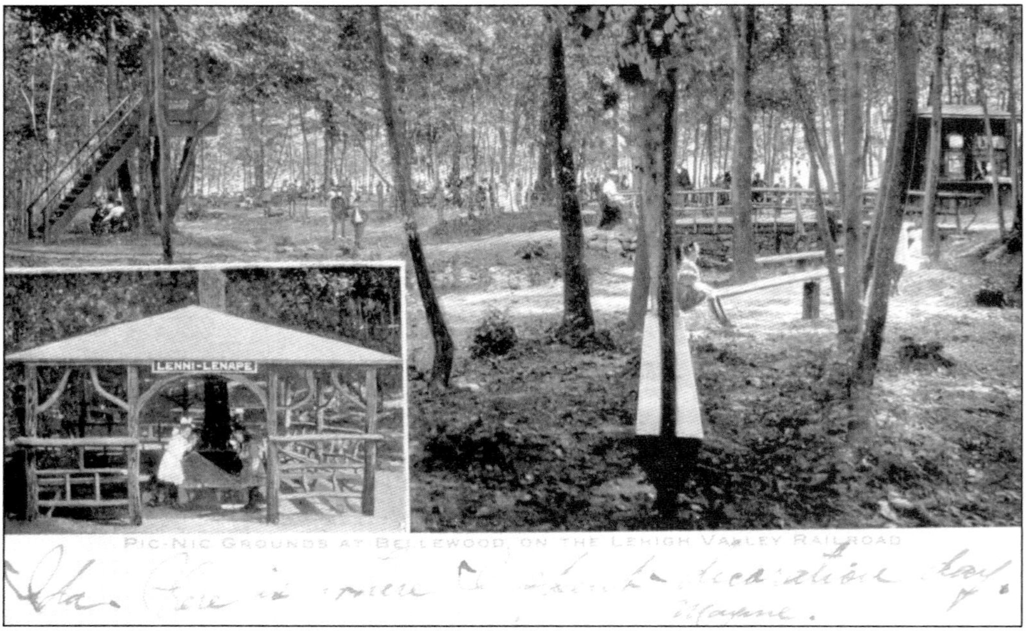

In this undated postcard view of the wooded groves of Bellewood Park, it is no wonder why people were so attracted to its beauty. The card reads, "Ida. Here is where I spent decoration day. Maryanne." Decoration Day was once the popular name for Memorial Day before 1882 but was still commonly used until shortly after World War II. This postcard was probably mailed sometime in June. (Courtesy of Richard Taylor.)

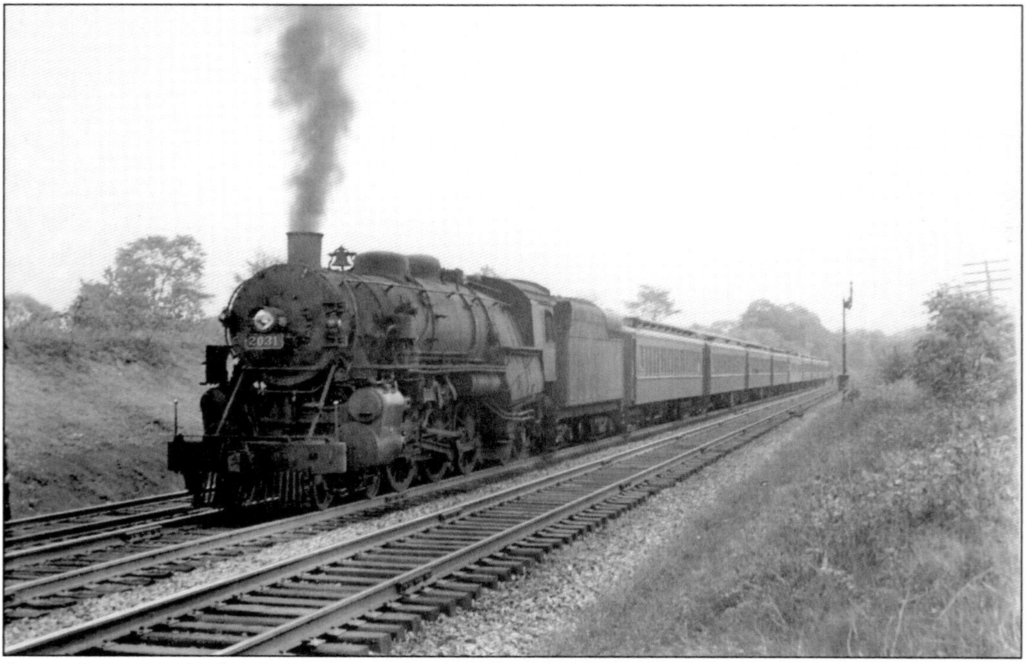

Somewhere near Jutland, this passenger train headed by engine No. 2031, a utilitarian 4-6-2 of the K-3 class built in the railroad's own Sayre shops between 1917 and 1921, is stopped on the eastbound main for some unidentified reason, possibly for a restricting signal or an unknown mechanical problem. (Courtesy of Richard Taylor.)

GEOGRAPHICAL LIST—(Continued).

MAIN LINE—NEW JERSEY AND LEHIGH DIVISION—(Continued).

on	Distance	Telegraph Calls	STATION	COUNTY	STATE	Class of Agency	AGENT OR WAYBILLING POINT	REMARKS
	From New York.							
58	57.7	DN	Landsdown (Jct Clinton and Pittstown Branches	Hunterdon	N. J.	F & T	E. R. Robinson....... J. S. Berkaw, Assistant	B.
60	59.1	....	Grandin	"	"	T	Sidney M. Smith.......	Y. W. L. P. at Hamden.
61	60.7	JN	Jutland	"	"	F & T	M. F. Behney...........	
64	63.6	BU	Pattenburg	"	"	F & T	A. K. Helman..........	D. S. P. D. S. W. P.
65	63.9	....	Bellewood (Summer Office)	"	"	Excursion Resort	Chas. Eaton, Park Sup't.............	F. Waybill to Pattenburg Prepaid.
66	65.8	WP	West Portal	"	"	F & T	W. J. Farley..........	D. S. P. at Valley.
69	68.7	BY	Bloomsbury	"	"	F & T	John H. Heaney........	D. S. W. P.
70	69.9	....	Musconetcong Jct. (Jct. Musconetcong Br.)	Warren	"	F	John H. Heaney (Bloomsbury)	
	Musconetcong Jct.		Musconetcong Br.					
73	1.8	....	Warren Paper Mills	Hunterdon	"	F	John H. Heaney (Bloomsbury)	P.
74	3.2	....	Hughesville	"	"	F	John H. Heaney (Bloomsbury)	P.
	From New York.							
72	71.9	....	Kennedy	Warren	"	F	....	S. P. Warren Paper Mills Prepaid.
74	73.7	....	Alpha	"	"	F T	John E. Smith, Phil'burg J. H. Hawk	P.
76	76.5	PD	Phillipsburg (Jct. Penna. R. R., C. R. R. of N. J., D., L. & W. R. R.)	"	"	F T	John E. Smith.......... G. R. Hallenbach.......	B. X. O. P.
77	77.0	Q	Easton (Jct. E. & N. Branch and L. & H. R. Ry.)	Northampt'n	Pa.	F T	H. S. Mattes............ G. J. Ealer.............	B. S. P.
78	77.8	....	South Easton	"	"	F T	H. S. Mattes, Easton.... W. J. Dinsmore.........	
78	77.9	NG	South Easton Engine House	"	"	F	H. S. Mattes, Easton....	B. O. W. L.
79	78.6	GY	Glendon	"	"	F	H. S. Mattes, Easton....	B.
81	80.1	....	Island Park	"	"	F	H. S. Mattes, Easton....	
83	83.0	RN	Redington	"	"	F & T	E. S. Bishop...........	B. P.
86	85.8	FR	Freemansburg	"	"	F & T	J. H. Ritter...........	D. S. P.
87	86.1	....	Florence	"	"	F	J. H. Ritter, Freemansburg	

This list is a page taken from a 1905 LVRR-issued *List of Officers, Agents, Stations, Equipment, and Facilities* book and shows all the pertinent station information such as agents in charge, hours of operation, and telegraph call letters that any employee might need to know in the course of his daily duties. The part of the railroad shown covers from Landsdown Junction, where the Clinton and Pittstown branches met the main line, and heading west along the railroad and into Pennsylvania to Florence Yard, which was located in Bethlehem, Pennsylvania, and adjacent to the mills of Bethlehem Steel. (Courtesy of Ralph A. Heiss.)

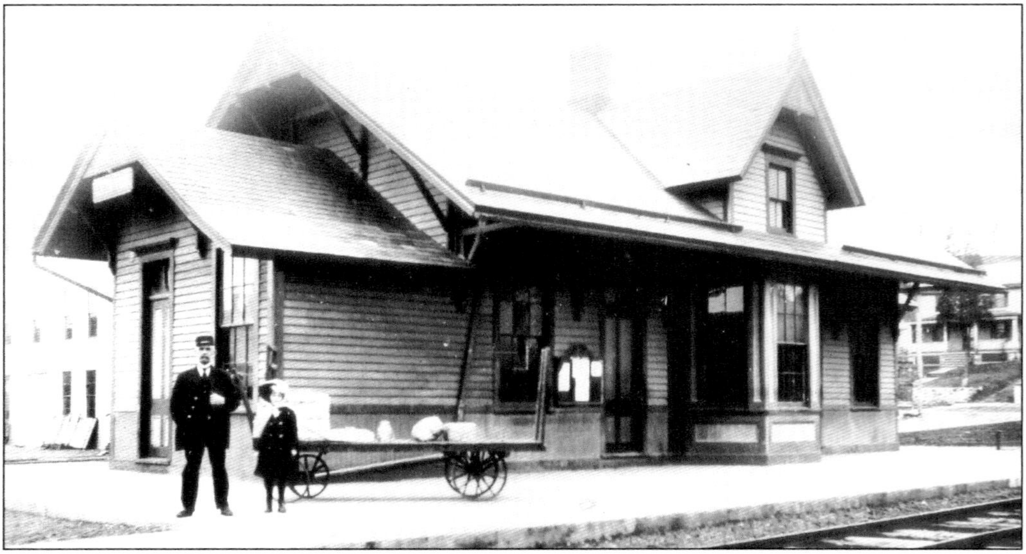

This *c.* 1905 view of the Clinton station shows a beautifully gable-roofed station with what appears to be the conductor of the local train posing with a young girl dressed in her best traveling attire. Small-town stations like this one were the main outlets to the outside world in the days before paved highways. (Courtesy of H. G. MacDonald.)

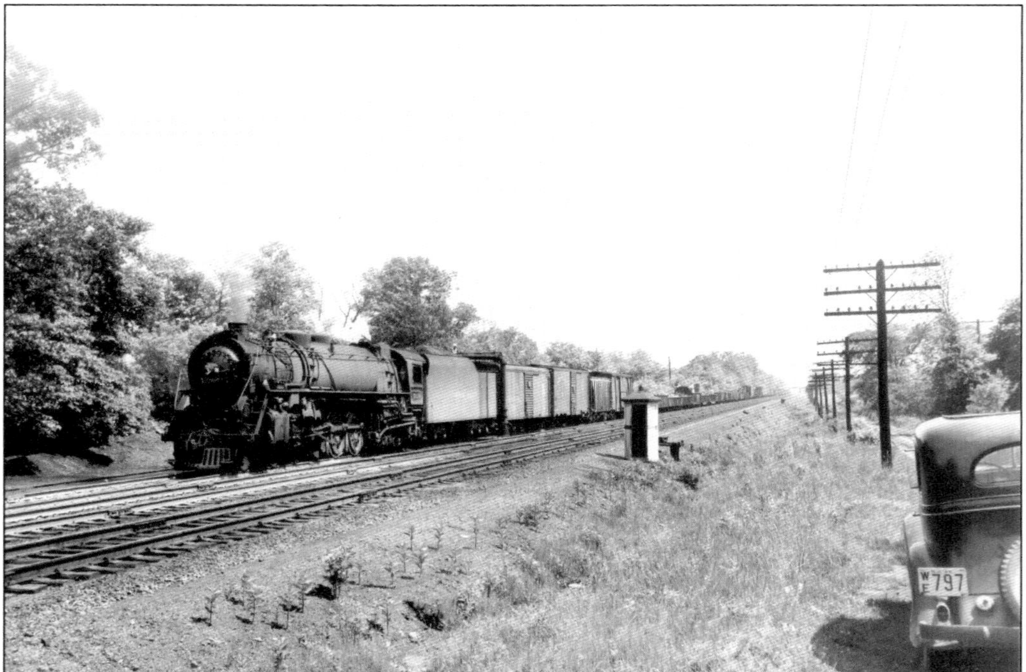

This westbound extra behind engine No. 5220 is making a stop at Flax Mill water station, located near Packers Island in May 1946. No. 5220 was the last of the T-2b class 4-8-4s built by the American Locomotive Company (ALCO) in 1943. The water station was in continuous use from 1875 until 1951, as it was located near the base of the ruling westbound grade that leads to the Musconetcong Tunnel. (Photograph by W. R. Osborne, courtesy of Richard T. Steinbrenner.)

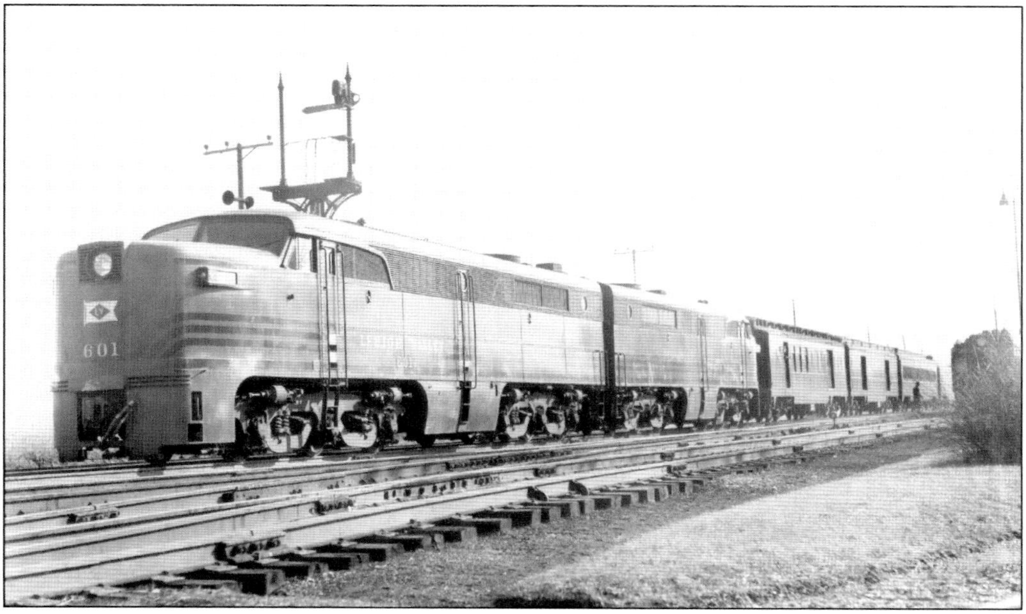

Flemington Junction was the connection with the 1.7-mile Flemington branch, built in 1884. Even though Flemington Junction had been adopted for the name of this location in 1876, it was another eight years before the branch was completed into the county seat of Hunterdon County. This view shows the station stop of the *Black Diamond* in charge of PA No. 601 and No. 602 on December 8, 1948. (Courtesy of Theodore F. Gleichmann Jr.)

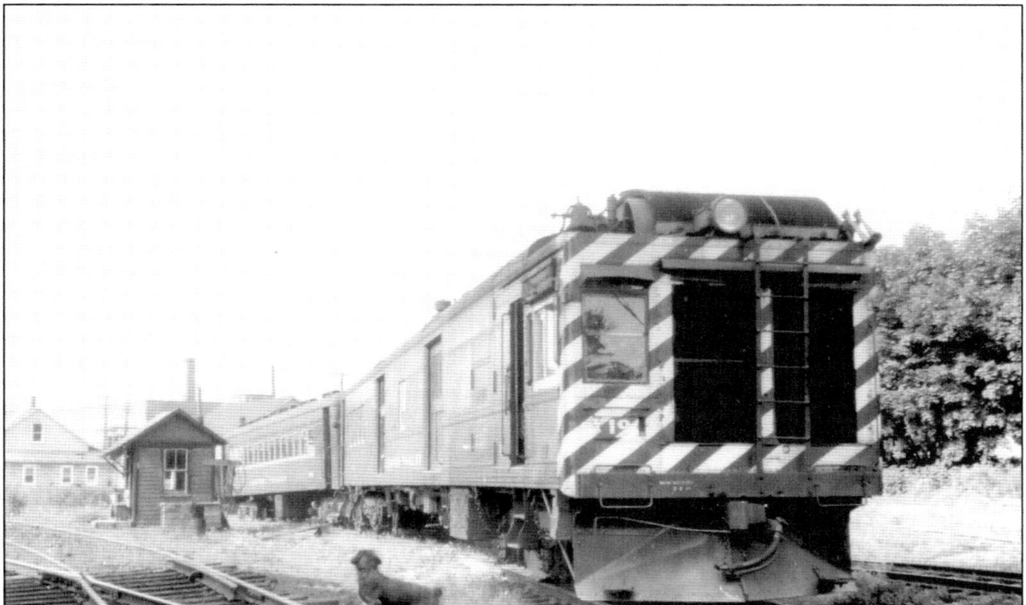

At the end of the branch in Flemington is self-propelled gas-electric motor car No. 19 coupled with trailer T-74 on August 7, 1949. A 1948 timetable shows 11 round-trips between Flemington and Flemington Junction, which took six minutes to complete in one direction. (Photograph by John Brinckmann, courtesy of Joel Rosenbaum/Tom Gallo.)

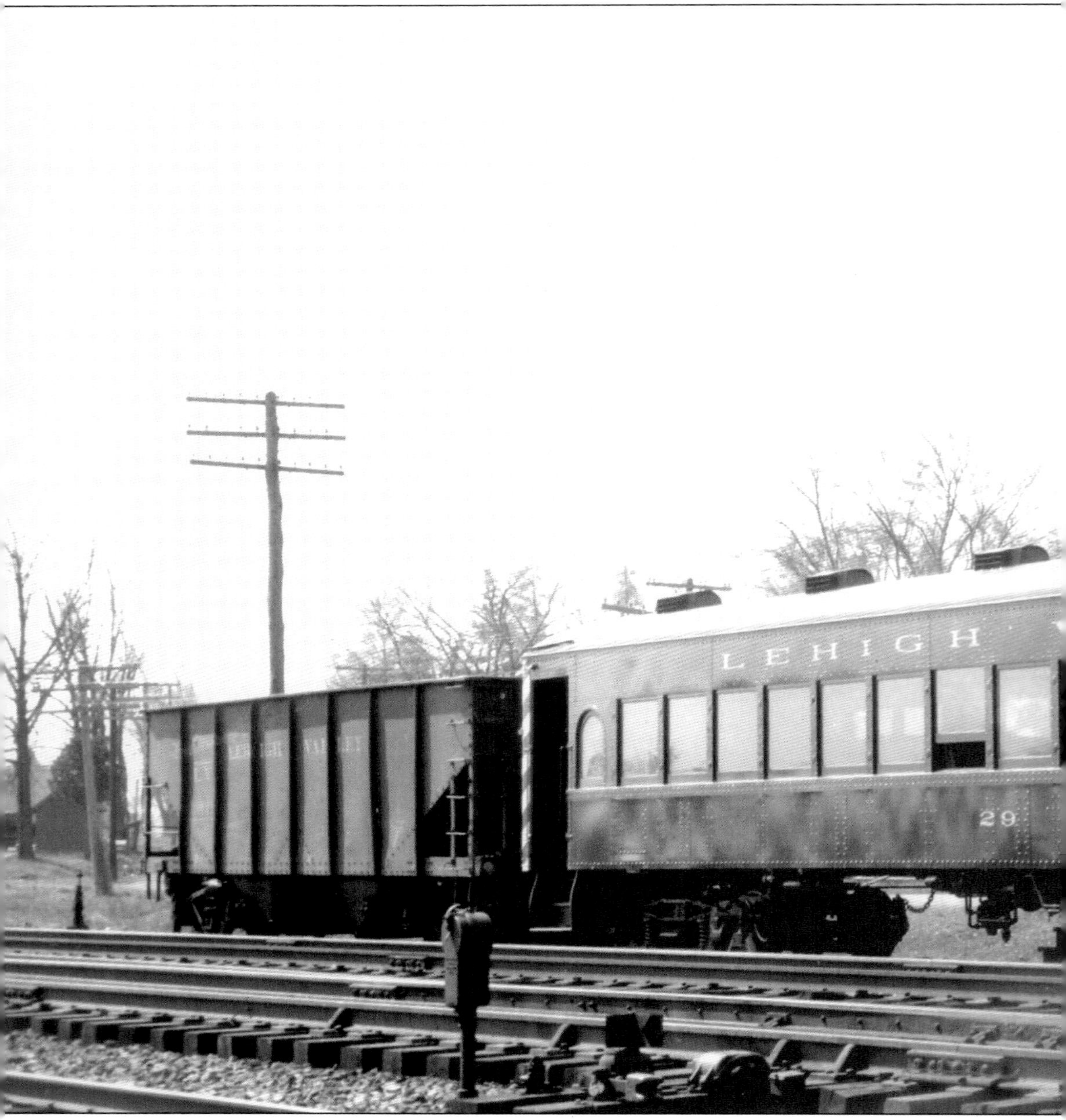

When one thinks of mixed trains, one usually envisions the classic image of a small steam engine trailing a few cars and followed up by the classic wood caboose on the rear. The LVRR was always a bit different, and here is a rare view of gas-electric motor car No. 29 pulling a 34-foot, two-bay coal hopper on the Flemington branch mixed train. No. 29's six-cylinder Winton engine could

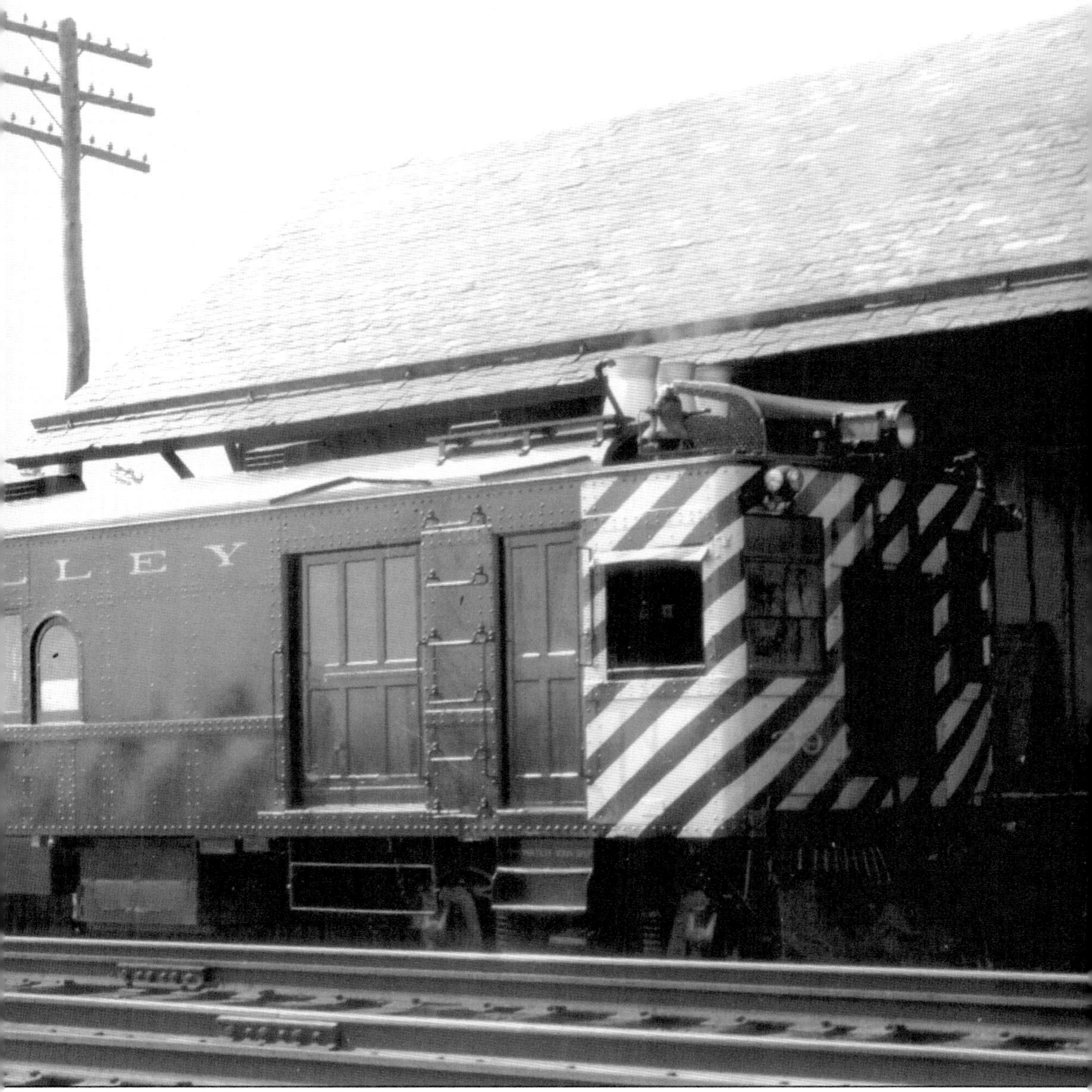

deliver 220 horsepower, enough to handle a few freight cars. The train is sitting in front of the Flemington Junction freight station, which was located just west of the passenger station. This eastward view was taken on April 14, 1936. (Photograph by George Votava, courtesy of Joel Rosenbaum/Tom Gallo.)

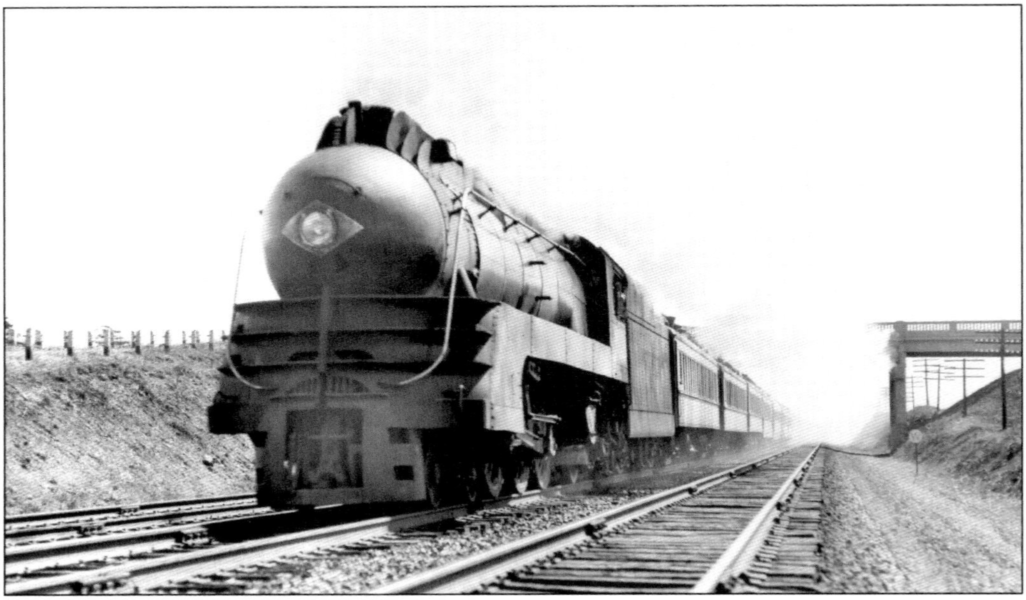

One of the classic streamlined 4-6-2s heads up the business end of the *Asa Packer* as it races westbound through Three Bridges and under the U.S. Route 202 highway bridge in March 1946. (Courtesy of Theodore F. Gleichmann Jr.)

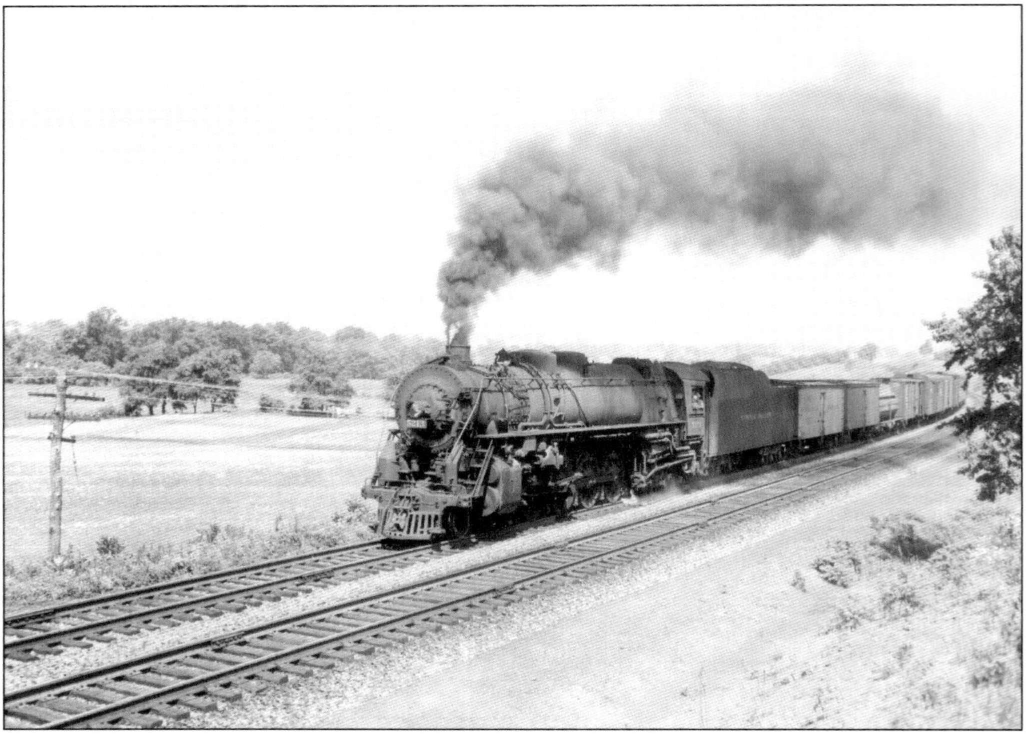

A 4-8-4, No. 5213, pounds the rails on its way east through Three Bridges in June 1946. From the crest of the ruling grade inside the Musconetcong Tunnel, the grade all the way to Perth Amboy was relatively all downgrade, allowing the heavy coal trains to quickly and easily roll eastward. (Photograph by W. R. Osborne, courtesy of Richard T. Steinbrenner.)

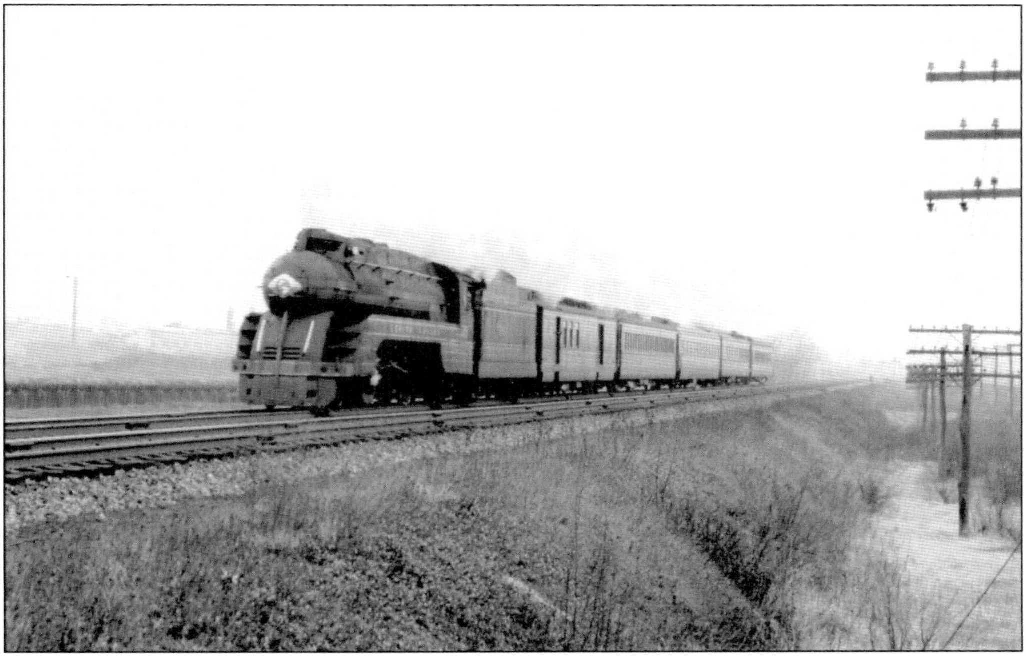

Train No. 9, the *Black Diamond*, highballs westbound along the Raritan River and past the Johns-Manville Asbestos Insulation plant in Manville, which provided many carloads of freight for the LVRR, on a cold and dreary day in January 1941. (Photograph by George Votava, courtesy of Joel Rosenbaum/Tom Gallo.)

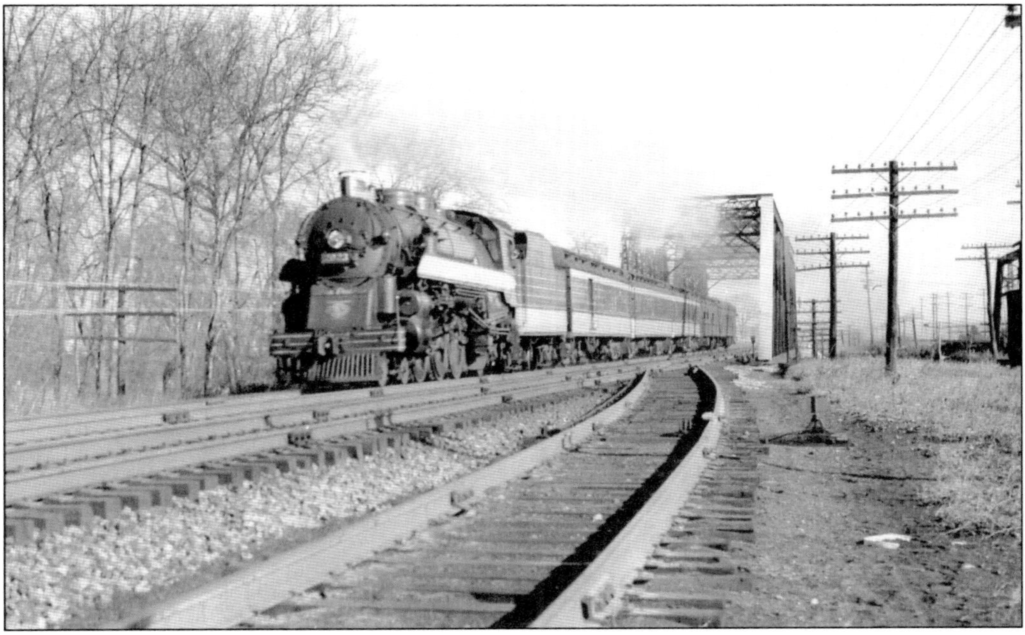

The westbound *Asa Packer* crosses the Raritan River with a five-car train on December 18, 1939. To the right of the train, the parallel Port Reading branch of the Reading Railroad (RDG) can be seen also crossing the river. Today both sets of tracks are used daily by the trains of CSX, Conrail Shared Assets, and the Norfolk Southern Railroad. (Photograph by George Votava, courtesy of Joel Rosenbaum/Tom Gallo.)

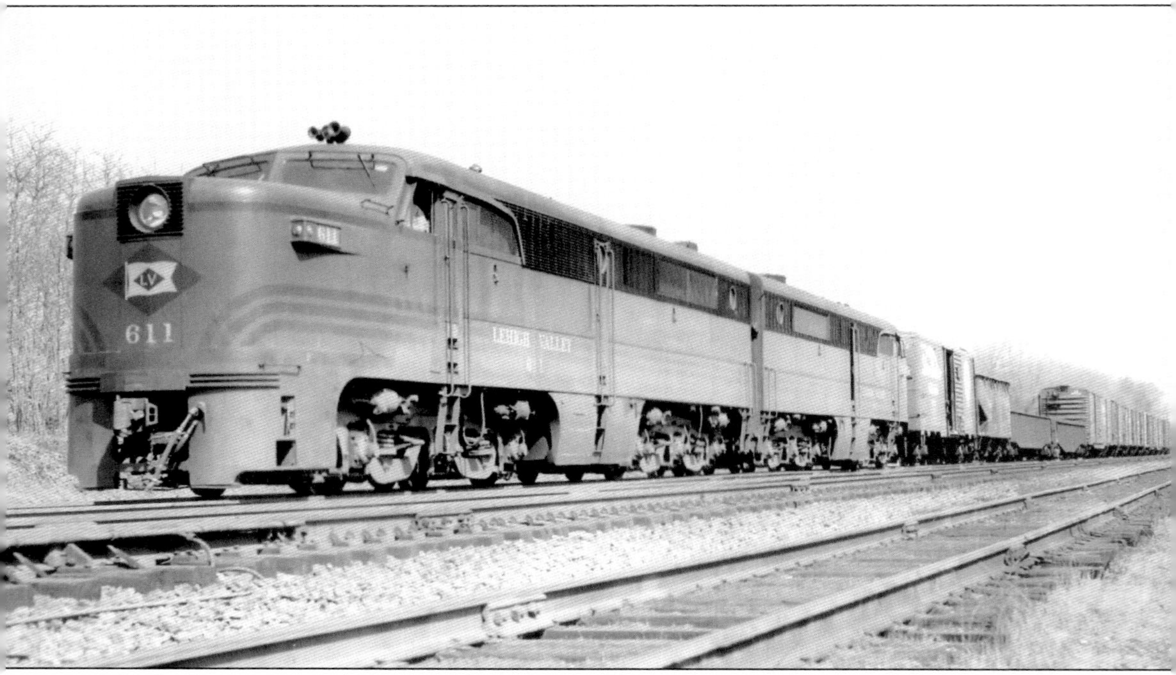

While the presence of passenger locomotives like PA-1s No. 611 and No. 605 on a westbound freight at Manville in March 1959 might seem strange, the LVRR was known for its excellent utilization of motive power while locomotives laid over at terminals at the end of their runs, and the PAs were no exception. After turning over their trains to the PRR at NK Tower in Newark, the engines were dispatched to Oak Island Yard and put on short turnarounds, or STAs as the LVRR called them, to South Plainfield or as far as Easton, Pennsylvania, if there was time to make the return trip. When all main line passenger trains were eliminated in 1961, the availability of the PAs became even more commonplace on freight trains on the New York division between Oak Island and Lehighton, Pennsylvania, until the eventual retirement of all the locomotives by 1964. (Photograph by Gene Collora.)

Two

BOUND BROOK TO PERTH AMBOY

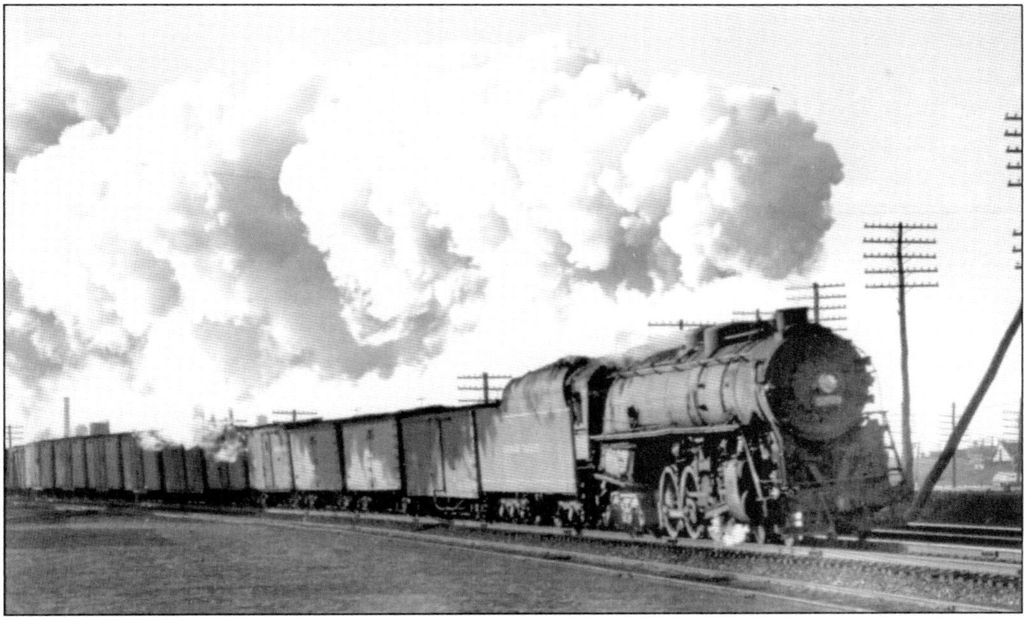

No. 5509, a 4-8-4 known as a Wyoming-type locomotive on the LVRR, has its throttle wide open passing eastbound through Bound Brook. The powerful 4-8-4s were almost always assigned to power the eastbound and westbound manifest trains, allowing the maximum amount of horsepower and tractive effort for the train. (Photograph by Wayne Brumbaugh, courtesy of Bob's Photos.)

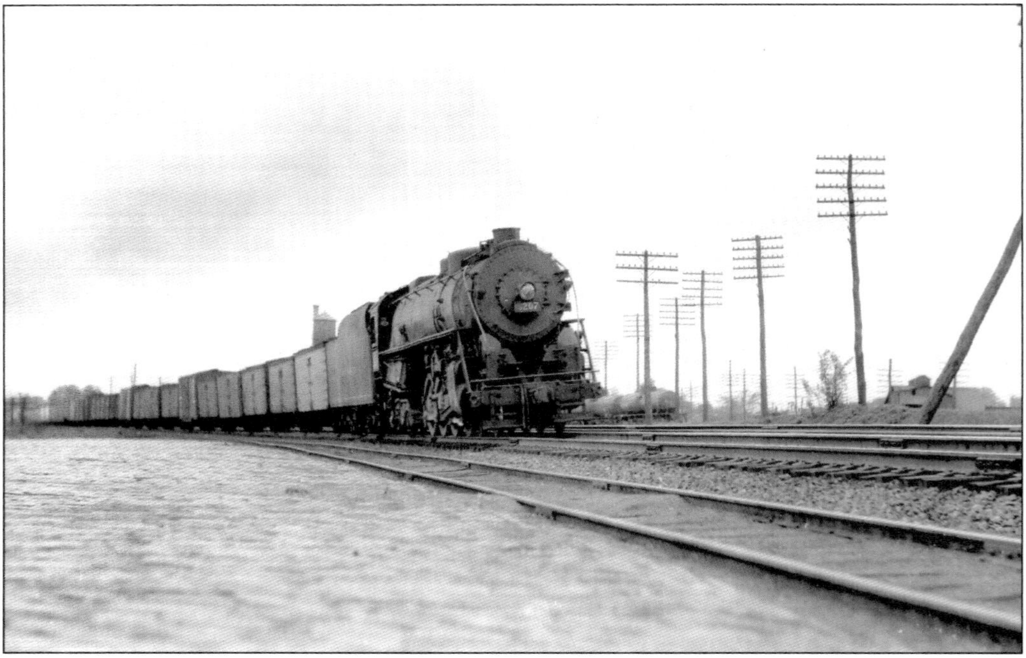

Another 4-8-4, this time No. 5207, rolls another eastbound manifest train at almost the same location in Bound Brook. The refers on the head end of the train may identify it as train BNE-2, which carried a large perishable block for the New Haven connection at Jersey City. (Photograph by Wayne Brumbaugh, courtesy of Bob's Photos.)

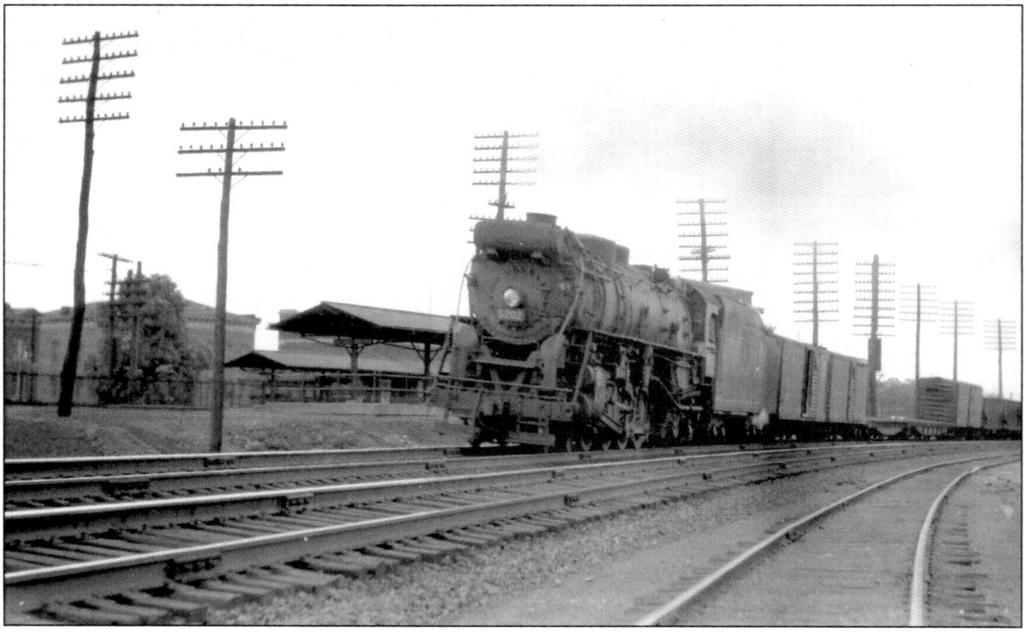

With its Elesco feedwater heater giving it a distinctive beetle-browed look, a T-2 class 4-8-4, No. 5202, rolls westbound with an extra freight. The 4-8-4 wheel arrangement was popular on the rival Delaware, Lackawanna and Western Railroad (DL&W) as well, which called its 4-8-4 Northern-type steam locomotives Poconos. (Photograph by Wayne Brumbaugh, courtesy of Bob's Photos.)

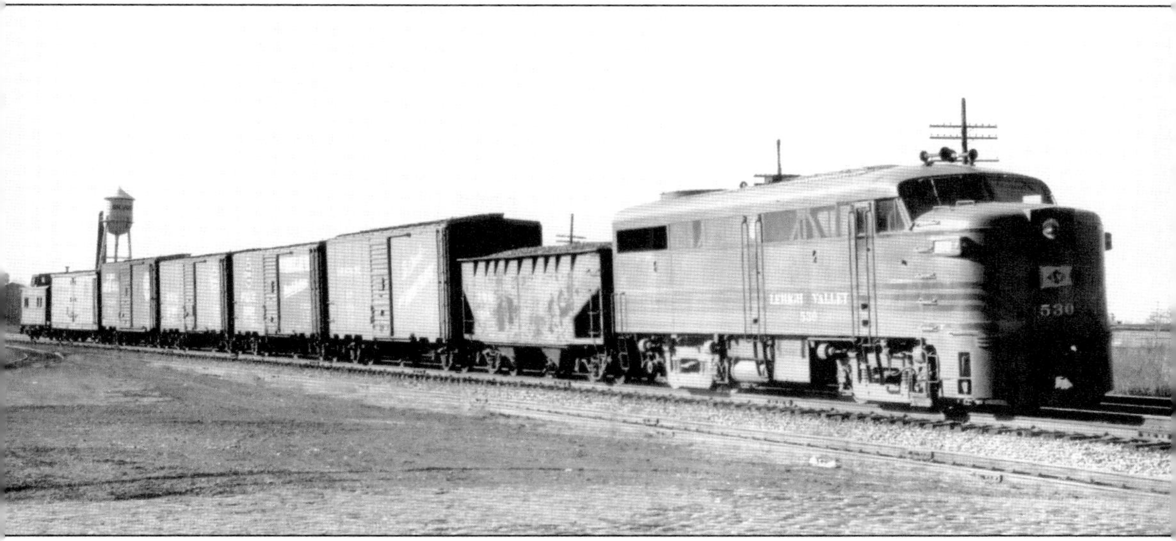

With only six freight cars and a caboose, ALCO FA-1 No. 530 leisurely rolls a local freight eastbound past the Belgian Block driveway of the Bound Brook freight station on a December 1959 day. As a general rule, cab units were not the best kind of locomotive to use on a local freight that did a good deal of switching en route due to its poor rear visibility when performing backup moves, but the LVRR utilized its locomotive fleet wisely, so there must have been a good reason that day to assign No. 530 on this train, even if its engineer and fireman did not necessarily agree with the management. (Photograph by Gene Collora.)

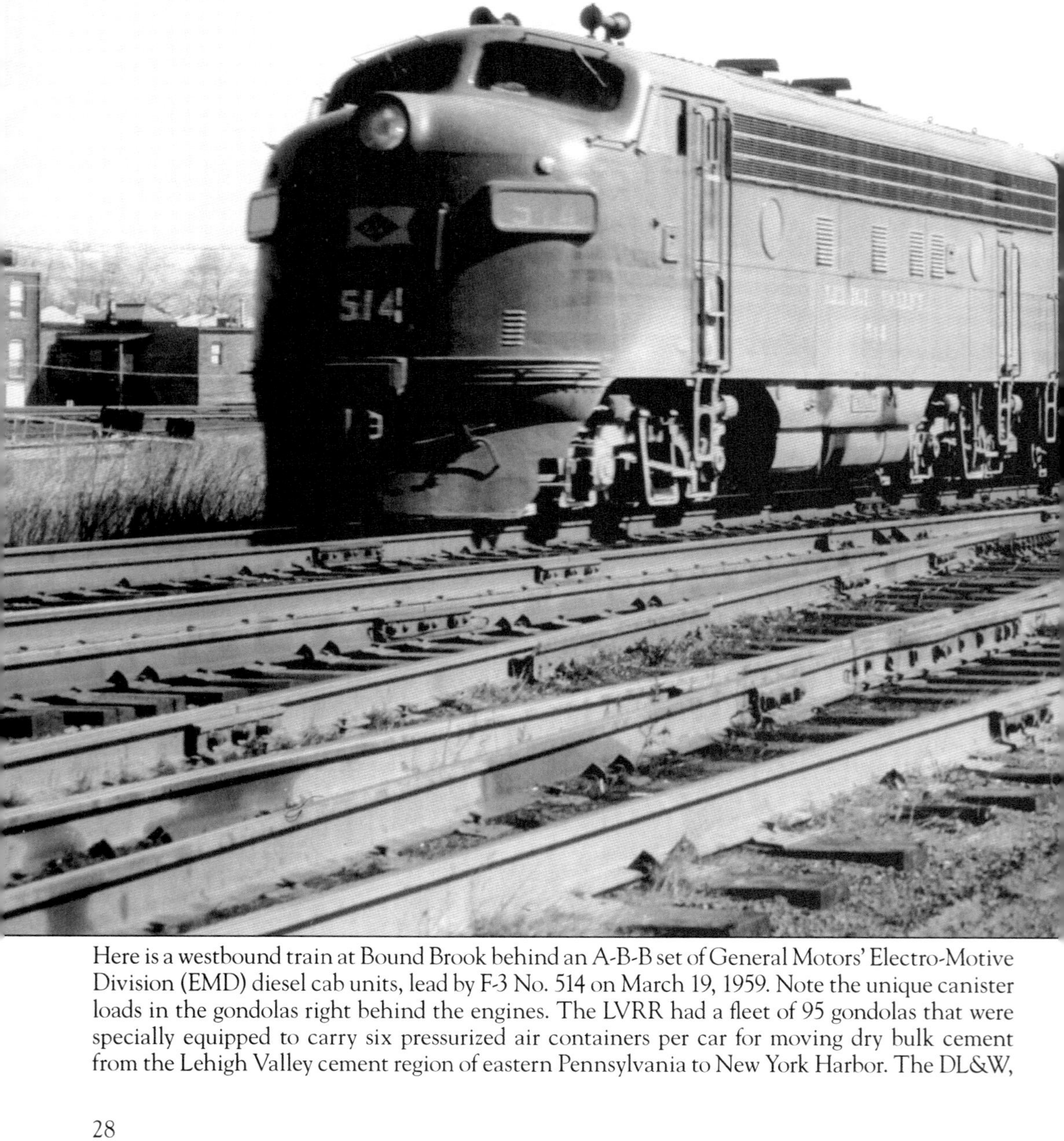

Here is a westbound train at Bound Brook behind an A-B-B set of General Motors' Electro-Motive Division (EMD) diesel cab units, lead by F-3 No. 514 on March 19, 1959. Note the unique canister loads in the gondolas right behind the engines. The LVRR had a fleet of 95 gondolas that were specially equipped to carry six pressurized air containers per car for moving dry bulk cement from the Lehigh Valley cement region of eastern Pennsylvania to New York Harbor. The DL&W,

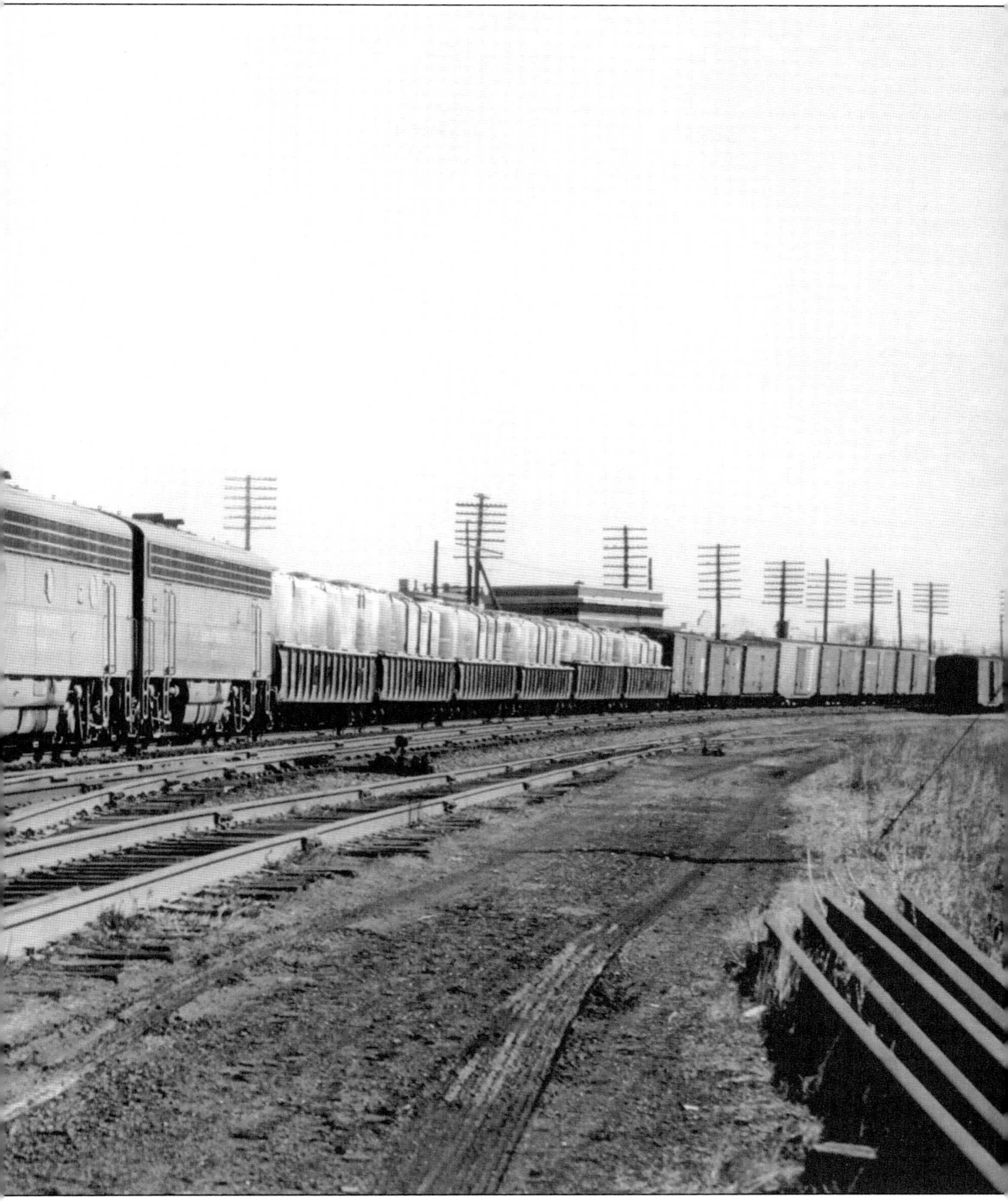

which also served the same cement region of Pennsylvania, had a similar fleet of cars, as did the New York Central Railroad (NYC) and the Delaware and Hudson Railroad (D&H). Upon arrival at Jersey City, they would be off-loaded via crane and floated around New York Harbor by barges to construction sites in and around New York Harbor. (Photograph by Gene Collora.)

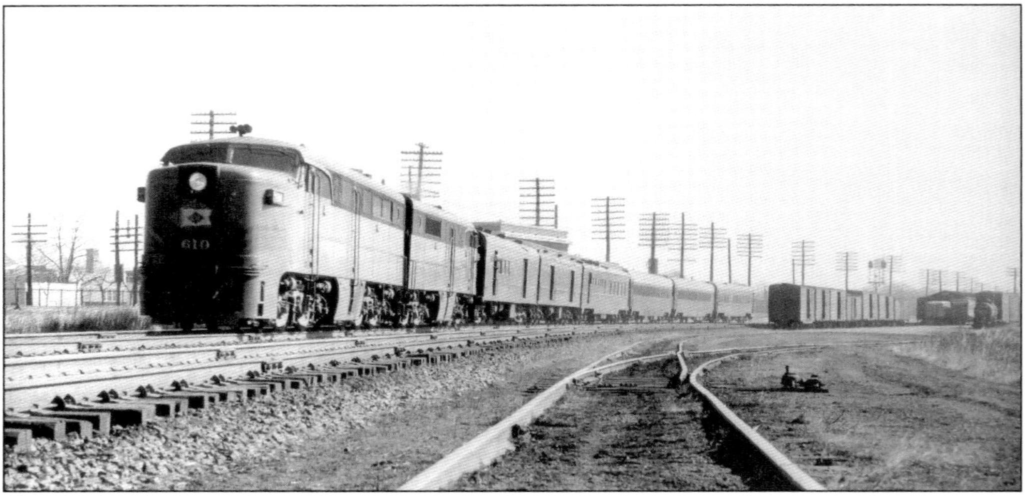

With LVRR PA-1 No. 610 in the lead, the *Black Diamond* rolls westbound as it passes through Bound Brook on the same March day in 1959. To the right of the locomotive are the team tracks of the Bound Brook freight house, and just peeking over the train is the roof of the CNJ's Bound Brook passenger station. In less than two months, this once grand train would be discontinued. (Photograph by Gene Collora.)

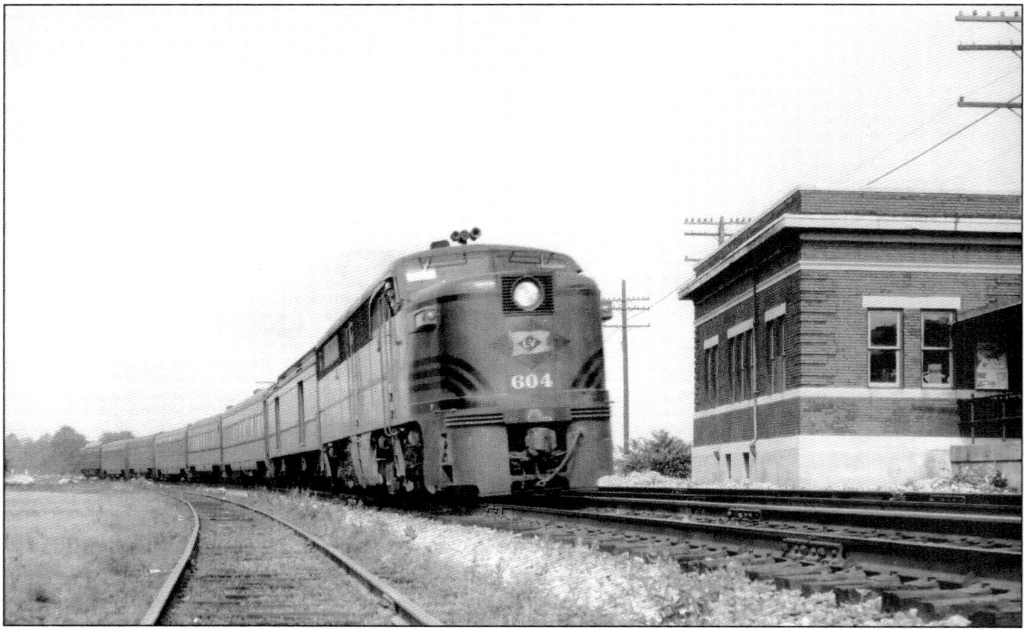

Faithfully performing its job during the last summer before all passenger train service on the entire railroad was to be discontinued, PA-1 No. 604 rolls its train eastbound past the Bound Brook station on July 7, 1960. The seven sets of PA-1 locomotives were purchased in 1948 to haul the main line passenger trains. (Photograph by Gene Collora.)

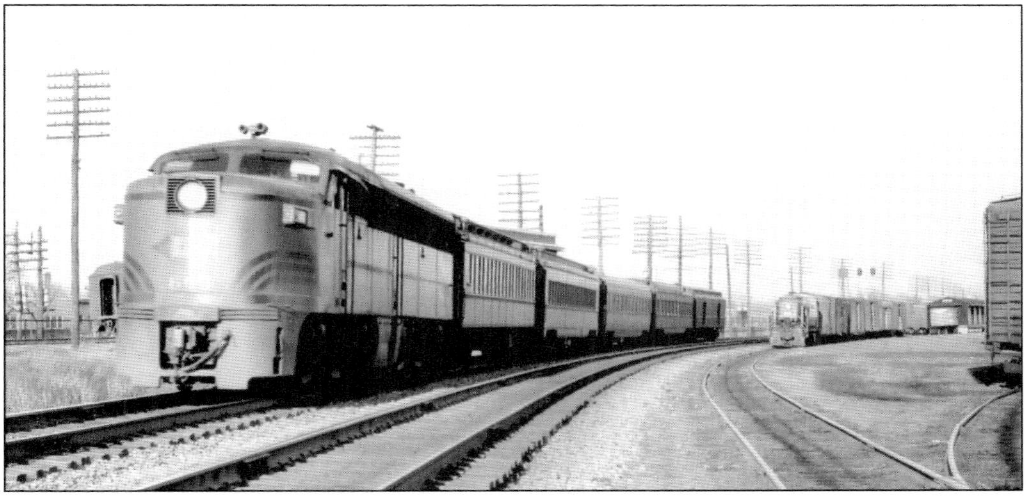

This train, behind a single PA, rounds the curve westbound behind engine No. 603. The short length of the train, while indicative of the declining fortunes of the LVRR's passenger service, also helps to identify it as being train No. 28, the *John Wilkes*, that ran from New York to Lehighton, Pennsylvania, on its daylight journey across New Jersey. Note the coach stopped at Bound Brook on the adjacent CNJ main line. (Photograph by Gene Collora.)

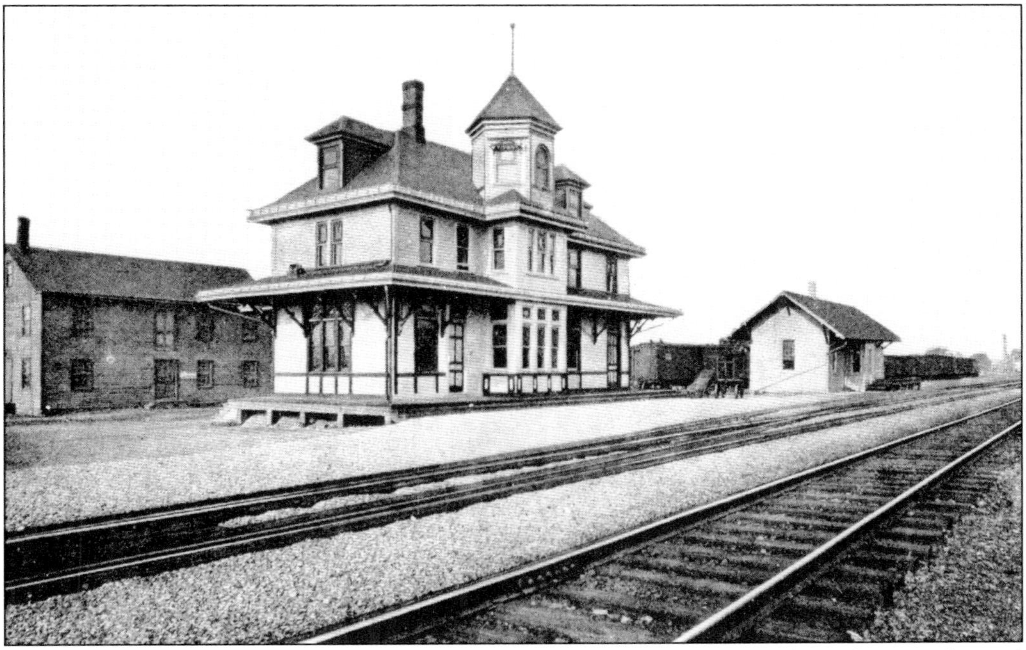

This *c*. 1905 view provides a glimpse of the original LVRR station at Bound Brook. It was located on the south side of the tracks adjacent to the freight station. The older stations along the route of the E&A tended to be very ornate in their architecture, and some even resembled Victorian dwellings. (Courtesy of H. G. MacDonald.)

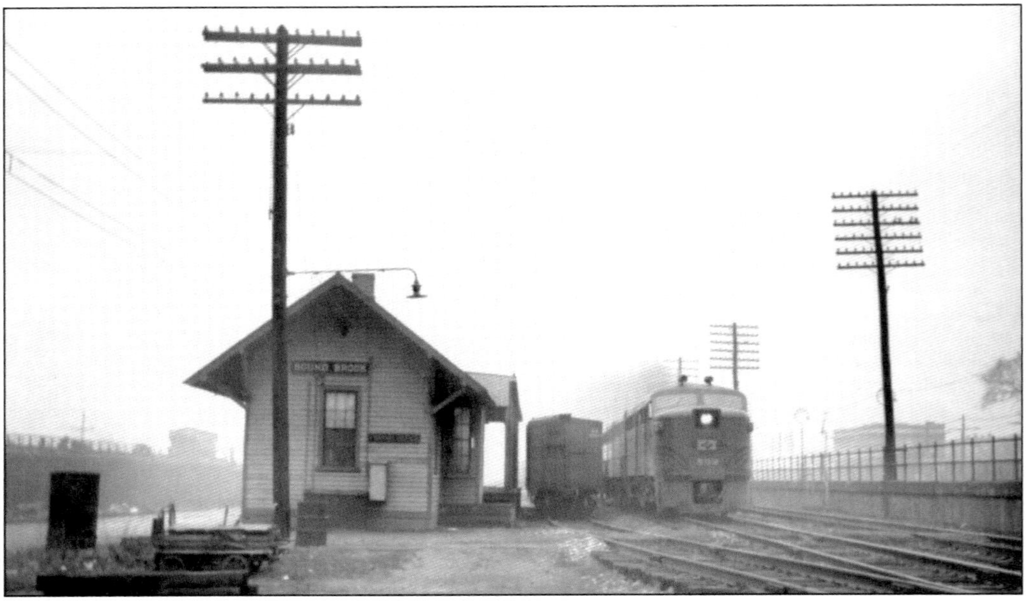

This undated view taken from the approximate location of the former passenger station shows a freight rolling eastbound at full throttle past the Bound Brook freight station with FA-1 No. 532 in the lead. Note the large coal trestle of Apgar Coal and Grain behind the freight station. (Courtesy of Gene Collora.)

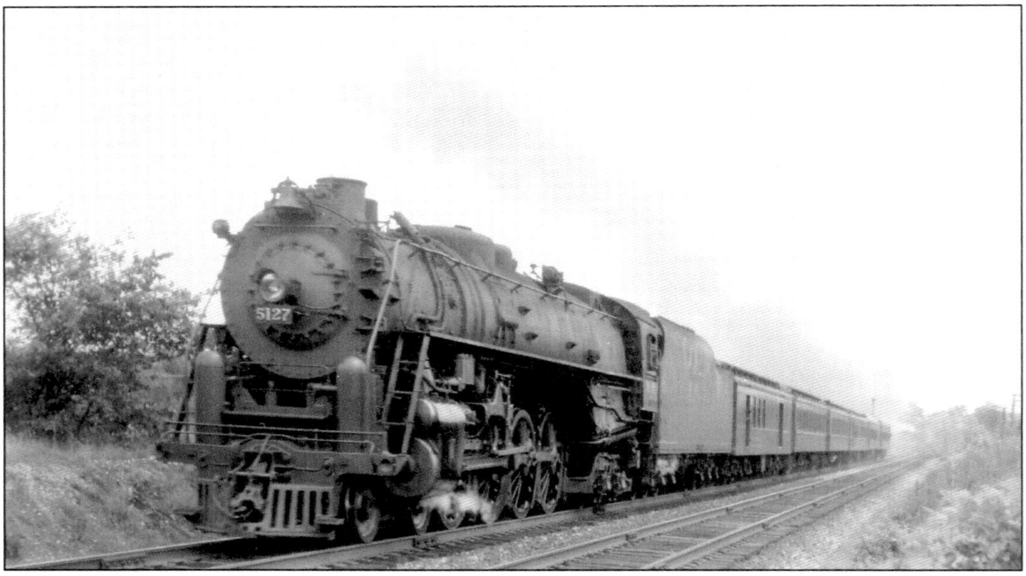

On this December 1943 day, train No. 9, the eastbound *Black Diamond*, has LVRR 4-8-4 No. 5127 in charge on the head end as it passes the photographer just outside Bound Brook. (Photograph by R. P. Morris, courtesy of Jack deRosset/Frank T. Reilly.)

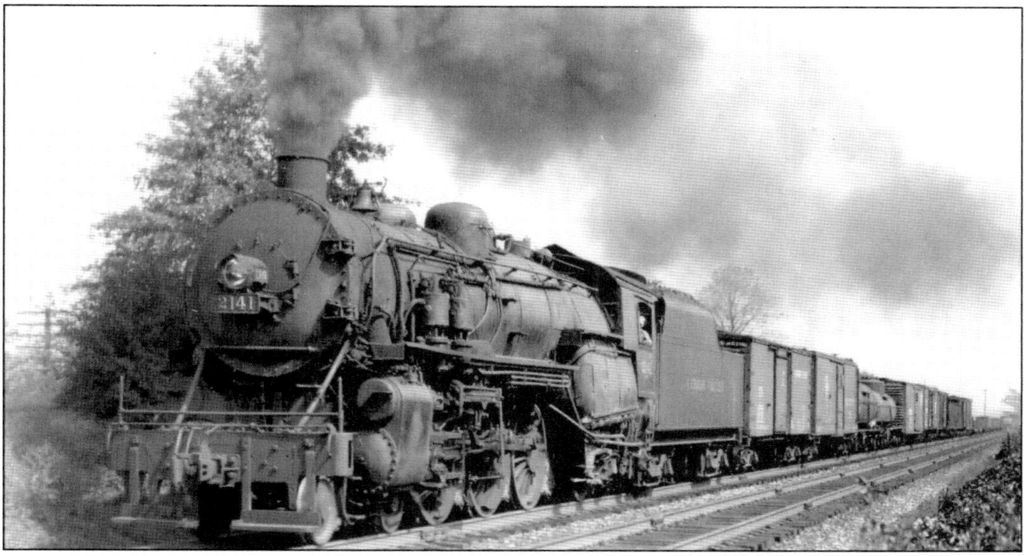

A Baldwin Locomotive Works (BLW) 4-6-2 of the K-4 class leads an eastbound freight near the same location behind engine No. 2141 in September 1936. (Photograph by R. P. Morris, courtesy of Jack deRosset/Frank T. Reilly.)

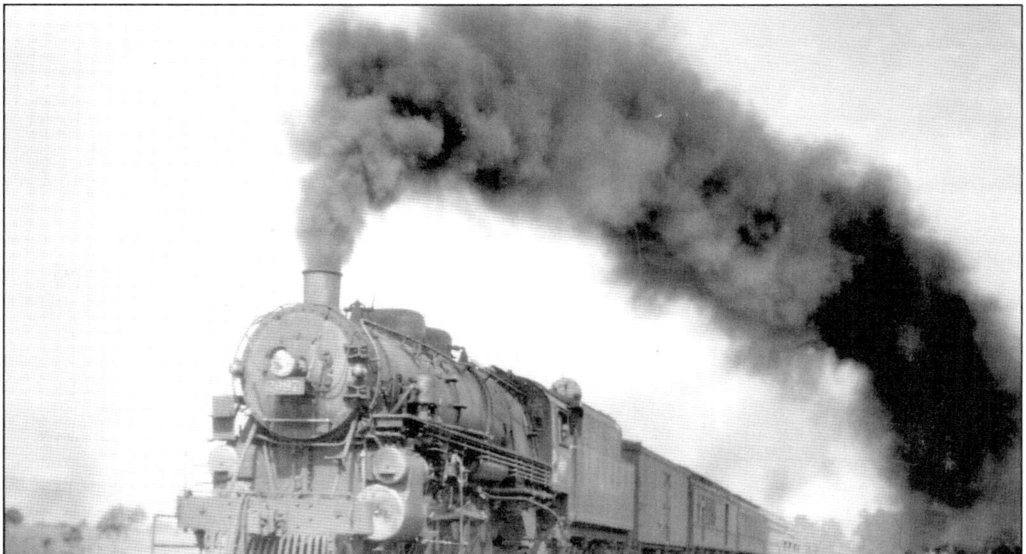

LVRR locomotive No. 2097 blackens the sky with train No. 2, the eastbound *Maple Leaf*, near the border of Bound Brook and Middlesex. As with most areas along the railroad, the CNJ and LVRR tracks were no more than a few yards away from each other. (Photograph by R. P. Morris, courtesy of Jack deRosset/Frank T. Reilly.)

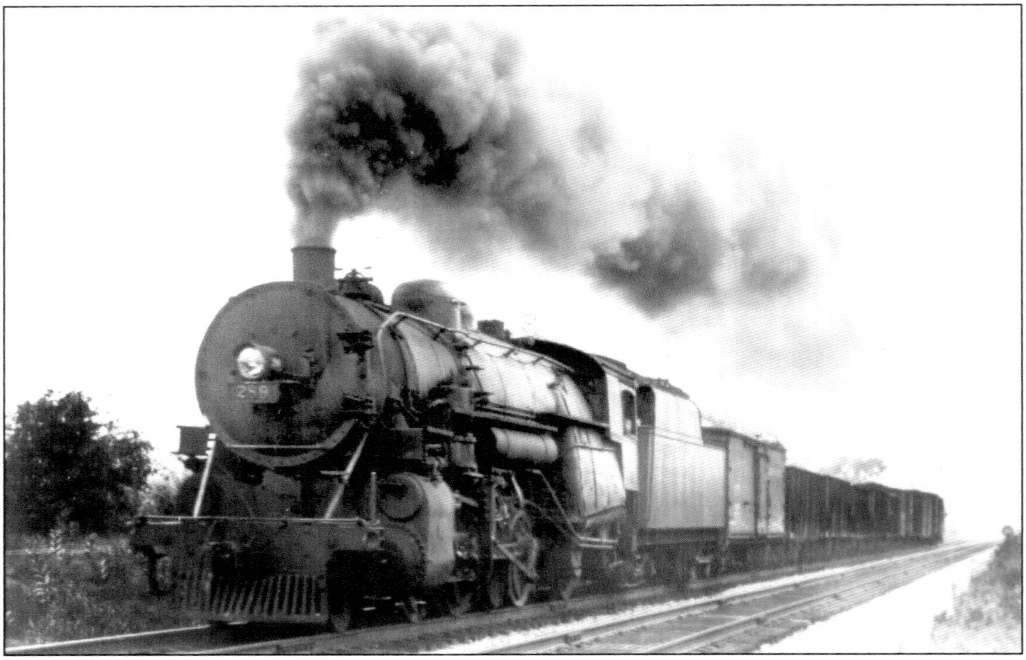

The 2-8-2 No. 289 rolls westbound just outside Bound Brook with a mixed freight on this August day in 1931. The 2-8-2 Mikado-type steam locomotives were generally suited to slower trains and were equipped with trailer boosters to give them a little extra kick on the steep grades in the Pennsylvania coal region. (Photograph by R. P. Morris, courtesy of Jack deRosset/ Frank T. Reilly.)

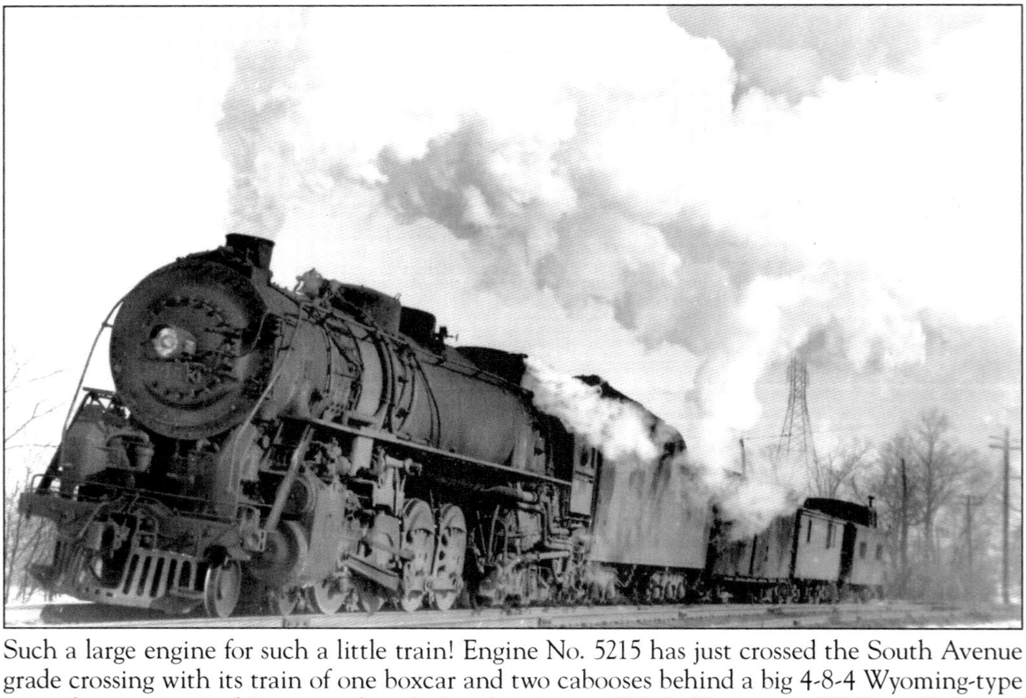

Such a large engine for such a little train! Engine No. 5215 has just crossed the South Avenue grade crossing with its train of one boxcar and two cabooses behind a big 4-8-4 Wyoming-type steam locomotive in this scene taken during the winter of 1940. (Courtesy of William Caloroso/ Cal's Classics.)

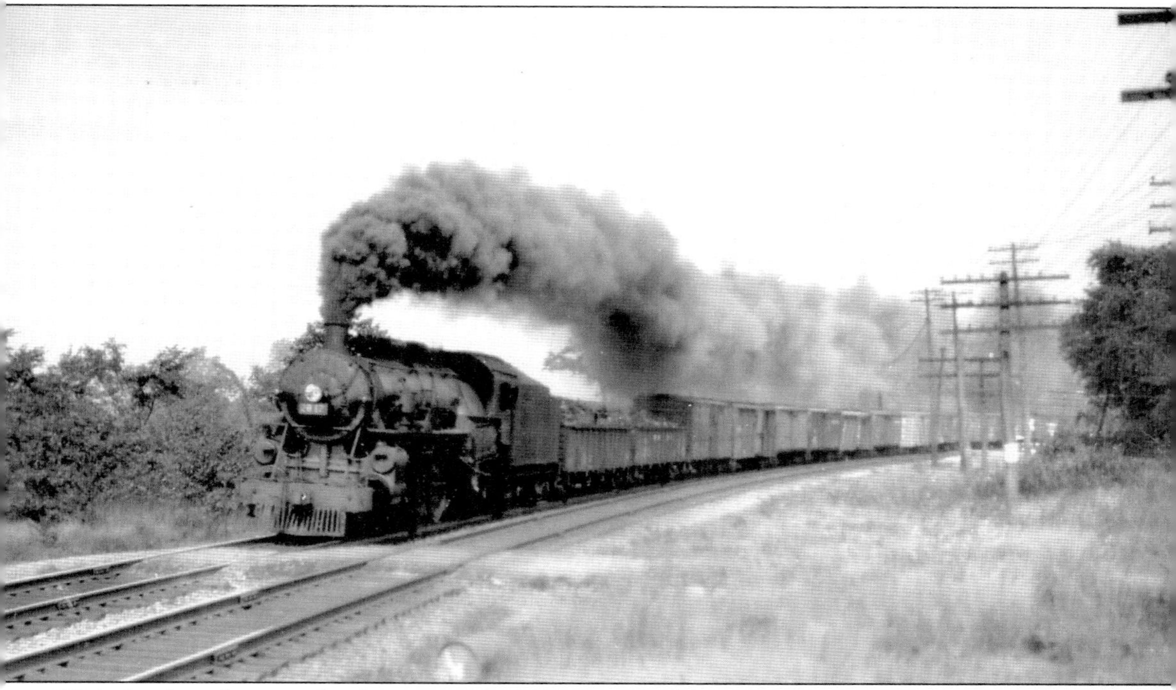

With the throttle opened wide, engine No. 2012, a 4-6-2 of the K-2½ class, crosses South Avenue at the same location, located on the border of Dunellen and New Market (Piscataway) in this undated photograph with its westbound freight. No. 2012 was built in the railroad's own shops in Sayre, Pennsylvania, in 1913. Just out of sight behind the trees to the left of the oncoming train are the tracks of the CNJ, which played tag with the LVRR from Jersey City all the way to Wilkes-Barre, Pennsylvania. (Photograph by R. P. Morris, courtesy of Jack deRosset/Frank T. Reilly.)

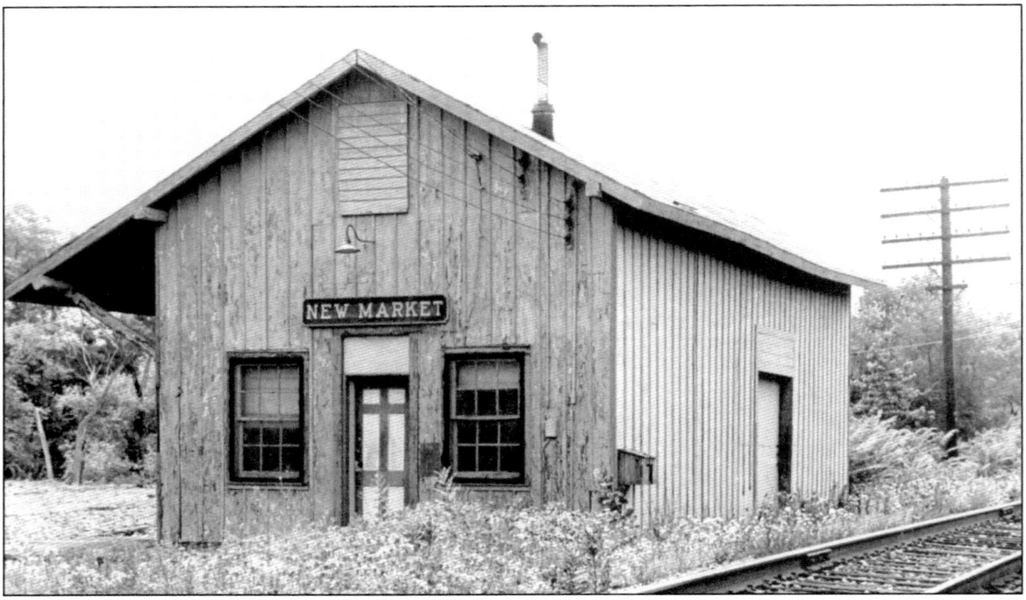

Here is the weather-beaten but well-cared-for New Market freight station in 1966. Located on the south side of the main line between the Prospect Avenue and New Market Road grade crossings, the agent here was responsible for several local industries that were located in the immediate area. The station burned down in 1968. (Photograph by Robert Pennisi.)

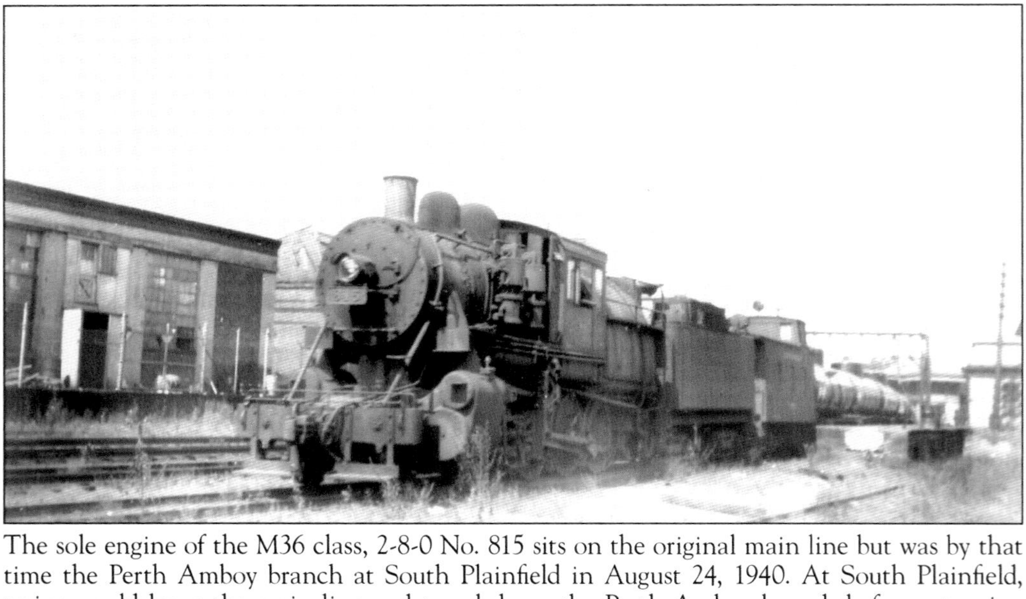

The sole engine of the M36 class, 2-8-0 No. 815 sits on the original main line but was by that time the Perth Amboy branch at South Plainfield in August 24, 1940. At South Plainfield, trains would leave the main line and travel down the Perth Amboy branch before returning to the main line extension and proceeding eastward toward Jersey City. (Photograph by John Brinckmann, courtesy of Joel Rosenbaum/Tom Gallo.)

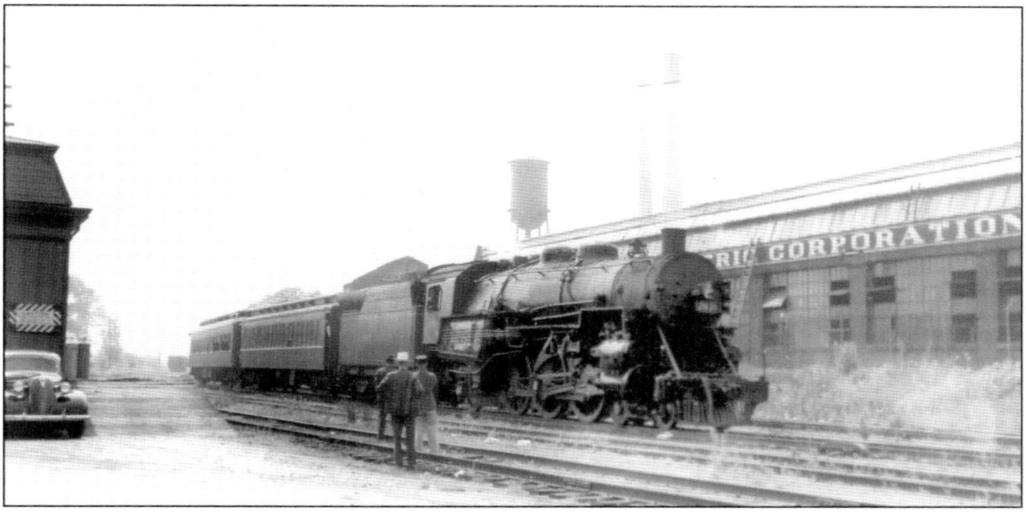

By the time this picture was taken in 1939, passenger trains on the original E&A had been discontinued for five years. Here LVRR president A. N. Williams's inspection train is seen stopped behind the South Plainfield station. The Cornell-Dublier Electric Corporation factory, which was torn down in 2007, sits behind the 4-6-2. (Photograph by John Brinckmann, courtesy of Joel Rosenbaum//Tom Gallo.)

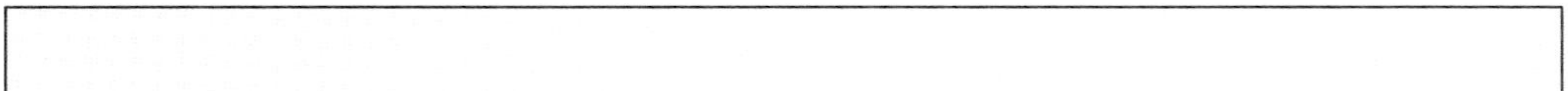

LVRR 2-8-2 No. 478 goes about switching some cars out of its train on the Perth Amboy branch in the South Plainfield yard on this August day in 1939. The 2-8-2's of the N class were the single-largest type of steam locomotive ever owned by the LVRR, with delivery beginning in 1903 and operation lasting until 1951 when all steam was retired. (Photograph by John Brinckmann, courtesy of Joel Rosenbaum/Tom Gallo.)

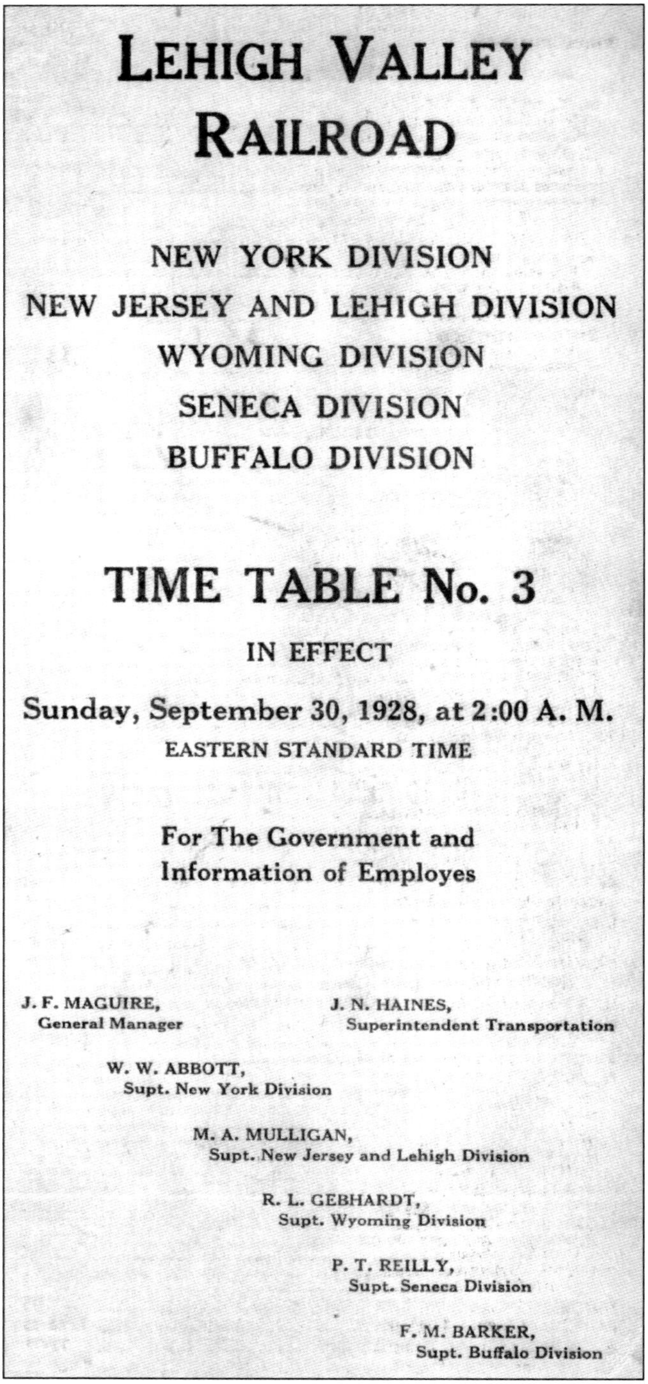

LEHIGH VALLEY RAILROAD

NEW YORK DIVISION
NEW JERSEY AND LEHIGH DIVISION
WYOMING DIVISION
SENECA DIVISION
BUFFALO DIVISION

TIME TABLE No. 3

IN EFFECT

Sunday, September 30, 1928, at 2:00 A. M.

EASTERN STANDARD TIME

For The Government and Information of Employes

J. F. MAGUIRE,
General Manager

J. N. HAINES,
Superintendent Transportation

W. W. ABBOTT,
Supt. New York Division

M. A. MULLIGAN,
Supt. New Jersey and Lehigh Division

R. L. GEBHARDT,
Supt. Wyoming Division

P. T. REILLY,
Supt. Seneca Division

F. M. BARKER,
Supt. Buffalo Division

Employee timetables (ETTs) were carried by every man in train service as a way to be aware of rules and other restrictions along the railroad. As seen here, they also used them to tell when opposing traffic was due, especially for second- and third-class freight trains to guard themselves against opposing first-class passenger trains, which have the right of way, so that they could then occupy the main track in accordance to their train orders and avoid a potentially catastrophic accident. (Courtesy of Ralph A. Heiss.)

16 **New York Division**

Perth Amboy Branch

Distance from New York	No. 3 STATIONS and Distances Between Stations	421	423	425	427	429
	WESTWARD — FIRST CLASS	See Note B Page 9	Daily	Daily	Daily	Daily Except Sunday
		A. M.	A. M.	A. M.	P. M.	P. M.
36.1	STATE STREET	5.45	7.30	9.06	12.05	4.17
	0.8					
35.3	PERTH AMBOY	s 5.49	s 7.34	s 9.10	s12.09	s 4.21
	1.5					
33.8	RARITAN JCT.	f 5.53	f 7.38	f 9.14	f12.13	f 4.25
	0.8					
33.0	FORDS	f 5.56	f 7.41	f 9.17	f12.16	f 4.28
	0.7					
32.3	VALENTINES	f 5.59	f 7.44	f 9.20	f12.19	f 4.31
	0.7					
31.6	PHOENIX	f 6.01	f 7.46	f 9.22	f12.21	f 4.33
	1.2					
30.4	METUCHEN, AMBOY AV.	s 6.04	s 7.49	s 9.25	s12.24	s 4.36
	0.5					
29.9	METUCHEN	s 6.06	s 7.51	s 9.27	s12.26	s 4.38
	2.4					
27.5	STORAGE GROUNDS	f 6.10	f 7.55	f 9.31	f12.30	f 4.42
	1.0					
26.5	SO. PLAINFIELD (Jct.) B	s 6.13	s 7.58	s 9.34	s12.33	s 4.45
		A. M.	A. M.	A. M.	P. M.	P. M.

Perth Amboy Branch

Distance from New York	No. 3 STATIONS and Distances Between Stations	424	426	428	430	432
	EASTWARD — FIRST CLASS	Daily	Daily Except Sunday	Sunday Only	Daily Except Sunday	Sunday Only
		A. M.	A. M.	A. M.	P. M.	P. M.
36.1	STATE STREET	s 8.48	s10.13	s10.47	s 1.13	s 5.23
	0.8					
35.3	PERTH AMBOY	s 8.45	s10.10	s10.44	s 1.10	s 5.20
	1.5					
33.8	RARITAN JCT.	f 8.42	f10.07	f10.41	f 1.07	f 5.17
	0.8					
33.0	FORDS	f 8.39	f10.04	f10.38	f 1.04	f 5.14
	0.7					
32.3	VALENTINES	f 8.36	f10.01	f10.35	f 1.01	f 5.11
	0.7					
31.6	PHOENIX	f 8.33	f 9.58	f10.32	f12.58	f 5.08
	1.2					
30.4	METUCHEN, AMBOY AV.	s 8.30	s 9.55	s10.29	s12.55	s 5.05
	0.5					
29.9	METUCHEN	s 8.27	s 9.52	s10.26	s12.52	s 5.02
	2.4					
27.5	STORAGE GROUNDS	f 8.23	f 9.48	f10.22	f12.48	f 4.58
	1.0					
26.5	SO. PLAINFIELD (Jct.) B	8.20	9.45	10.19	12.45	4.55
		A. M.	A. M.	A. M.	P. M.	P. M.

Raritan River Branch

WESTWARD		Distance from New York	No 3 STATIONS and Distances Between Stations	EASTWARD	
		33.8	RARITAN JCT.		
			0.8		
		34.6	KEASBYS		
			3.7		
		38.3	NIXON		
			1.4		
		39.7	GREENSAND		

On this page, taken from the same September 30, 1928, ETT, the schedules of 10 of the 13 passenger trains that ran between Perth Amboy and the main line at South Plainfield are shown. It also lists the station stops made by each train along the route of the entire branch, complete with the milepost distances from New York. Even the short seven-mile Raritan branch, which served the giant U.S. Army Raritan Munitions Arsenal along the Raritan River in what was then Raritan Township (known as Edison since 1954) is shown, although no scheduled trains ran on this branch. The Raritan branch is today operated by the short line Raritan Central Railroad, which serves the sprawling Raritan Center Industrial Park, located near four major highway arteries, and is bordered by the Raritan River. The branch is no longer accessed by the Perth Amboy branch, which was removed by Conrail in the 1996, but by a former PRR Bonhamton branch that also served the arsenal at one time. (Courtesy of Ralph A. Heiss.)

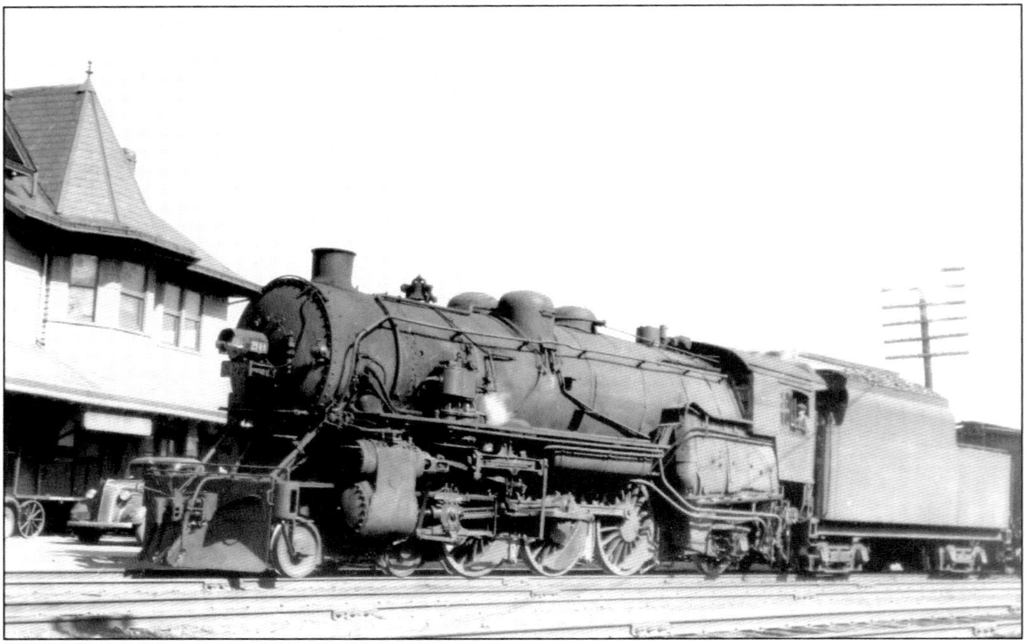

A local freight with engine No. 2144 sits beside the South Plainfield station in this March 1940 photograph. This train may be YK-1, which ran between South Amboy and Packerton Yard in Lehighton, Pennsylvania. Note the classic automobile hiding just behind the engine. (Photograph by John Brinckmann, courtesy of Joel Rosenbaum/Tom Gallo.)

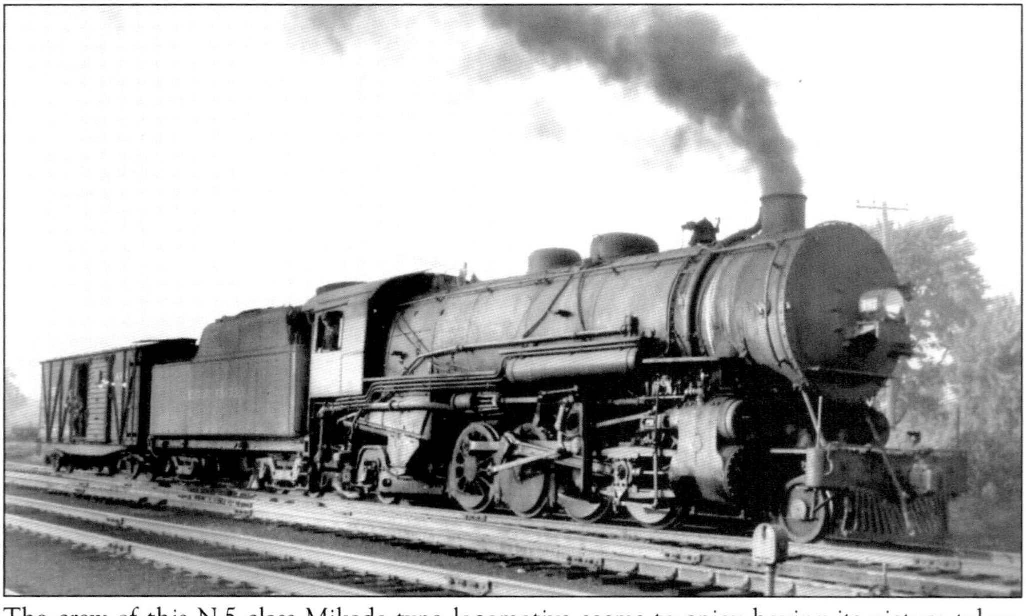

The crew of this N-5 class Mikado-type locomotive seems to enjoy having its picture taken, as evidenced by the engineer in the cab window and the brakeman in the door of the NH boxcar in this 1939 photograph. (Photograph by John Brinckmann, courtesy of Joel Rosenbaum/Tom Gallo.)

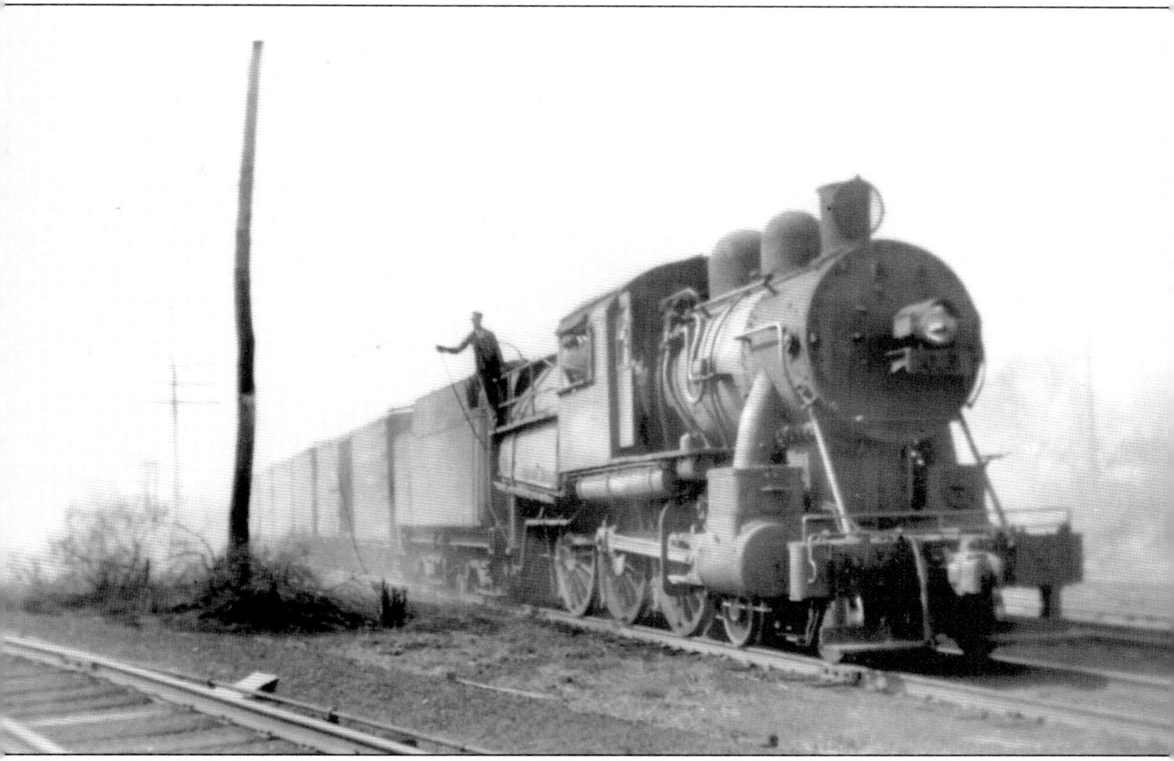

Sparks from steam locomotives were always a fire hazard, as evidenced in this 1939 photograph of the fireman of engine No. 1605 putting out a small brush fire. He appears to be using his squirt hose that he used to wet down the coal in the tender to reduce dust. It is entirely possible that the engine even started the fire, as evidenced by the fact that the circular screen seen hanging down in front of the smokestack is not doing its job of catching sparks! This is but one reason the railroads and the general public were happy to see the passing of the steam engine from everyday life, even though it did make watching trains far more interesting. (Photograph by John Brinckmann, courtesy of Joel Rosenbaum/Tom Gallo.)

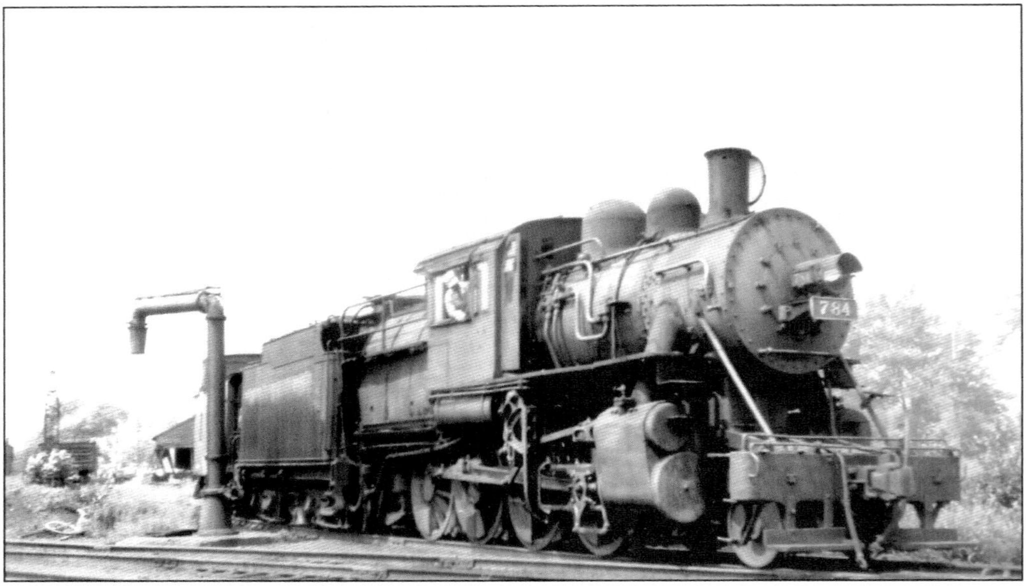

Engine No. 784 is changing directions by turning itself and its caboose on one of the wye tracks located around the South Plainfield yard in this June 1939 photograph. Wye tracks were a way to turn engines in the opposite direction without having to use a turntable, although they did take up considerably more space. (Photograph by John Brinckmann, courtesy of Joel Rosenbaum/Tom Gallo.)

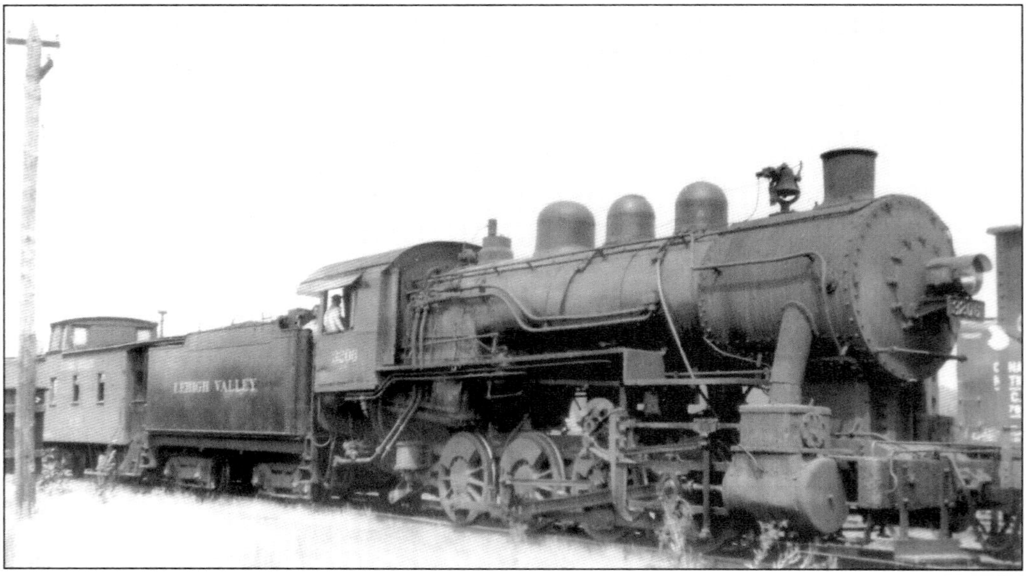

Before departing the South Plainfield yard and continuing east toward Perth Amboy, one finds LVRR engine No. 3206 working on an August day in 1939. The yards at South Plainfield were constructed within a giant wye, with at least four other small wyes contained within the yard trackage. (Photograph by John Brinckmann, courtesy of Joel Rosenbaum/Tom Gallo.)

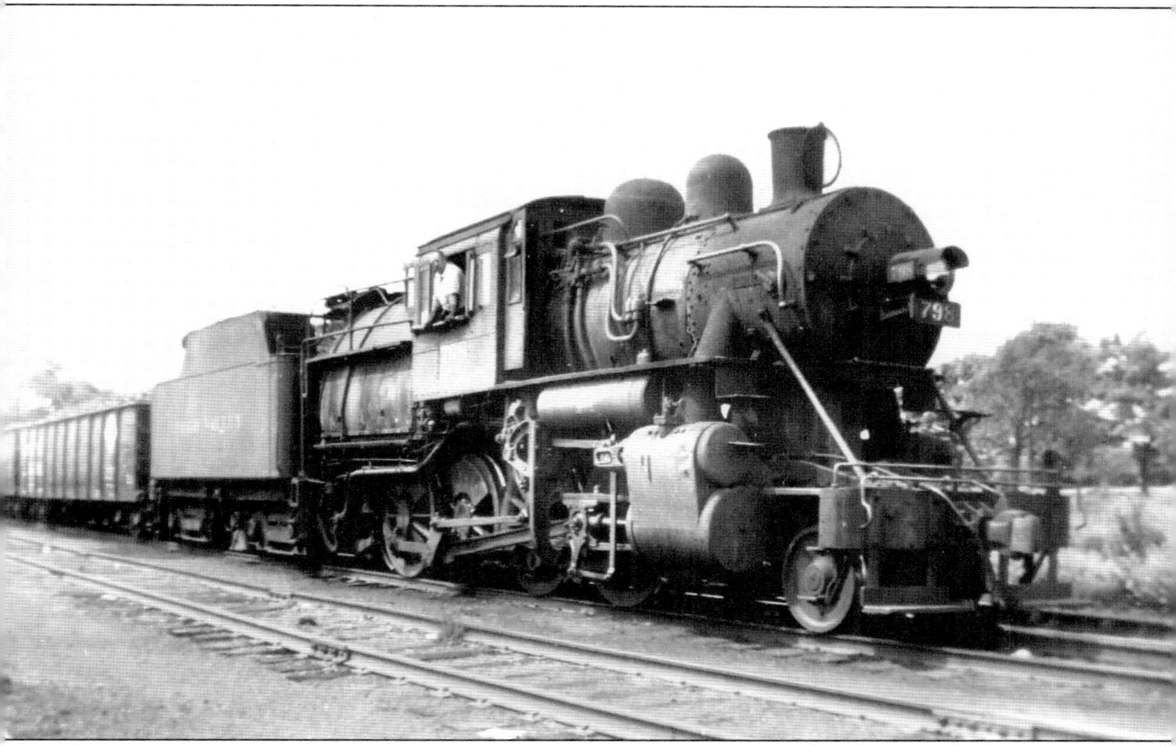

The engineer of camelback No. 798, an early-20th-century Baldwin, seems to be wondering just who is taking a photograph of him and his locomotive. Note the Erie Railroad gondolas that appear to be loaded with coal. When the E&A was first built, an open area at South Plainfield then known as New Brooklyn was used as a 100,000-ton-capacity coal storage yard. Coal was moving so fast out of Pennsylvania that there was not enough room at the coal docks in Perth Amboy to store it while awaiting loading into barges and schooners, so large piles of coal were stored here awaiting further transshipment. By the time this photograph was taken in June 1938, the storage yard had been abandoned for five years. Today the area is an industrial park. (Photograph by John Brinckmann, courtesy of Joel Rosenbaum/Tom Gallo.)

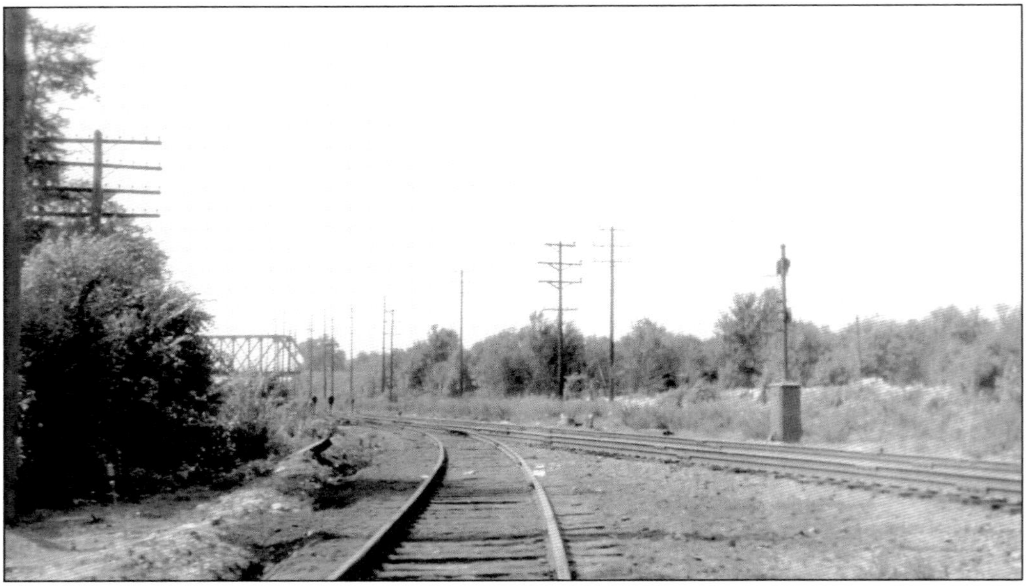

As the railroad enters Metuchen and looking west back toward South Plainfield, the photographer is standing on the westbound wye track that leads to the RDG connection to Camp Kilmer in Edison. The camp was built as a staging camp for U.S. Army troops leaving for the European theater, and the LVRR, RDG, and PRR all had access to it. In the background, the overhead crossing of the Port Reading branch can be seen. (Photograph by John Brinckmann, courtesy of Joel Rosenbaum/Tom Gallo.)

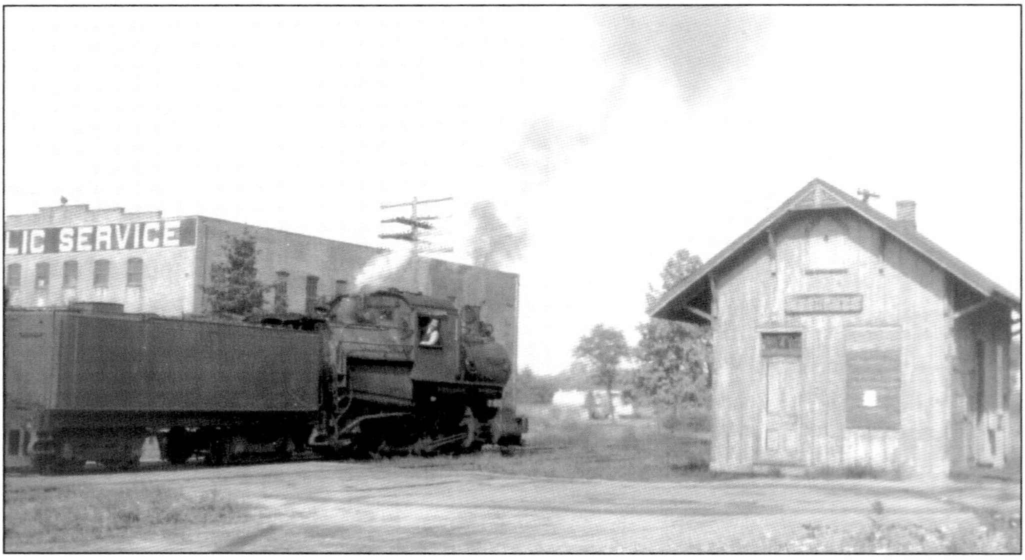

Passing the Durham Avenue station in Metuchen, LVRR No. 3170 switches the large Celotex plant in this 1939 photograph. Note the public service substation building at left. Today a mini-mart sits in the general location of this building, and it is hard to believe a railroad even crossed the road here at one time. (Photograph by John Brinckmann, courtesy of Joel Rosenbaum/Tom Gallo.)

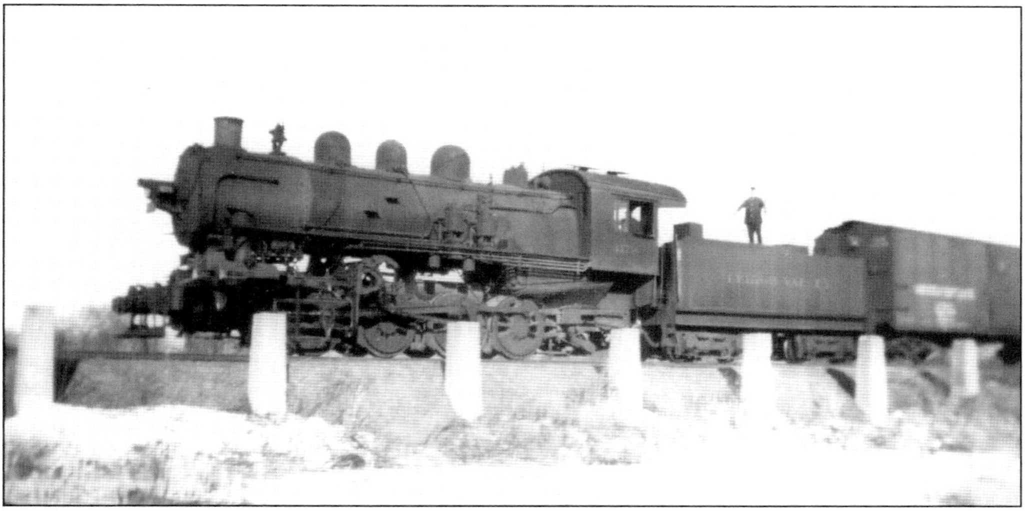

An L-5½ class 0-8-0 switches the Celotex plant in Metuchen in this March 1939 photograph, as the head-end brakeman appears to be watching the photographer, and not his train! Celotex was a manufacturer of an asbestos-based gypsum wallboard and was one of Metuchen's larger industries and provided many car loadings for the railroad. (Photograph by John Brinckmann, courtesy of Joel Rosenbaum/Tom Gallo.)

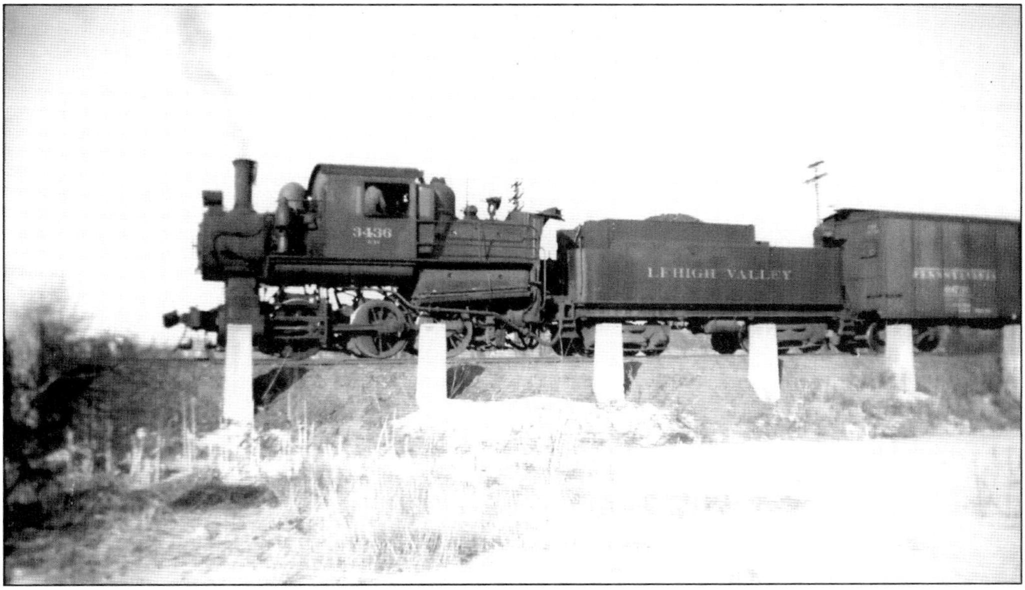

A diminutive 0-6-0 steam switching locomotive, in this case No. 3436, works the same switching job taken only a month after the previous photograph in this April 1939 scene. Interestingly enough, both engines seem to be switching a PRR boxcar of the same design. Metuchen's large factories required very frequent switching in order to meet production schedules. (Courtesy of Richard Chapin.)

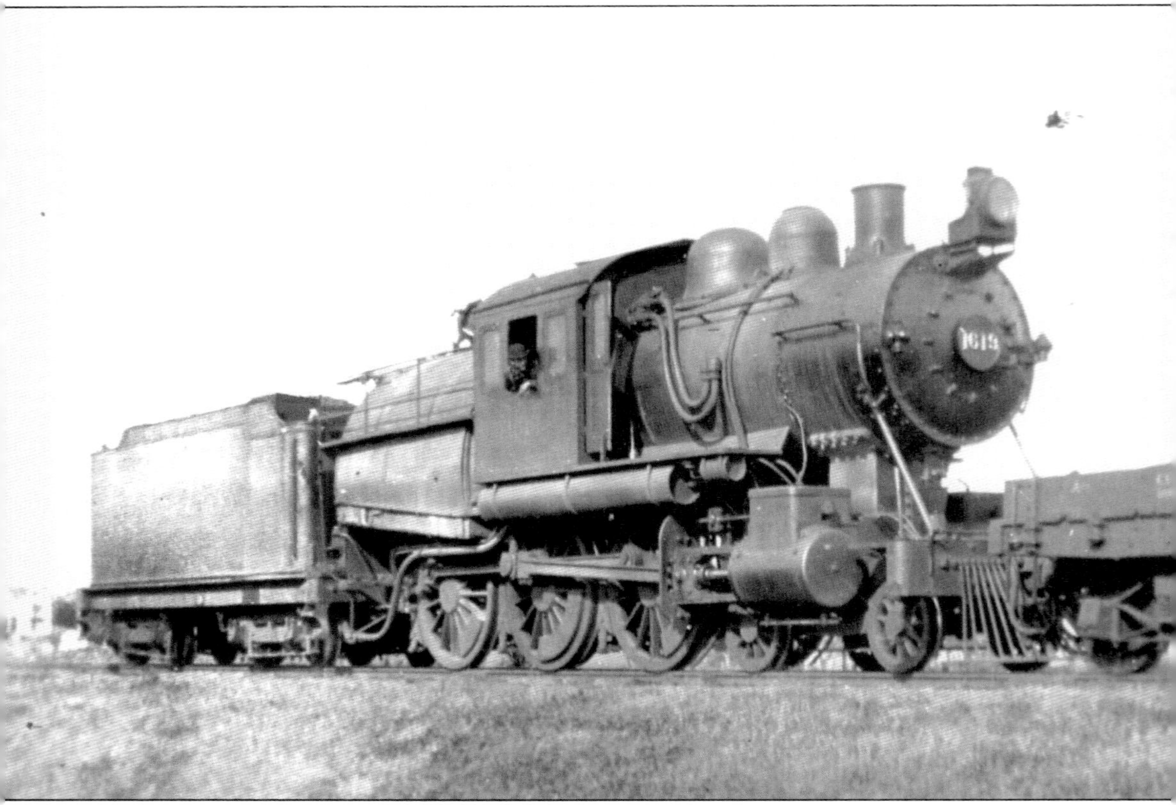

This classic photograph shows almost brand-new 4-6-0 No. 1619 pushing a flatcar with arch bar trucks up the PRR passenger train connection at Metuchen. When the LVRR first built eastward, this elevated ramp allowed its passenger trains to enter the PRR main line just west of the PRR's Metuchen station for the trip east to the Exchange Place terminal in Jersey City. Through passenger trains stopped using this connection in 1891 when the main line extension was completed to West Newark Junction on the PRR at Newark. Today most of this ramp still exists nearly 100 years after it was first constructed. (Courtesy of John Brinckmann.)

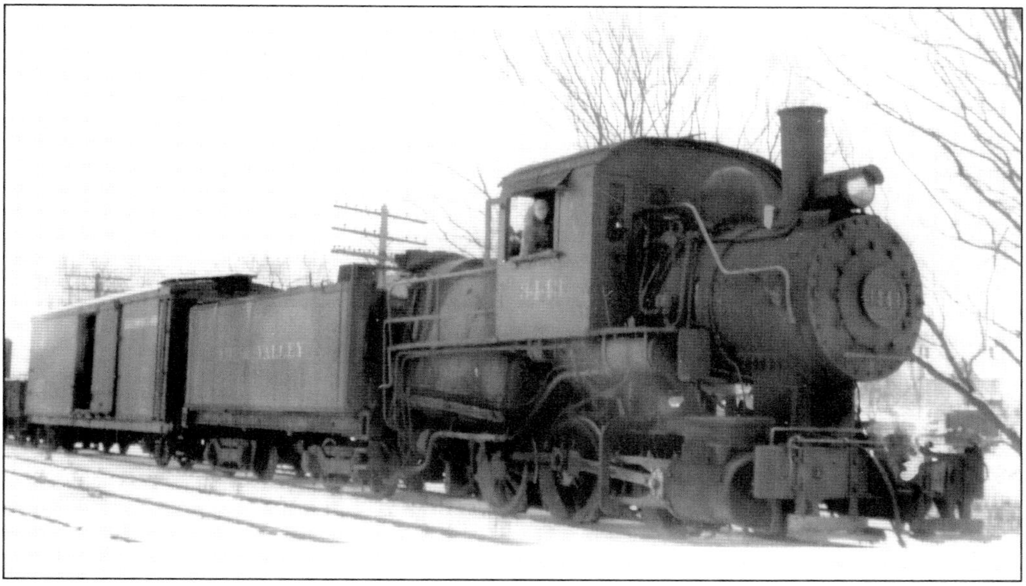

On a cold March 1940 day, engine No. 3443, a BLW design built in the LVRR Sayre shops in the early 1900s, switches industries at Metuchen. The reality of a job working on the railroad being tough could not be more apparent here, as rain, snow, and other unpleasant weather required employees to brave the elements no matter what in the course of their jobs. (Photograph by John Brinckmann, courtesy of Joel Rosenbaum/Tom Gallo.)

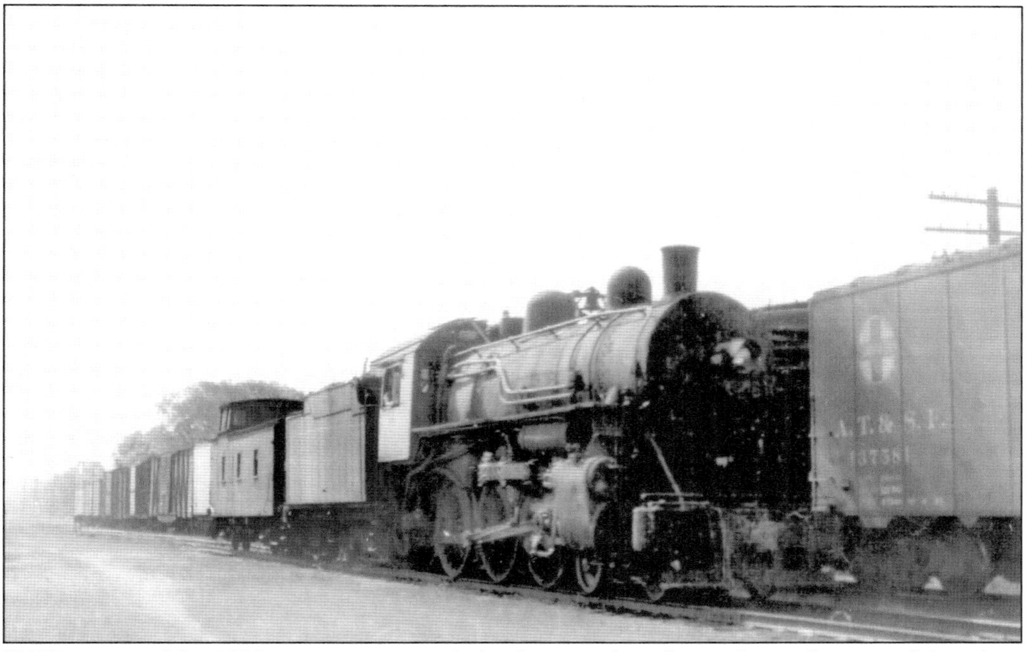

LVRR engine No. 1820 is seen moving light (no train) with a caboose between Metuchen and South Plainfield in this 1940 photograph. The Atchison, Topeka and Santa Fe Railway (commonly known as the Santa Fe) boxcar on the second track appears to be sitting on the eastbound track. The Perth Amboy branch produced many car loadings for the LVRR all the way to the end of the railroad in 1976. (Photograph by John Brinckmann, courtesy of Joel Rosenbaum/Tom Gallo.)

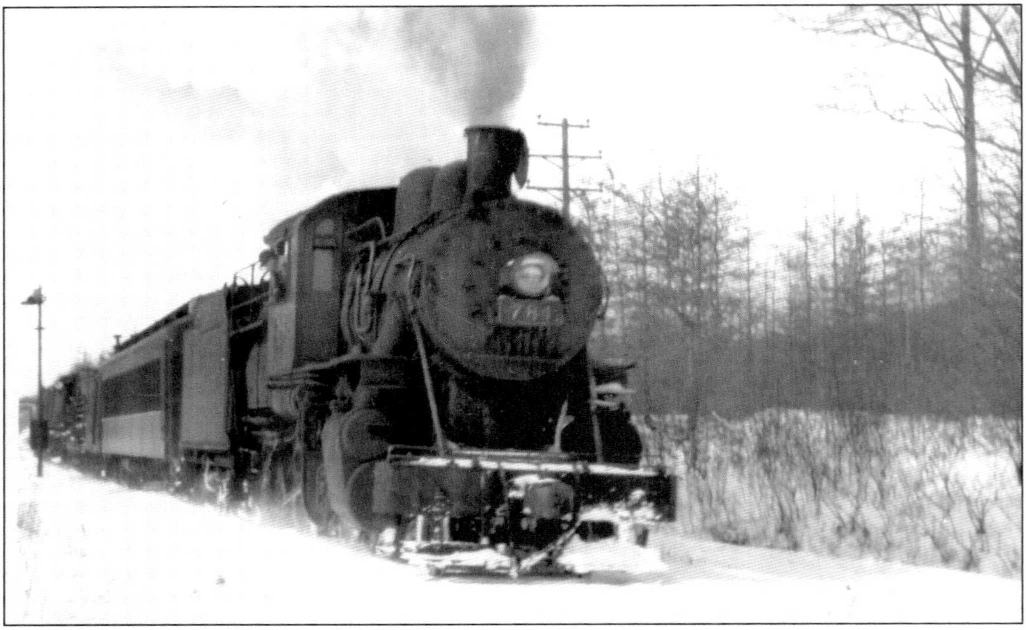

LVRR engine No. 784 powers a work train past Hillside Cemetery on a snowy February day in 1940. Even though it was there only to provide protection for the work crew, passenger cars were a rare sight on the branch by this time, as all passenger service had been gone for five years at the time this photograph was taken. (Photograph by John Brinckmann, courtesy of Joel Rosenbaum/Tom Gallo.)

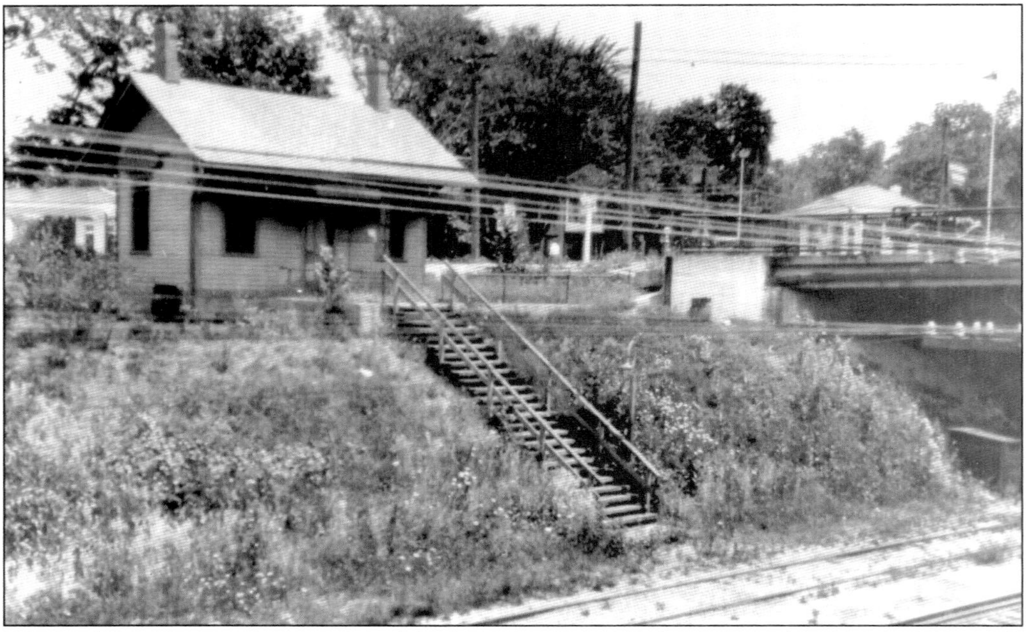

Here is the Amboy Avenue station of the LVRR in 1932. By this time, only one round-trip each way with a gas-electric car remained to serve passengers on the branch, down from 13 trains only four years previous. The cutbacks in passenger service would continue across the entire railroad until the passenger service renaissance of the late 1930s. (Photograph by John Brinckmann, courtesy of Joel Rosenbaum/Tom Gallo.)

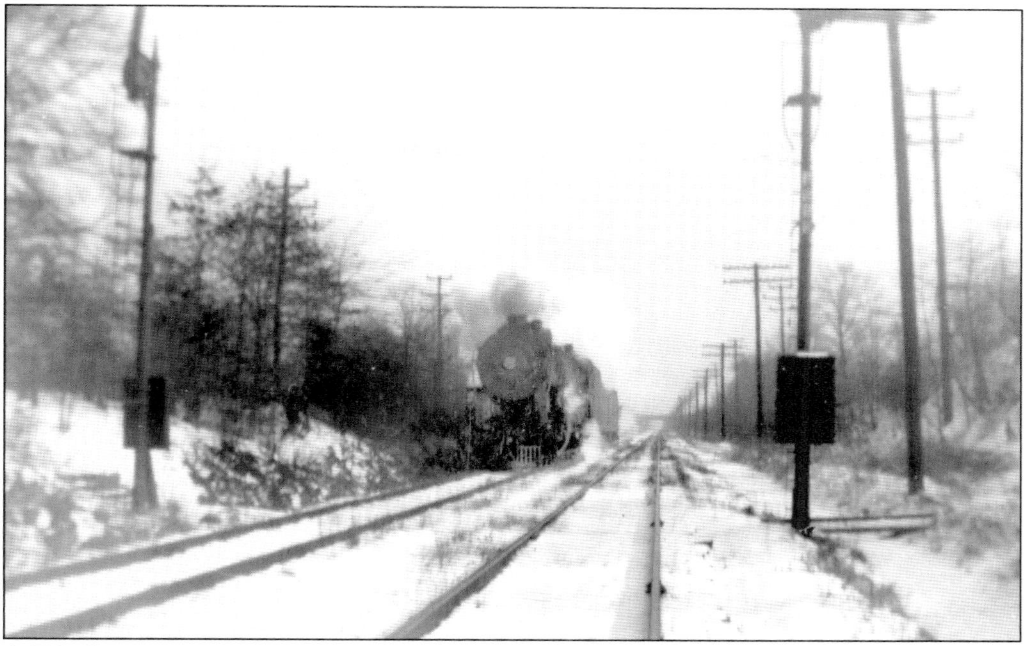

A T-2 class 4-8-4 is seen running light with a caboose westbound through Metuchen in this January 1940 photograph, probably after having delivered its coal train at Perth Amboy. If there was no return train from Perth Amboy, the 4-8-4 would be dispatched to run light back to Oak Island Yard for servicing. (Photograph by John Brinckmann, courtesy of Joel Rosenbaum/Tom Gallo.)

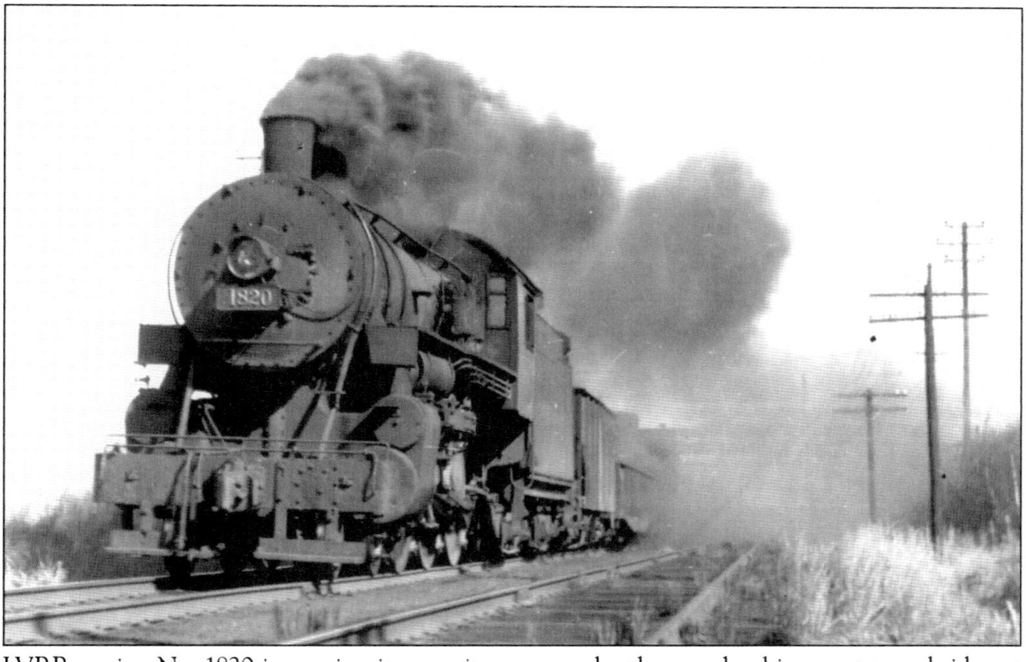

LVRR engine No. 1820 is pouring it on as it passes under the wooden king post truss bridge at Pierson Avenue on the east end of Metuchen in 1940. Today in this location, the Pierson Avenue bridge has been removed and filled in across the roadbed, and the railroad is nothing more than a shallow ditch. (Photograph by John Brinckmann, courtesy of Joel Rosenbaum/Tom Gallo.)

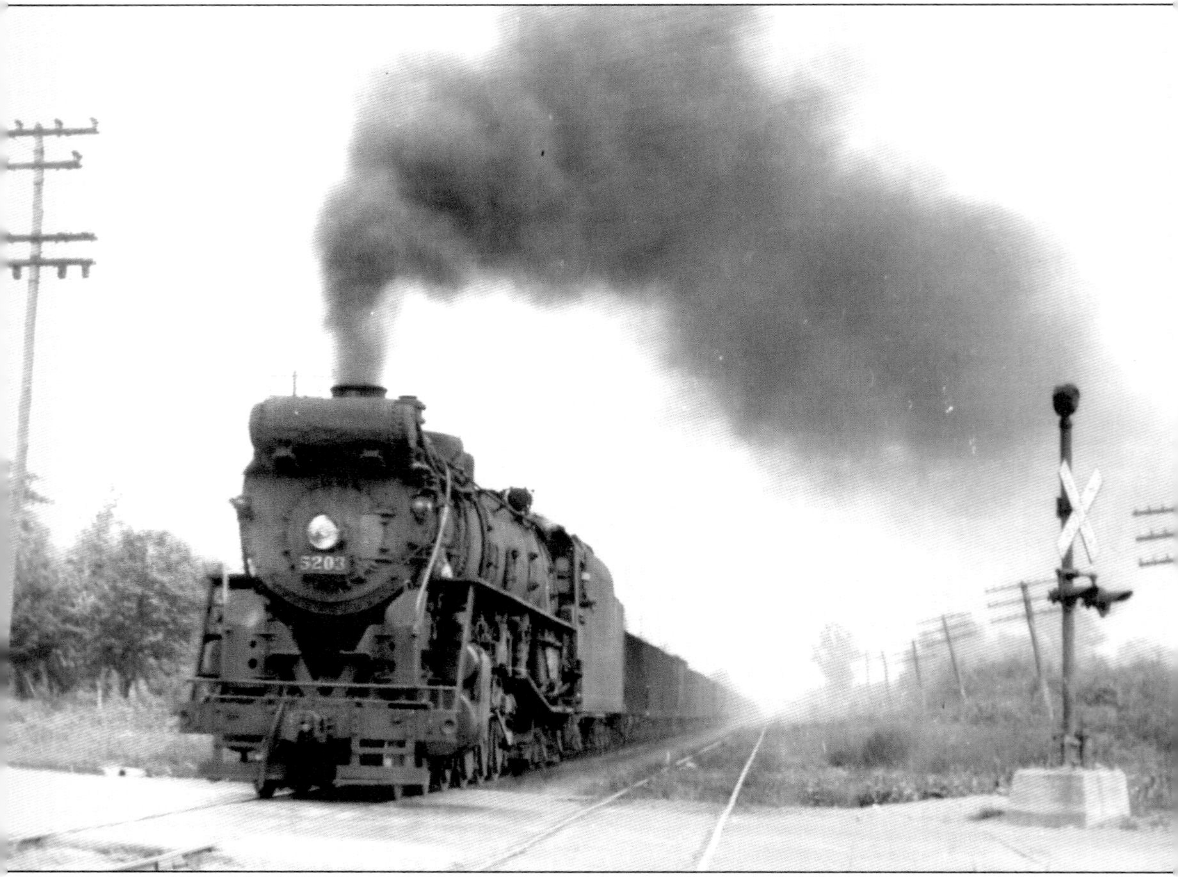

After delivering its trainload full of coal to the docks at Perth Amboy, Wyoming-type locomotive No. 5203 passes westbound with a string of empty cars through the Phoenix section of Edison in 1939. Wyoming-type 4-8-4s needed to be backed down the entire nine-mile length of the Perth Amboy branch from South Plainfield in reverse when assigned to a large coal train, as the engine facilities at Perth Amboy did not have a turntable large enough to spin a 4-8-4 steam locomotive until one was installed in the late 1940s. The power for these heavy trains would be dispatched out of Oak Island Yard in Newark. (Photograph by John Brinckmann, courtesy of Joel Rosenbaum/Tom Gallo.)

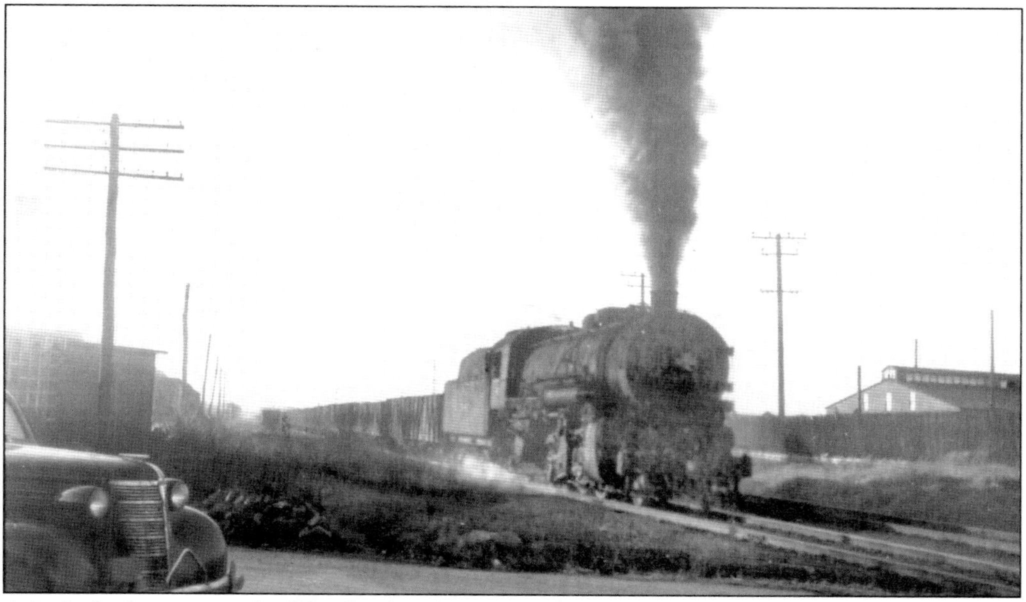

A little farther east at the Woodbridge Avenue grade crossing, 2-8-2 No. 467 hauls a long train full of coal hoppers for the piers at Perth Amboy. In the background can be seen one of the many pottery factories in this part of Middlesex County, which lent the local name of Ceramics to this part of town. (Photograph by John Brinckmann, courtesy of Joel Rosenbaum/Tom Gallo.)

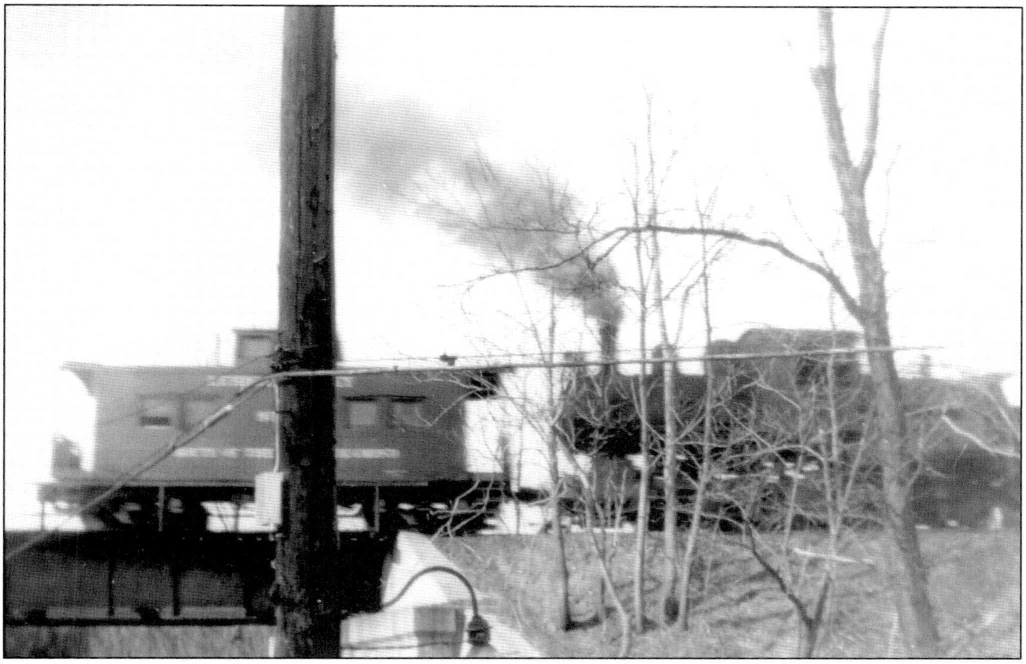

Near the very end of the Raritan branch at the area known as Greensand, an unidentified 0-8-0 and a modern steel caboose displaying the "Route of the Black Diamond" slogan have just crossed over the Silver Lake Avenue bridge in this undated photograph. While the tracks of the Raritan branch no longer reach this far, the bridge still remains at the time of this writing. (Photograph by William E. Christian, courtesy of John Brinckmann.)

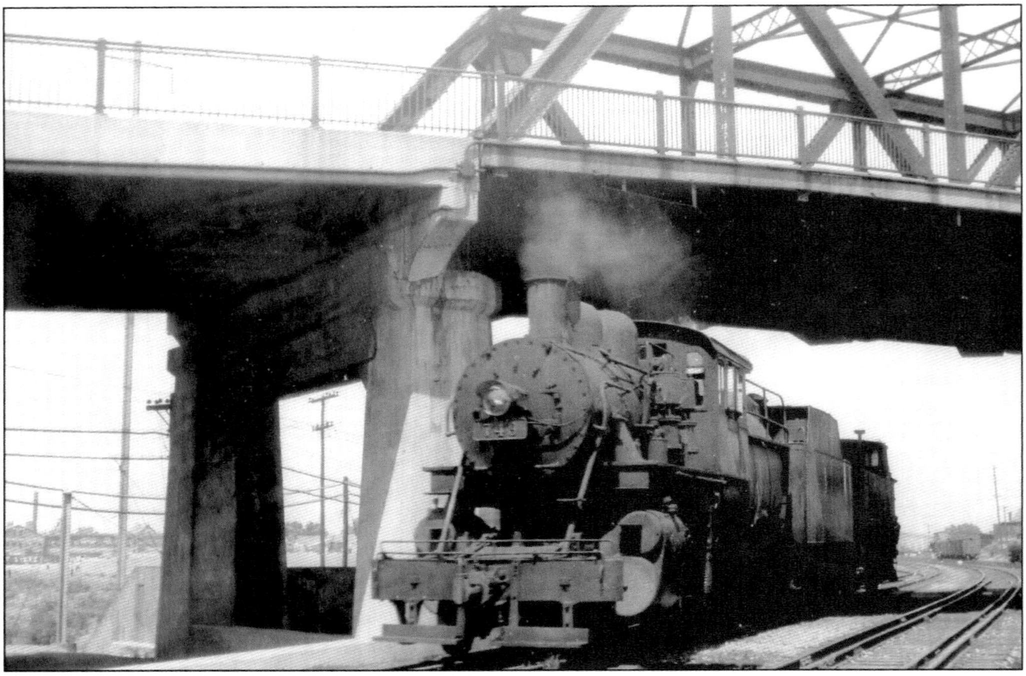

LVRR engine No. 749 passes under the Washington Street bridge at the same time it passes over the CNJ tracks leading to the Jersey Shore at Perth Amboy in this June 1940 view. (Photograph by John Brinckmann, courtesy of Joel Rosenbaum/Tom Gallo.)

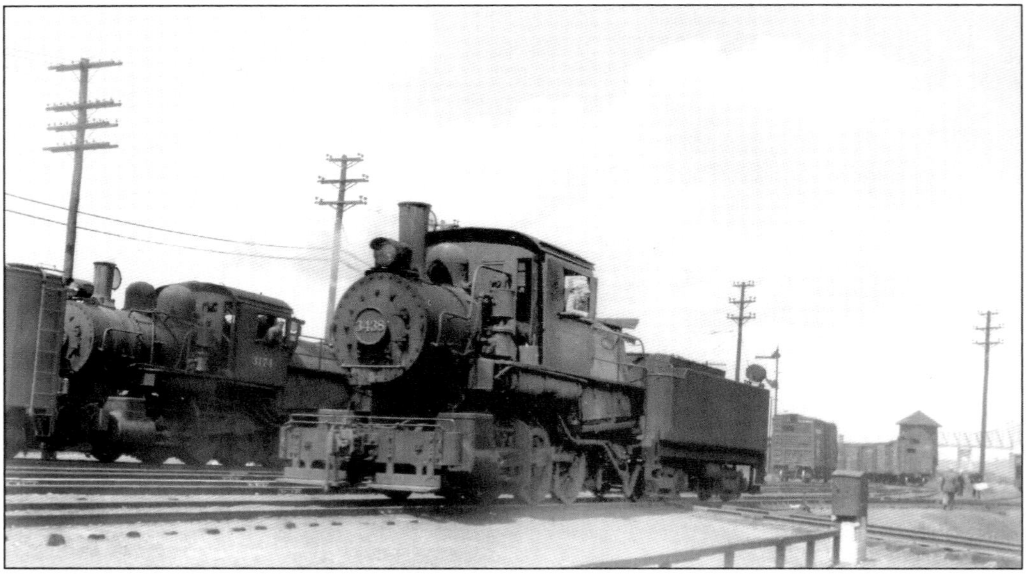

In this busy photograph, tiny 0-6-0 No. 3438 waits to make another switching move as its tender sits across the diamond of the Perth Amboy and Woodbridge (PA&W) branch of the PRR. In the background, the Outerbridge Crossing between Perth Amboy and Staten Island can be seen in this June 1940 photograph. (Photograph by John Brinckmann, courtesy of Joel Rosenbaum/Tom Gallo.)

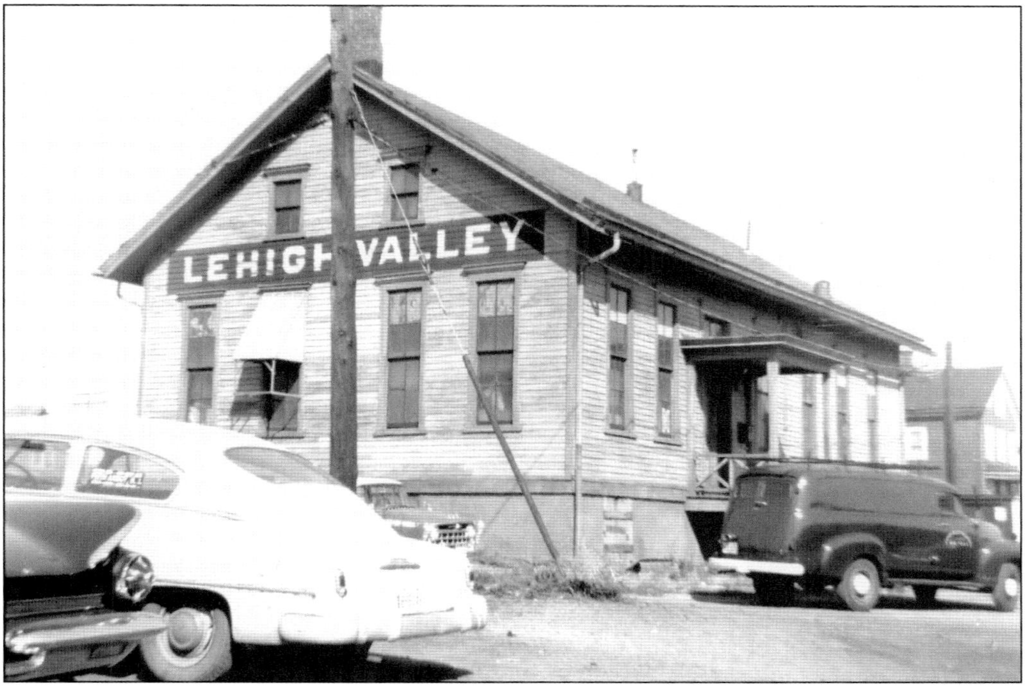

This photograph, taken sometime in the 1960s, shows the "nerve center" for the operations of the branch, the Perth Amboy freight station, located along State Street just north of downtown. (Courtesy of H. G. MacDonald.)

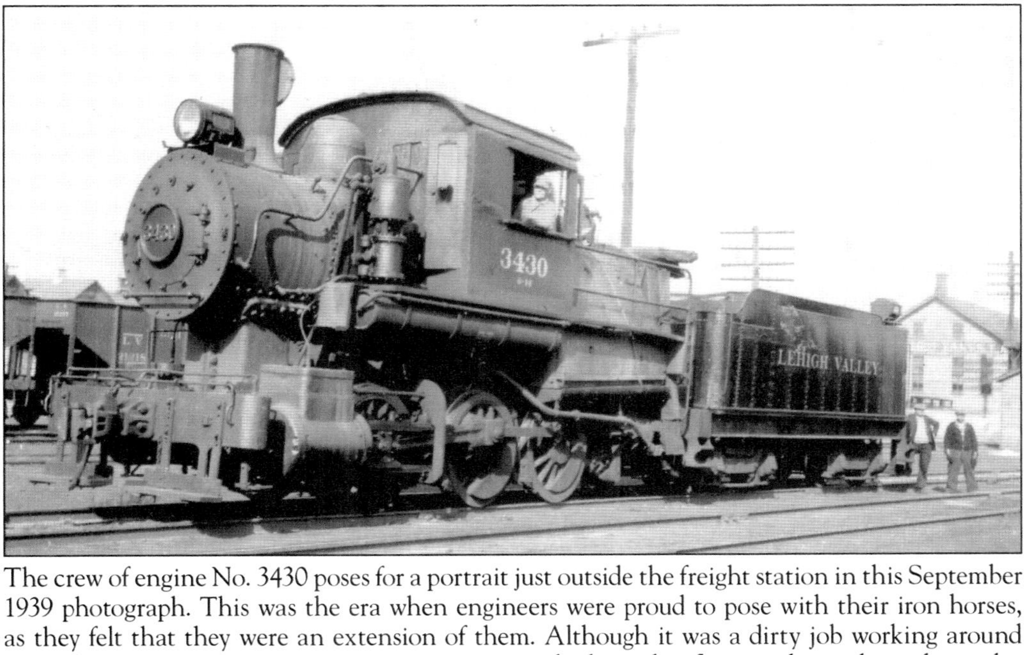

The crew of engine No. 3430 poses for a portrait just outside the freight station in this September 1939 photograph. This was the era when engineers were proud to pose with their iron horses, as they felt that they were an extension of them. Although it was a dirty job working around steam locomotives, most engineers were very smartly dressed, reflecting the pride in their jobs. (Photograph by R. P. Morris, courtesy of Jack deRosset/Frank T. Reilly.)

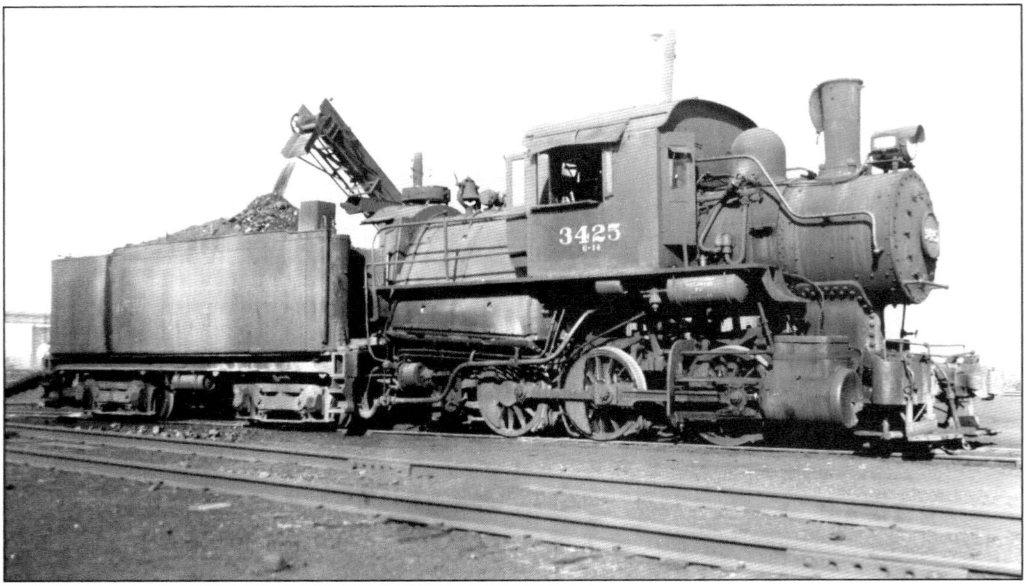

A hard day of switching can even make a locomotive hungry, and here the tender of engine No. 3425 is getting fed after a hard day's work at Perth Amboy on April 2, 1940. After the opening of the main line east of South Plainfield, the importance of Perth Amboy as a terminal expectedly declined, and even more so after coal traffic died off. (Photograph by John P. Scharle, courtesy of Richard Taylor.)

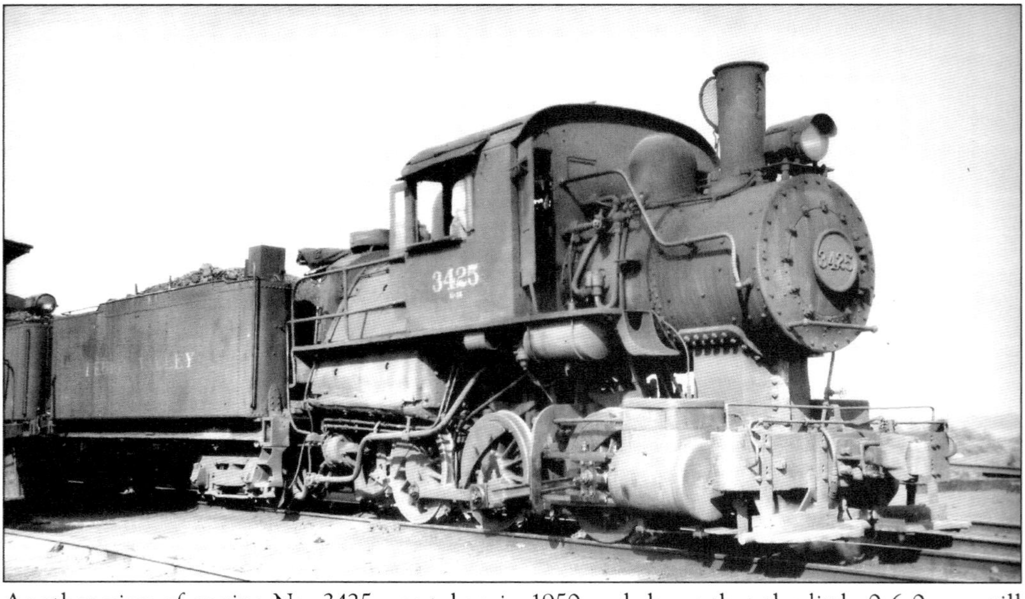

Another view of engine No. 3425 was taken in 1950 and shows that the little 0-6-0 was still hard at work after many years of faithful service to the LVRR, having first been built sometime around 1908. Smaller locomotives like this tended to be assigned to one location for many years, even becoming the "personal property" of their crews. (Courtesy of Richard Chapin.)

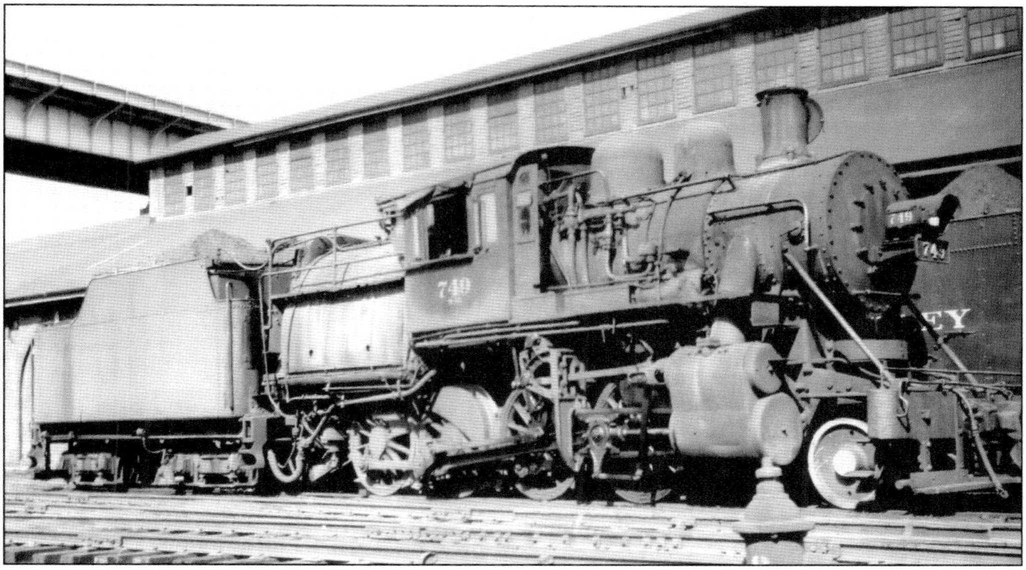

LVRR locomotive No. 749 rests alongside the Perth Amboy engine house in the shadow of the approach viaduct to the Outerbridge Crossing between Perth Amboy and Staten Island in this 1947 photograph. The Outerbridge Crossing was named after Eugenius H. Outerbridge, the then chairman of the New York Port Authority, the agency that built the bridge in 1928. (Courtesy of Gene Collora.)

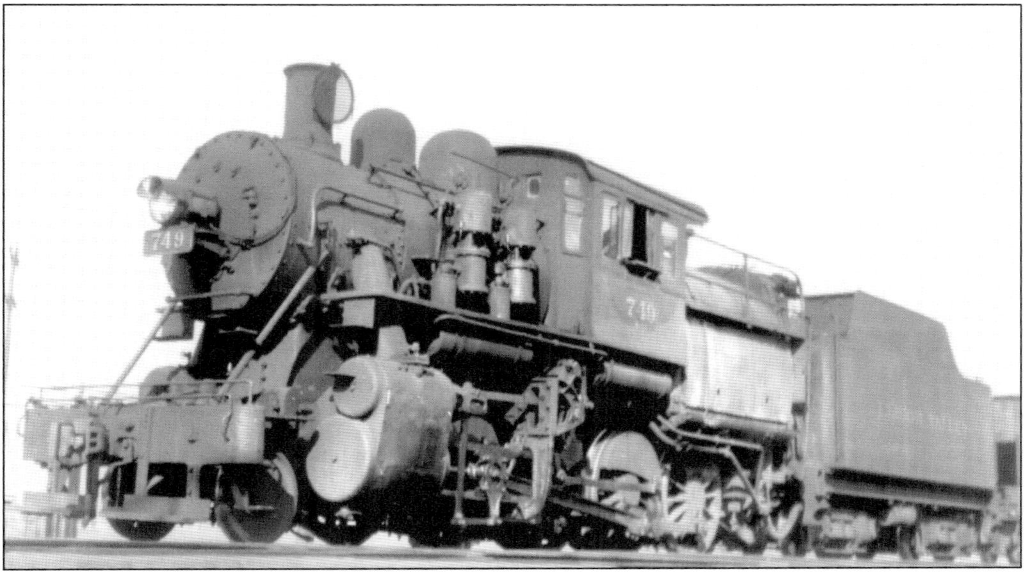

This low-angle photograph of camelback 2-8-0 No. 749 was taken at the yards in Perth Amboy in February 1940 and very nicely accentuates the bulk of these brutish BLW locomotives, built around the dawn of the 20th century and rebuilt just before World War I. (Photograph by John Brinckmann, courtesy of Joel Rosenbaum/Tom Gallo.)

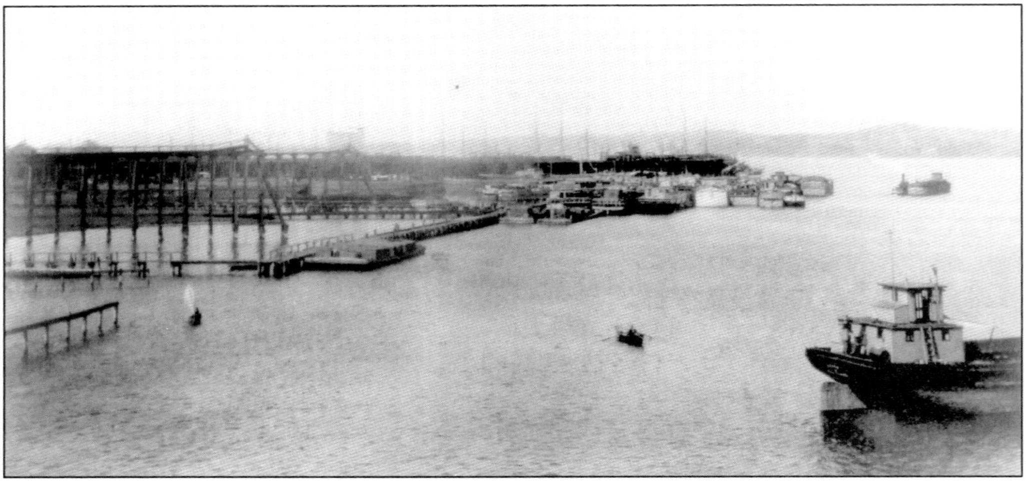

In this undated vintage photograph, the mass of coal barges can be seen lined up awaiting another load of black diamonds at the Perth Amboy coal wharves. The spindly looking trestle work on the left side of the photograph is the kickback tracks for the coal dumpers that were located here. (Courtesy of John Brinckmann.)

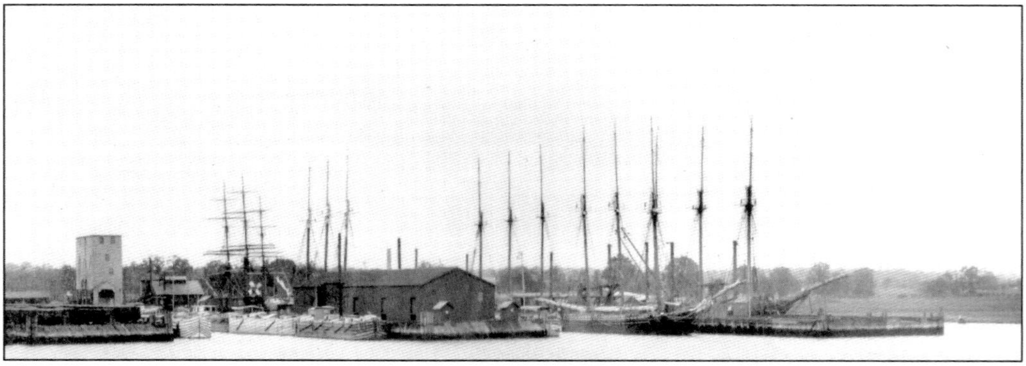

This 1895 view shows canal-type coal barges and large three-masted coal schooners laid up waiting to make another trip up the Arthur Kill and Kill Van Kull to New York Harbor. Note the apparently bucolic shoreline adjacent to this busy waterfront port, a far cry from what the area would become in the 20th century, At one time the waterfront here was considered a popular beach area. (Photograph by William H. Rau, courtesy of Theodore F. Gleichmann.)

Three

SOUTH PLAINFIELD TO NEWARK

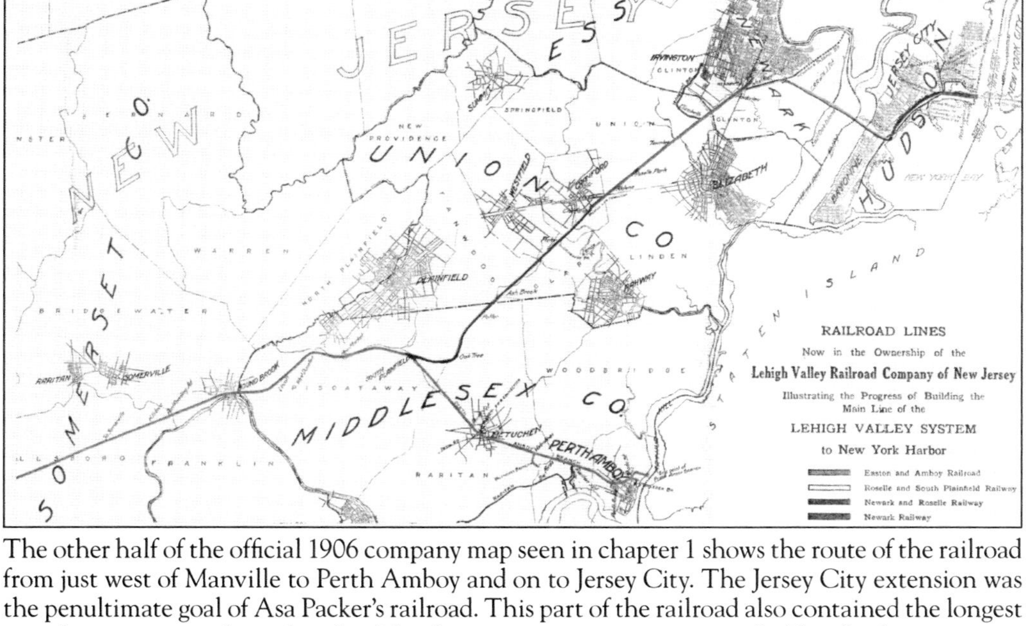

The other half of the official 1906 company map seen in chapter 1 shows the route of the railroad from just west of Manville to Perth Amboy and on to Jersey City. The Jersey City extension was the penultimate goal of Asa Packer's railroad. This part of the railroad also contained the longest straight tangent on the railroad in New Jersey, measuring approximately 12 miles from just east of Oak Tree (Edison) to Clark. (Courtesy of Ralph A. Heiss.)

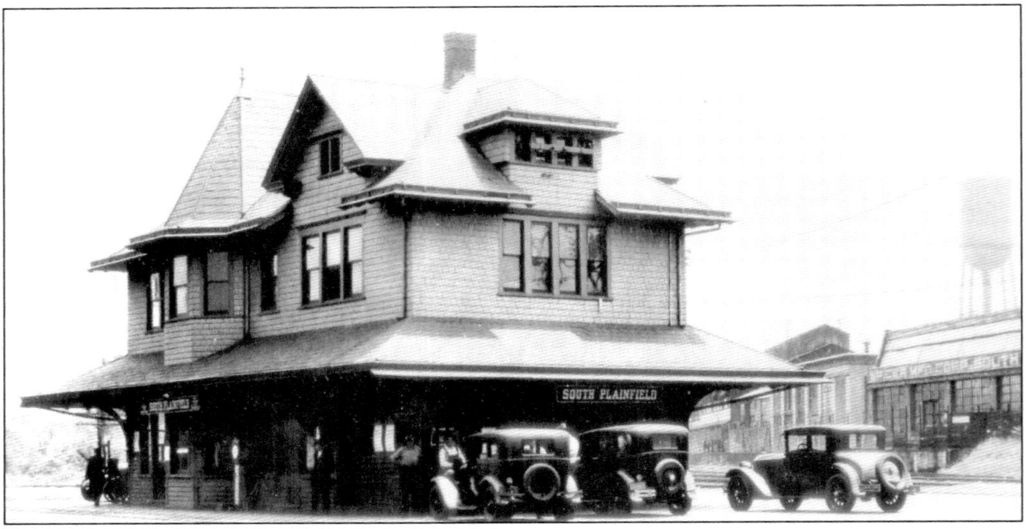

Returning to the main line at South Plainfield, this 1920s view of the South Plainfield station shows off the classic gabled rooflines of the building. Classic automobile fans will rejoice at the vehicles parked here, and the factory seen in the last chapter is seen here as occupied by its original owner, the Spicer Manufacturing Corporation, where the first automotive universal joint coupling for transmissions was manufactured. (Courtesy of H. G. MacDonald.)

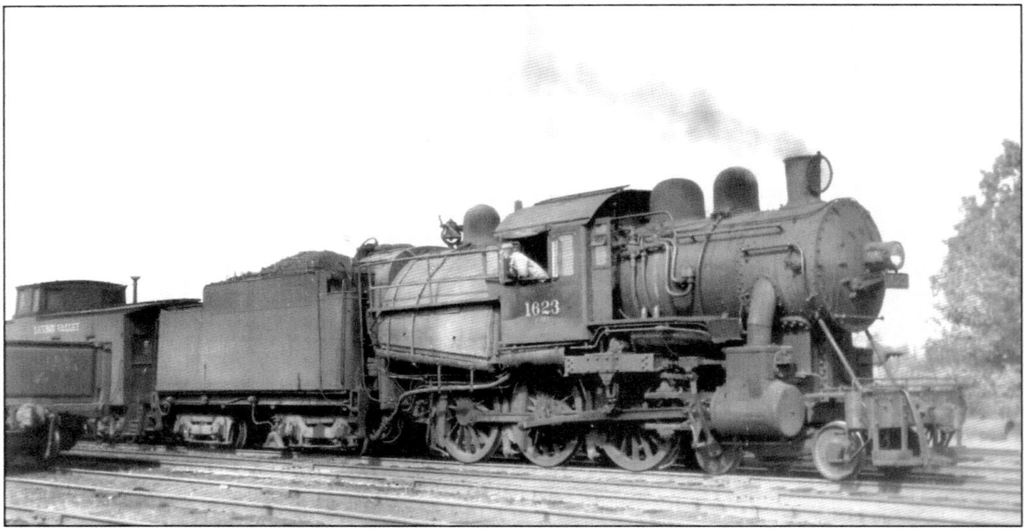

The 4-6-0 camelback No. 1623 shifts a caboose around the South Plainfield main line yard for placement on an outbound train on October 10, 1940. (Photograph by John Brinckmann, courtesy of Joel Rosenbaum/Tom Gallo.)

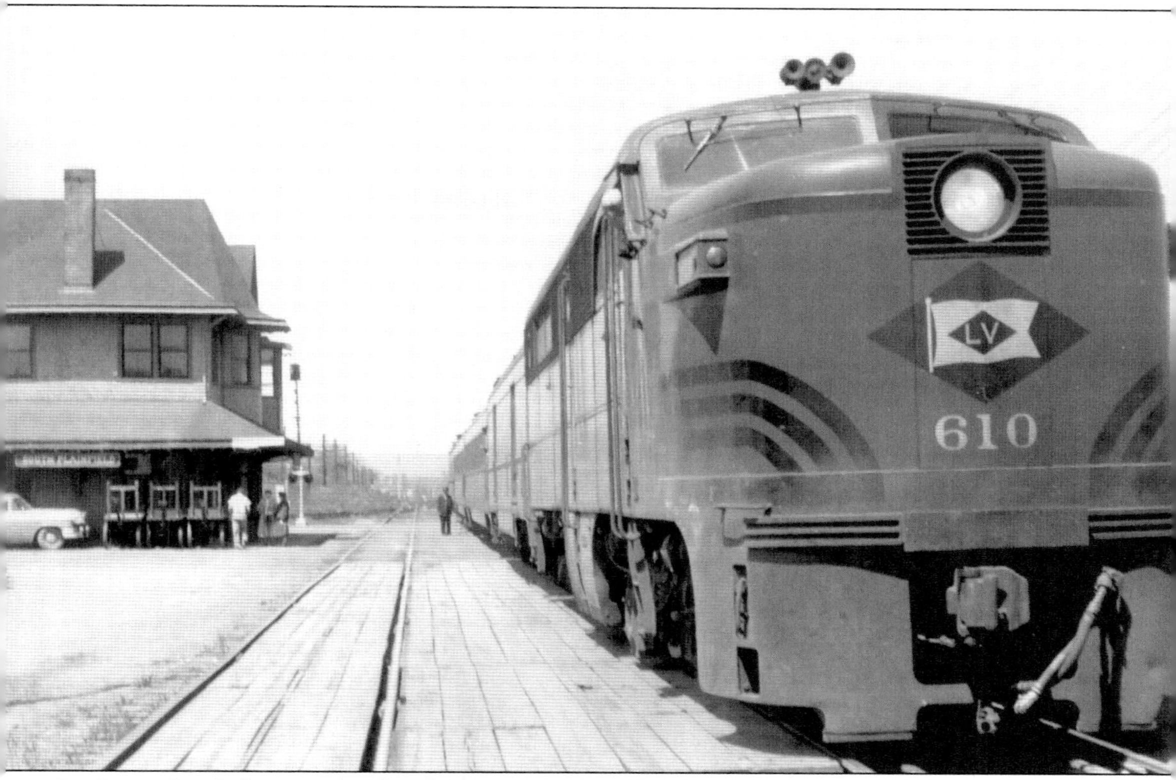

In this undated photograph taken looking west along the railroad, the engineer of PA-1 No. 610 looks back along his train for the signal from his conductor for the all clear to depart South Plainfield. Today this view has changed in more than one way. The Hamilton Boulevard bridge, which was constructed in 1974 to eliminate a grade crossing, cuts across the rear of this scene. The rustic South Plainfield station is also long gone, having been torn down in 1977. The station survives in spirit, however, as a lawyer's office in town was built to a very similar design, only a few blocks away from the original. (Courtesy of the North Jersey Electric Railway Historical Society.)

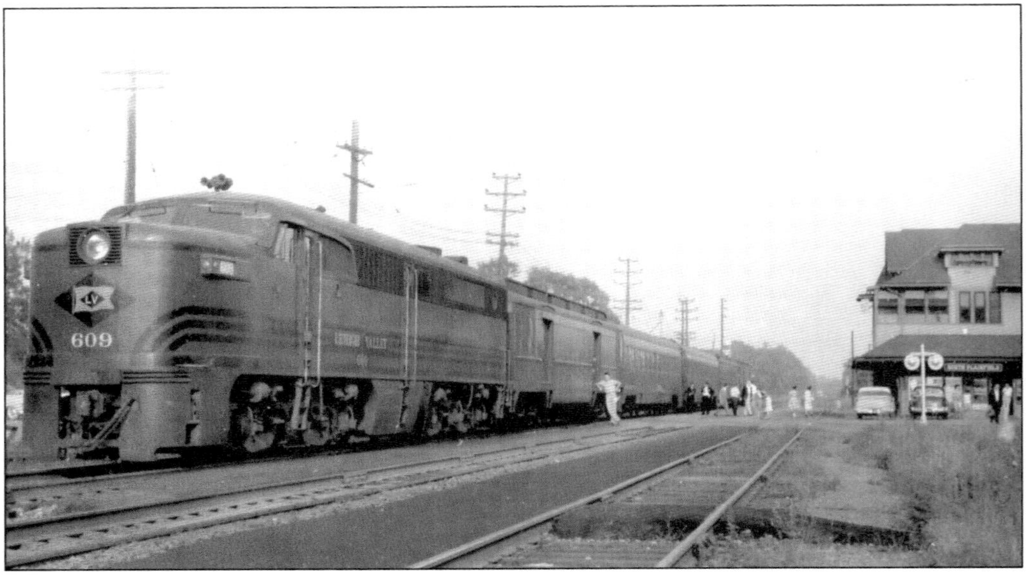

A westbound passenger train straddles the Hamilton Avenue grade crossing in this summer 1958 photograph during a station stop. All main line and local passenger trains stopped at South Plainfield until the cessation of service in 1961. (Courtesy of Robert Pennisi/Railroad Avenue Enterprises.)

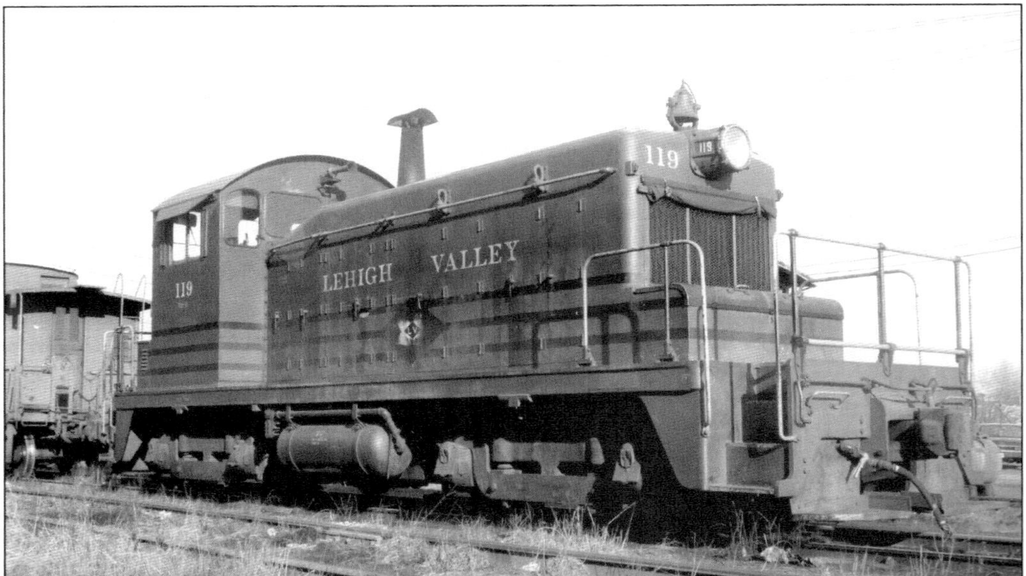

LVRR No. 119, an EMD model SW-1 diesel switcher, sits in the yard between assignments at South Plainfield on Pearl Harbor Day, December 7, 1968. (Courtesy of William Nixon.)

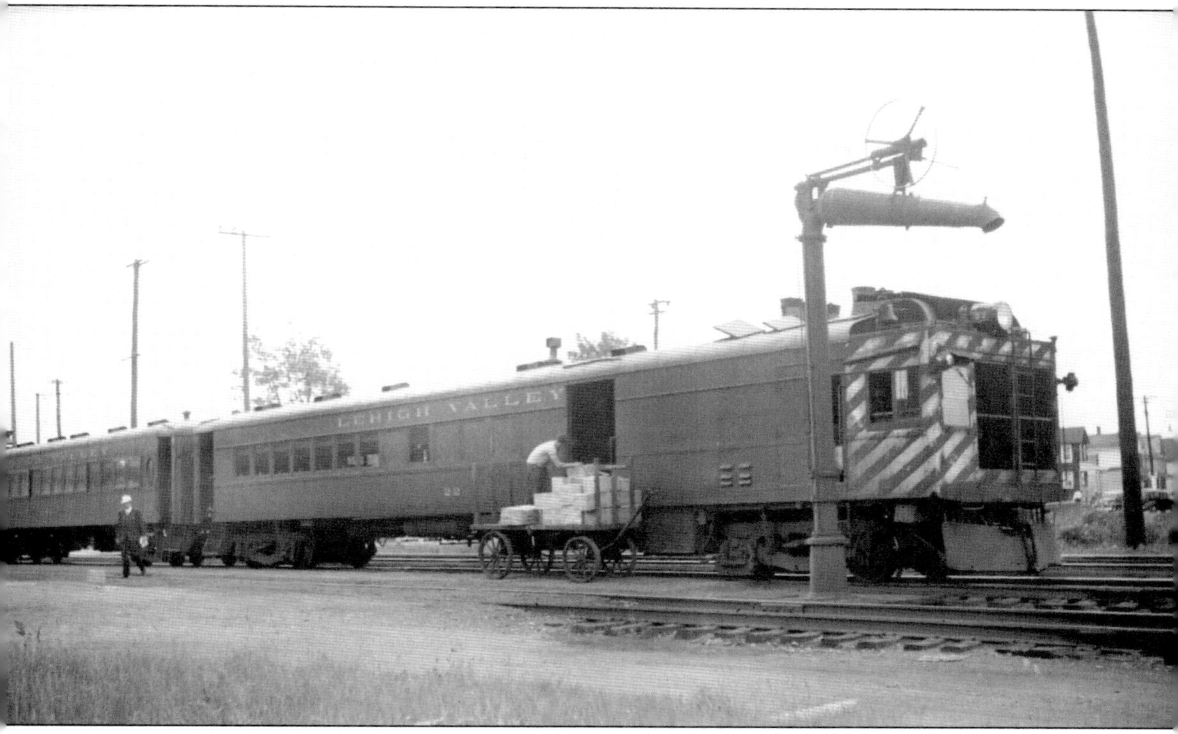

Gas-electric motor car No. 22, built by Osgood-Bradley in 1927, unloads some less-than-carload lot (LCL) freight during its South Plainfield stop in 1939. At one time, before services like UPS and FedEx, LCL freight delivery was the only way for people in rural areas to receive goods made in the city, and rural small-town life revolved around the local depot. Before going to the shopping mall was a quick ride in the family car, this was how a new washing machine, tractor, or rocking chair was delivered by way of the depot. (Photograph by John Brinckmann, courtesy of Joel Rosenbaum/Tom Gallo.)

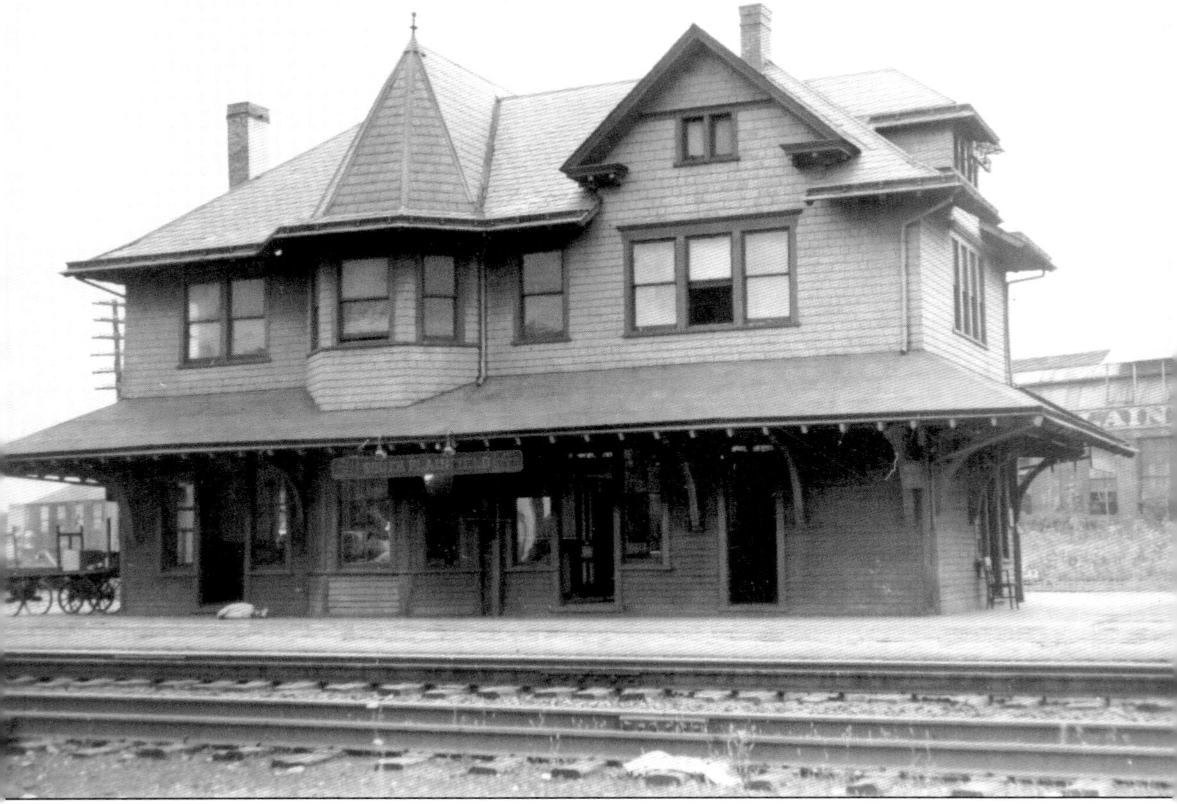

Here is another view of the South Plainfield station, taken in January 1950. The station seen here was built in 1892 when the E&A built northeast toward Jersey City. It was torn down in 1977 after years of deferred maintenance, as its services were no longer required after the LVRR had been absorbed into Conrail in 1976. It is truly a shame the station could not be saved to serve as a window to the past honoring a railroad that helped shape the town's development. (Courtesy of Richard Taylor.)

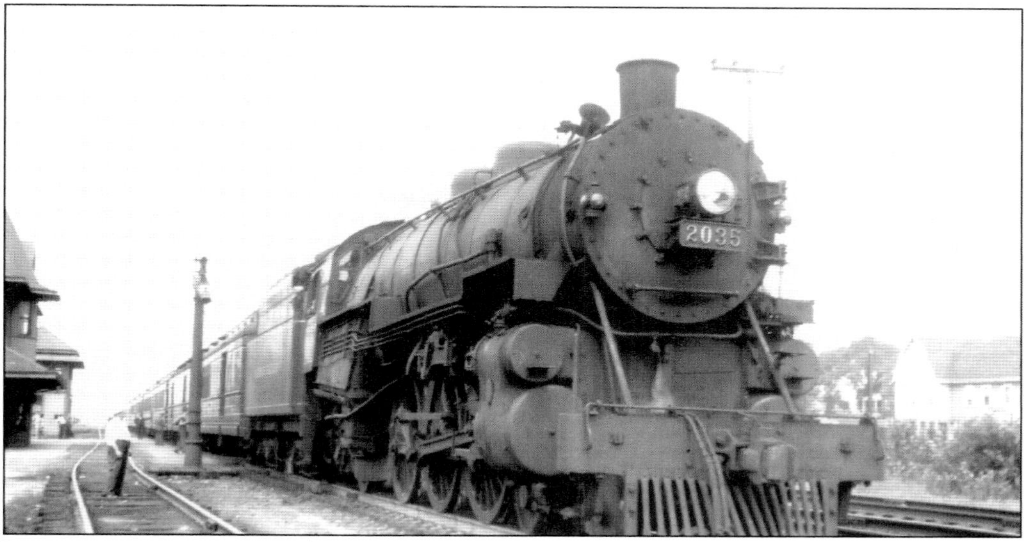

Locomotive No. 2035 is ready to depart town with train No. 28, the eastbound *John Wilkes*, on July 7, 1939. (Photograph by John Brinckmann, courtesy of Joel Rosenbaum/Tom Gallo.)

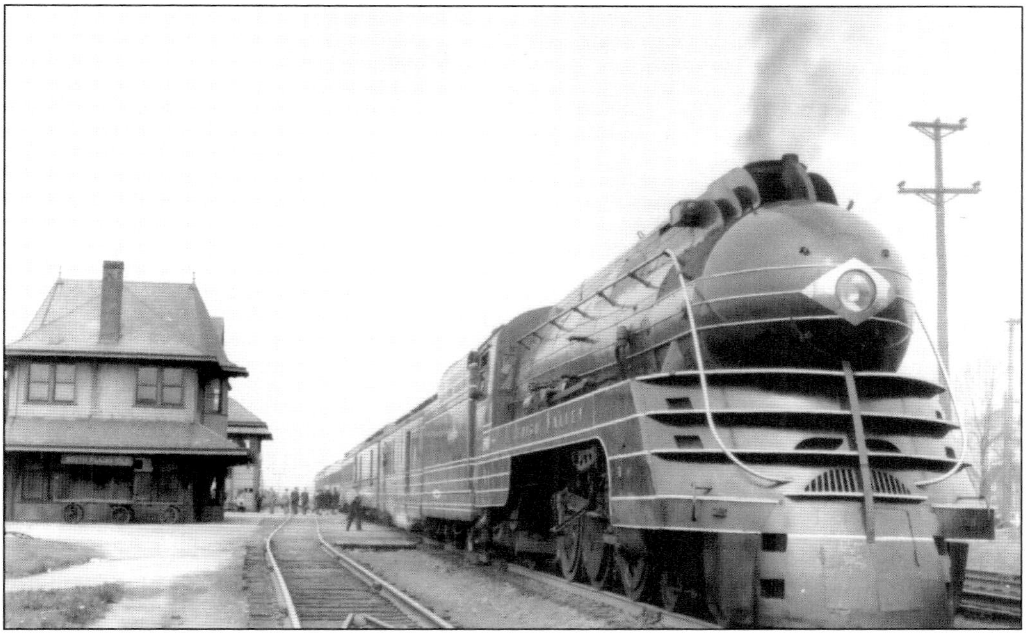

A year later, the *John Wilkes* is headed by handsomely streamlined 4-6-2 locomotive No. 2035 on May 18, 1940. Note that during the last year, the water plug at the end of the platform has been removed. (Photograph by John Brinckmann, courtesy of Joel Rosenbaum/Tom Gallo.)

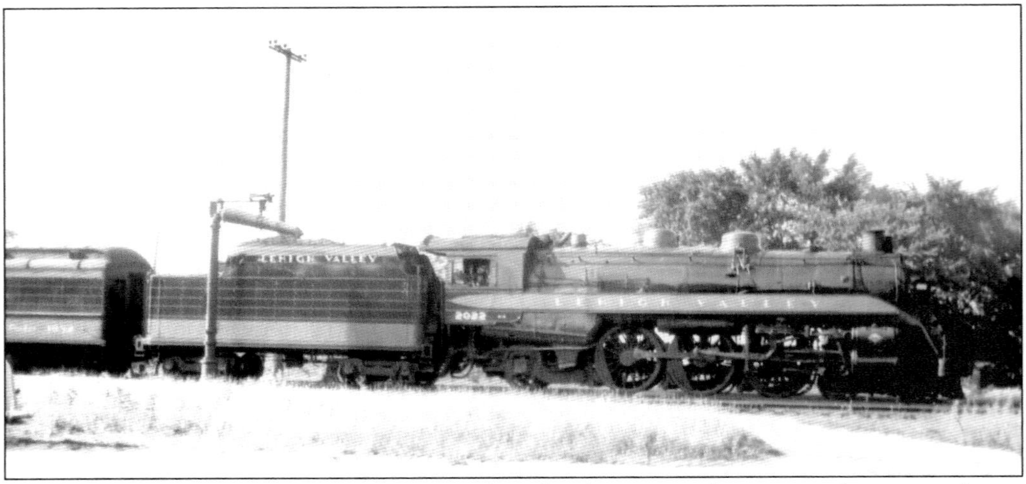

Stream-styled 4-6-2 No. 2022, fitted out to handle the *Asa Packer*, sits at the water plug at the South Plainfield station awaiting its departure time in July 1939. (Photograph by John Brinckmann, courtesy of Joel Rosenbaum/Tom Gallo.)

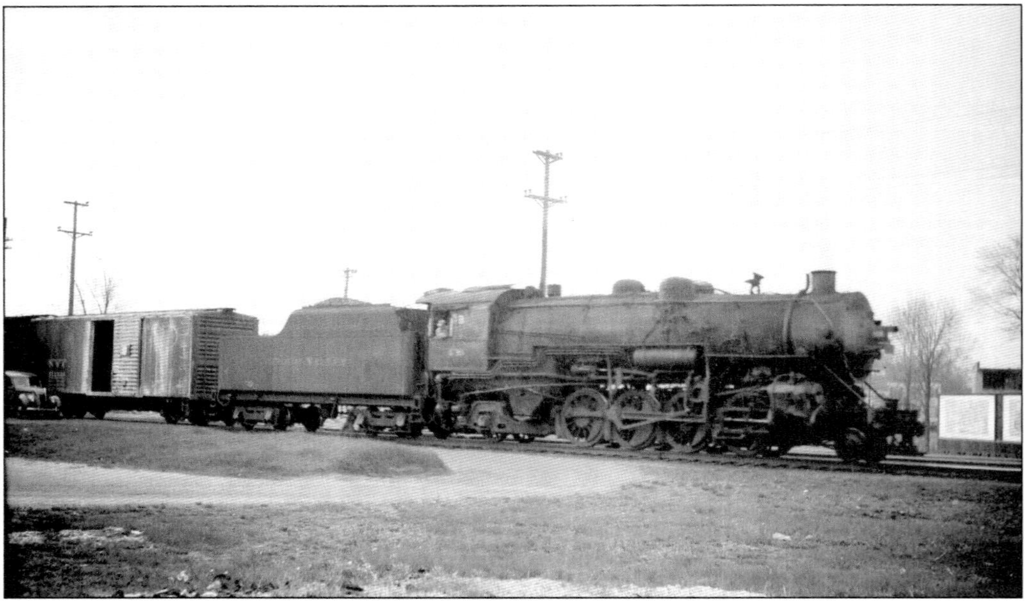

On May 8, 1940, locomotive No. 430, a rather beaten-looking N-4 class 2-8-2, is seen on a local freight train at South Plainfield. (Photograph by John Brinckmann, courtesy of Joel Rosenbaum/Tom Gallo.)

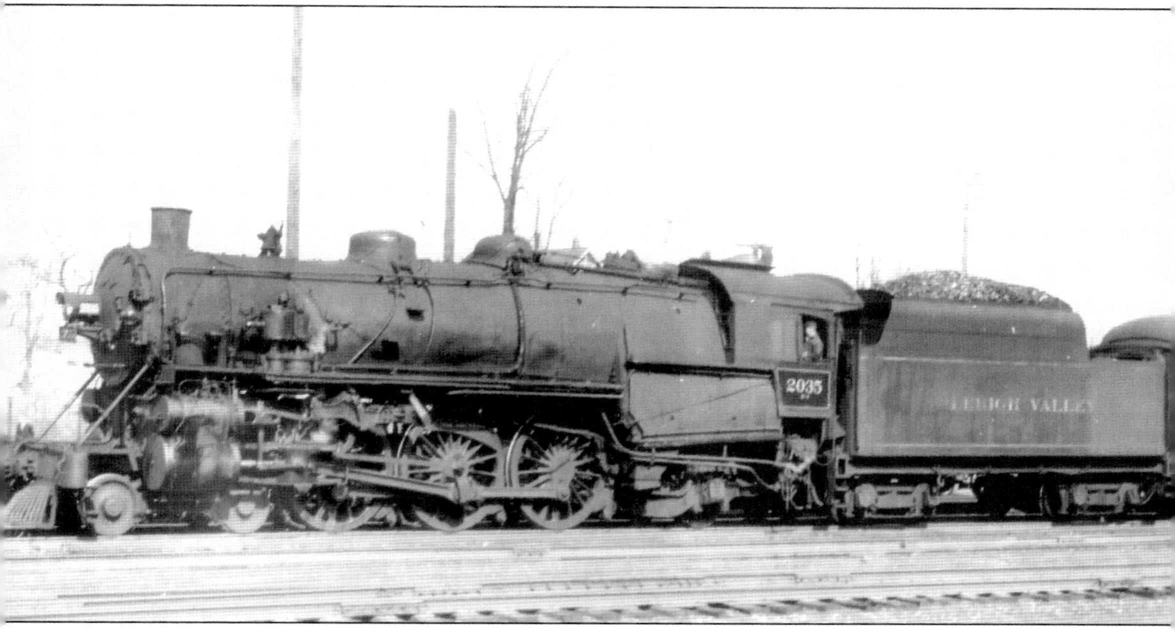

A 4-6-2 Pacific-type steam locomotive and final locomotive of the K-3 class gets ready to depart with a heaping tender full of coal for its four-and-a-half-hour journey westbound to Coxton, Pennsylvania, as it waits to proceed behind locomotive No. 2035 at South Plainfield with train No. 25, the *Asa Packer*, on March 3, 1940. The trains with purpose-built steam locomotives like the *Asa Packer*, *John Wilkes*, and *Black Diamond* did not always get to have their specific engines assigned to their trains, as breakdowns and scheduled maintenance could cause "regular" locomotives to have to pinch-hit for them at any given time. (Photograph by John Brinckmann, courtesy of Joel Rosenbaum/Tom Gallo.)

LEHIGH VALLEY RAILROAD COMPANY

Jersey City, N.J. March 10, 1958.

ALL TOWERMEN:

It has become the practice of some Towermen in the performance of their duties to be lax in reporting trains and the change of weather conditions as they occur at the various locations.

I wish to call your attention to Rules 222 and 803 in the Book Of Rules governing the conditions outlined above and caution all concerned that the rules quoted above, as well as other rules governing Towermen, must be complied with at all times.

There is no excuse of any kind that can be offered by any Towermen for their failure to comply with the rules quoted above, as well as all rules under which they are governed.

R.C.BECKER

Supervising Agent

Company memorandums from the management are nothing new, as evidenced by this official company bulletin dated March 10, 1958. Posted all over the railroad where employees of the operations department were sure to see it, it warns employees who man the interlocking towers to make sure they report any trains "on sheet" (OS) as they pass their locations as well as any weather changes in accordance with the company rule book. It was very important to get this information to the chief dispatcher on a timely basis so he could plan his next move and avoid any traffic tie-ups or, even worse, accidents. Across New Jersey alone, there were five such interlocking towers. (Courtesy of Ralph A. Heiss.)

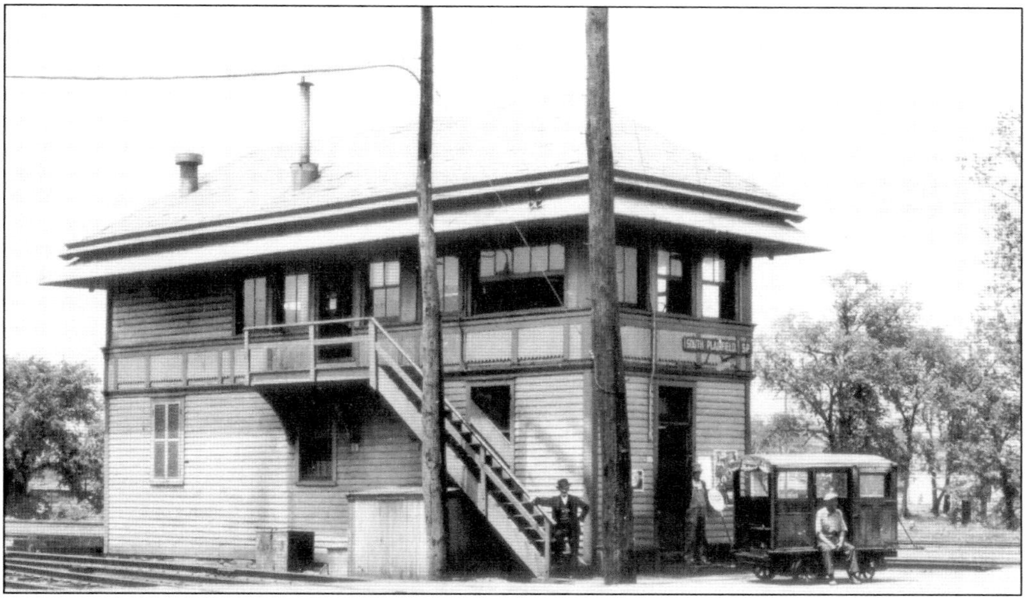

It is very possible that one of the towers addressed by that letter was the South Plainfield tower seen in this photograph, taken sometime in the 1920s. The interlocking tower guarded the junction of the main line and the Perth Amboy branch. It was later moved inside the station building in 1953, and the tower was torn down not long afterward. (Courtesy of H. G. MacDonald.)

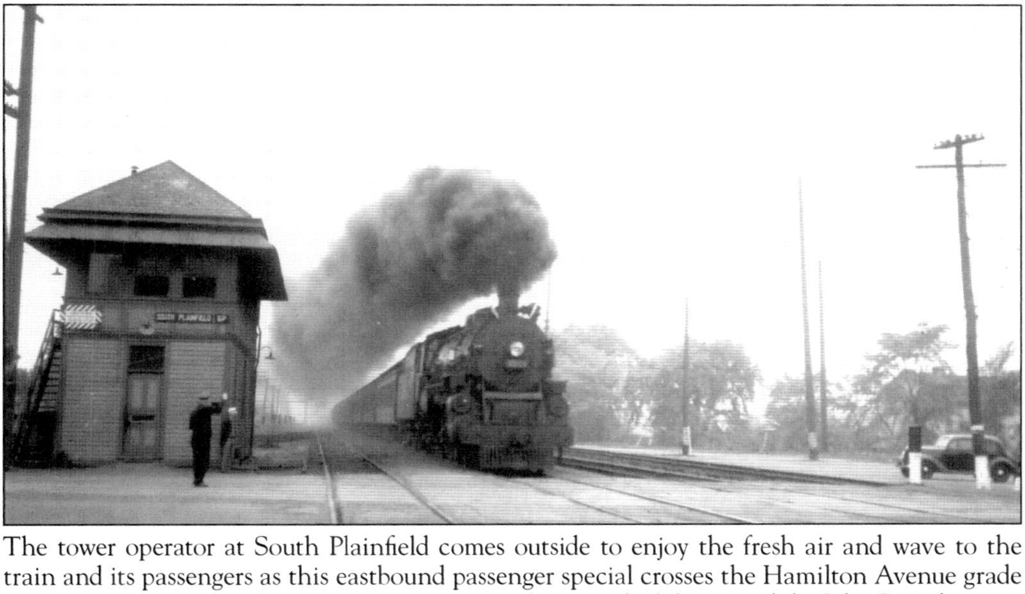

The tower operator at South Plainfield comes outside to enjoy the fresh air and wave to the train and its passengers as this eastbound passenger special crosses the Hamilton Avenue grade crossing at a high rate of speed in this May 1939 photograph. (Photograph by John Brinckmann, courtesy of Joel Rosenbaum/Tom Gallo.)

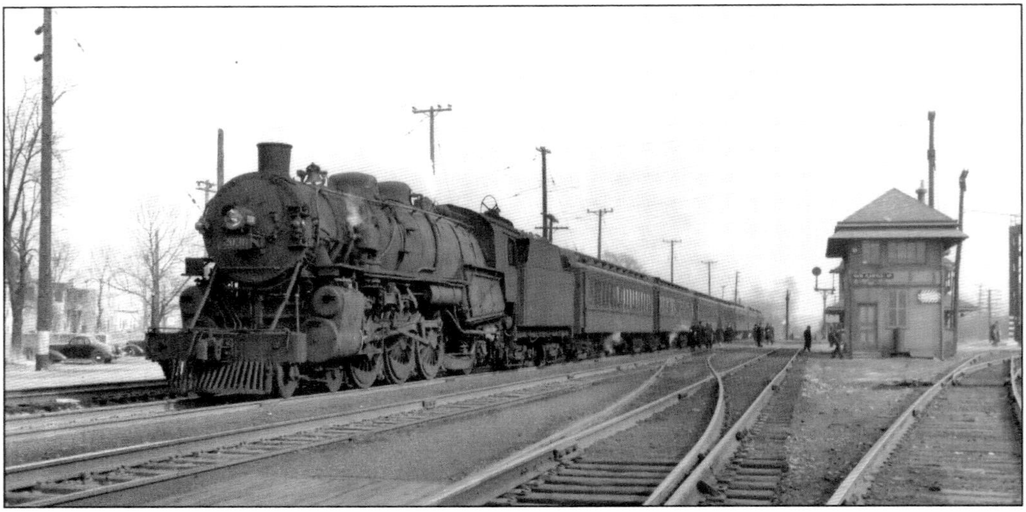

Its train time on a February morning in 1939 as people get ready to board train No. 31, a Saturday-only train to Pittston, Pennsylvania. By this time the following year, the train would be cut back to Mauch Chunk (Jim Thorpe), Pennsylvania, and by 1949 off the schedule for good. (Photograph by George Votava, courtesy of Joel Rosenbaum/Tom Gallo.)

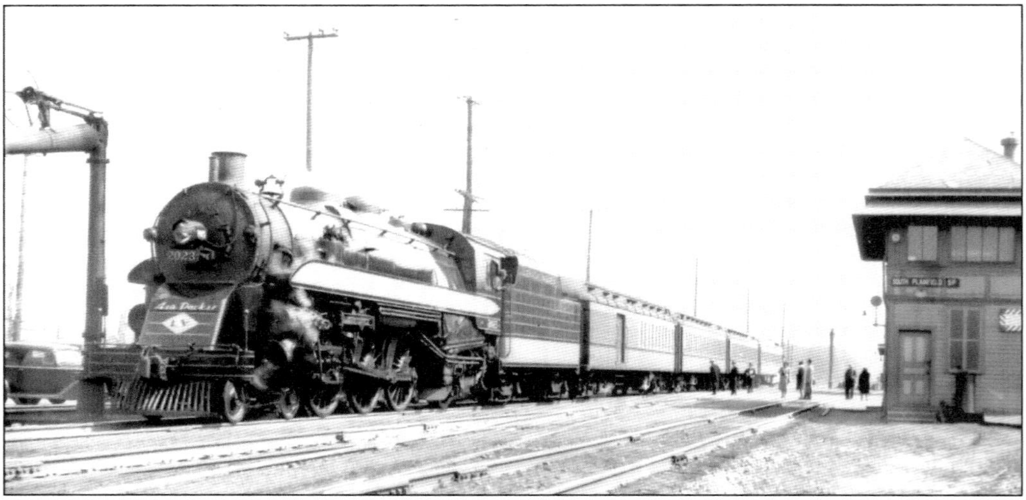

The westbound *Asa Packer*, resplendent in its flashy orange and black paint scheme, gets ready for departure on March 3, 1939. The *Asa Packer* proved to be a resounding success for boosting the railroad's dying passenger service and ran for 20 years before being discontinued. (Photograph by John Brinckmann, courtesy of Joel Rosenbaum/Tom Gallo.)

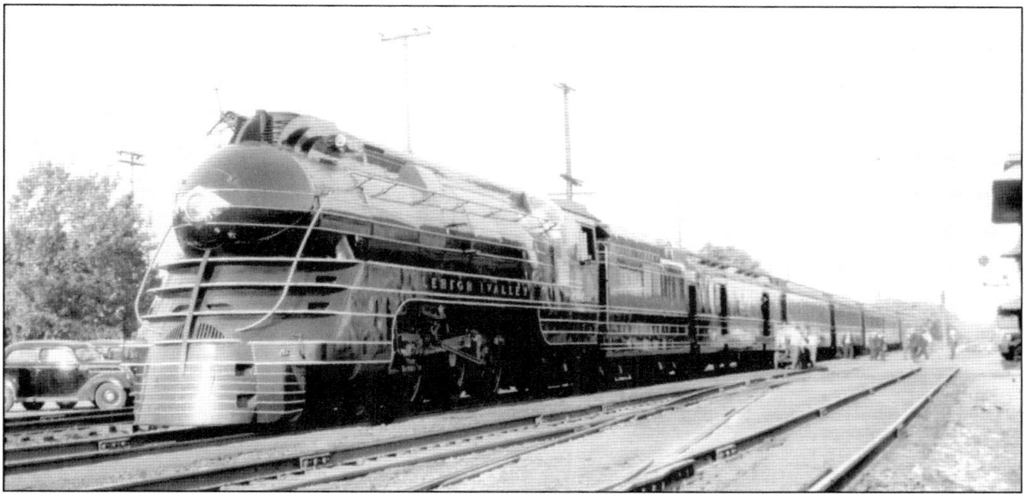

This early summer of 1939 view shows the *John Wilkes* making its stop to unload its cargo, both human and otherwise, at the South Plainfield station. The *John Wilkes* was scheduled to arrive at South Plainfield at 5:37 p.m. daily except Sundays, traveling westbound. (Photograph by John Brinckmann, courtesy of Joel Rosenbaum/Tom Gallo.)

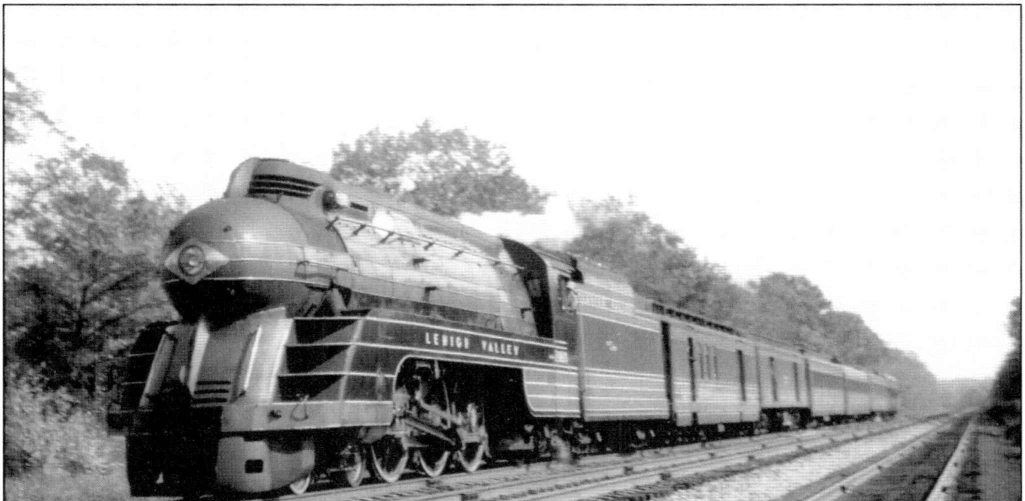

The westbound *Black Diamond* is seen here breaking hard for its 7:49 a.m. station stop at South Plainfield in 1940. It appears the skirting on the *Black Diamond*'s baggage car does not quite match the rest of the train. (Photograph by John Brinckmann, courtesy of Joel Rosenbaum/Tom Gallo.)

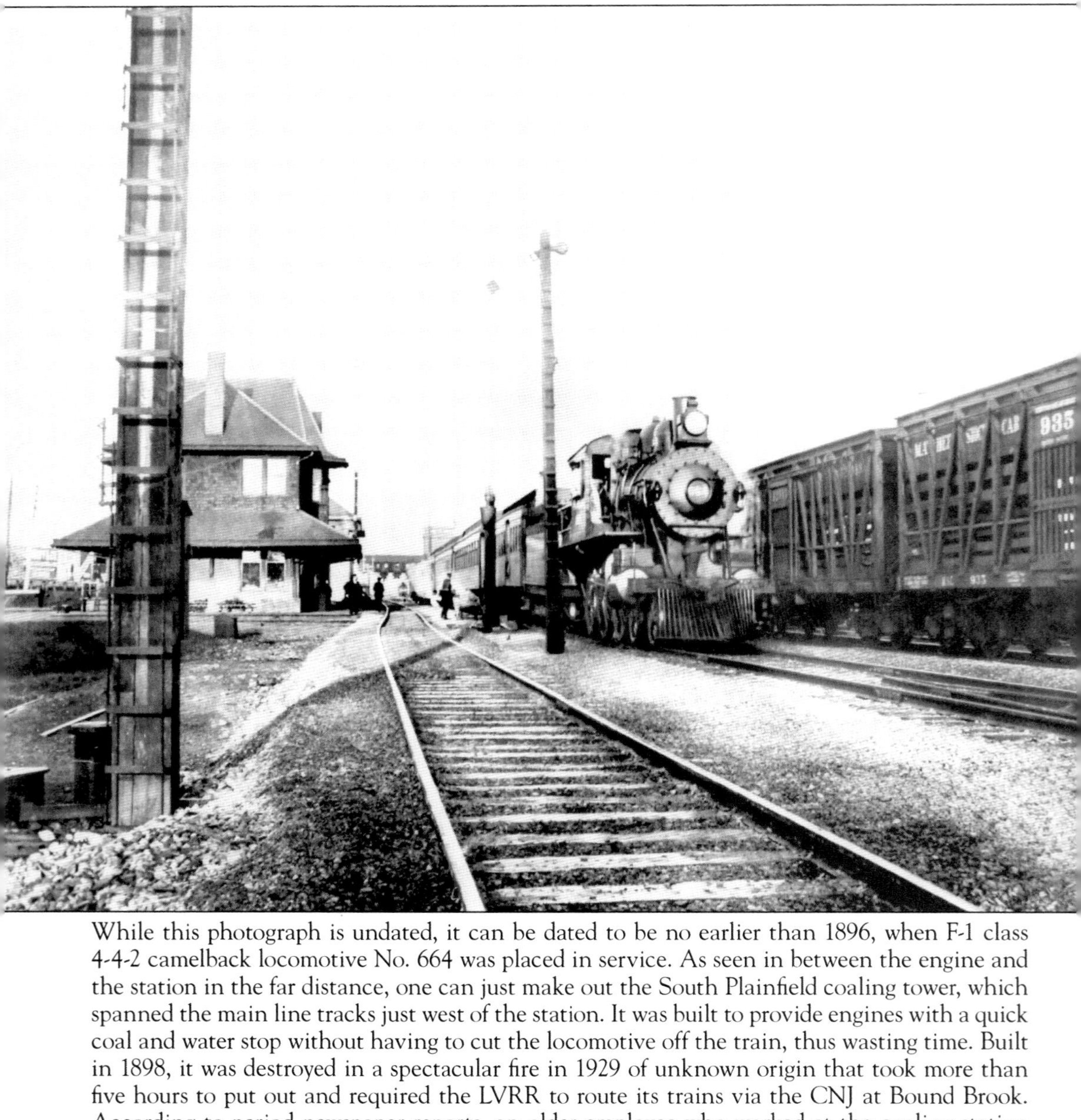

While this photograph is undated, it can be dated to be no earlier than 1896, when F-1 class 4-4-2 camelback locomotive No. 664 was placed in service. As seen in between the engine and the station in the far distance, one can just make out the South Plainfield coaling tower, which spanned the main line tracks just west of the station. It was built to provide engines with a quick coal and water stop without having to cut the locomotive off the train, thus wasting time. Built in 1898, it was destroyed in a spectacular fire in 1929 of unknown origin that took more than five hours to put out and required the LVRR to route its trains via the CNJ at Bound Brook. According to period newspaper reports, an older employee who worked at the coaling station went home despondent over the prospect of losing his job and committed suicide. (Courtesy of Theodore F. Gleichmann Jr.)

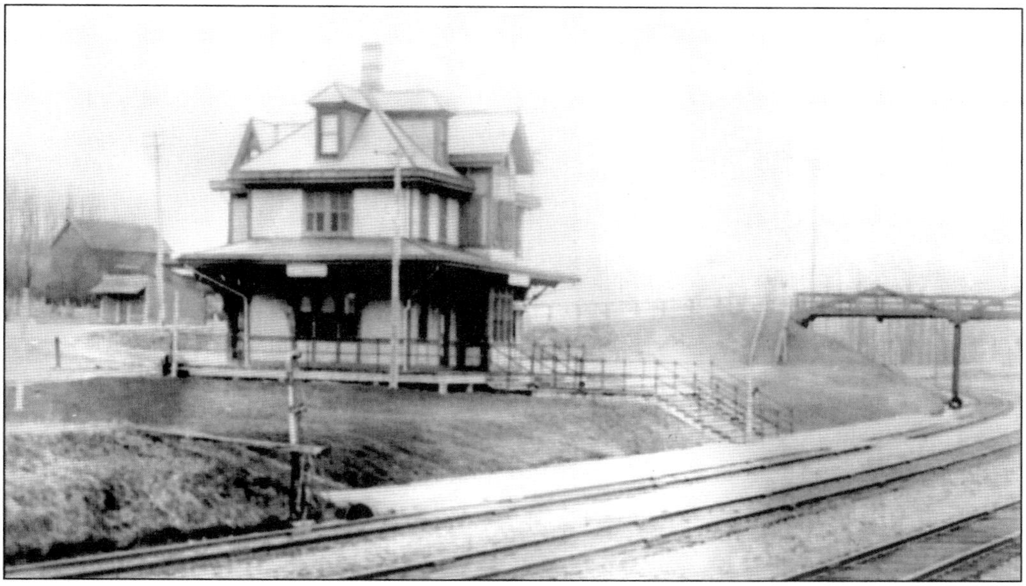

In this rare undated view of the Oak Tree station, one can see the bridge carrying Oak Tree Road over the railroad, on the eastern border of South Plainfield and Edison. The bridge is still in place today, although replaced with a modern steel span. (Courtesy of John Brinckmann.)

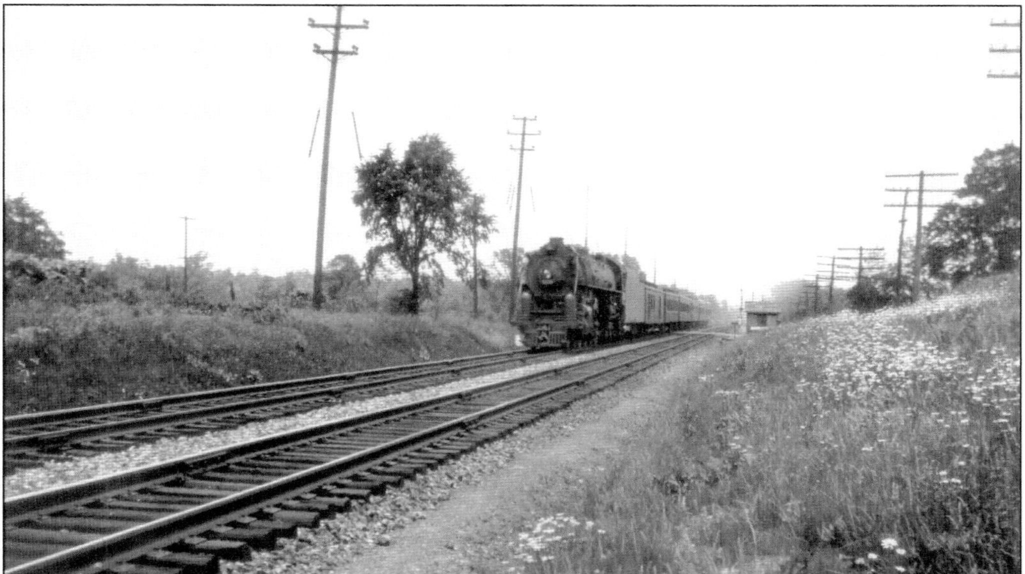

The *Black Diamond* rolls westbound at Goodmans Crossing behind T-3 class 4-8-4 No. 5127 on June 5, 1935. Located in Scotch Plains, the road bearing the location's name remains to this day, although a bridge over the railroad has long since replaced the crossing itself. (Photograph by John Brinckmann, courtesy of Joel Rosenbaum/Tom Gallo.)

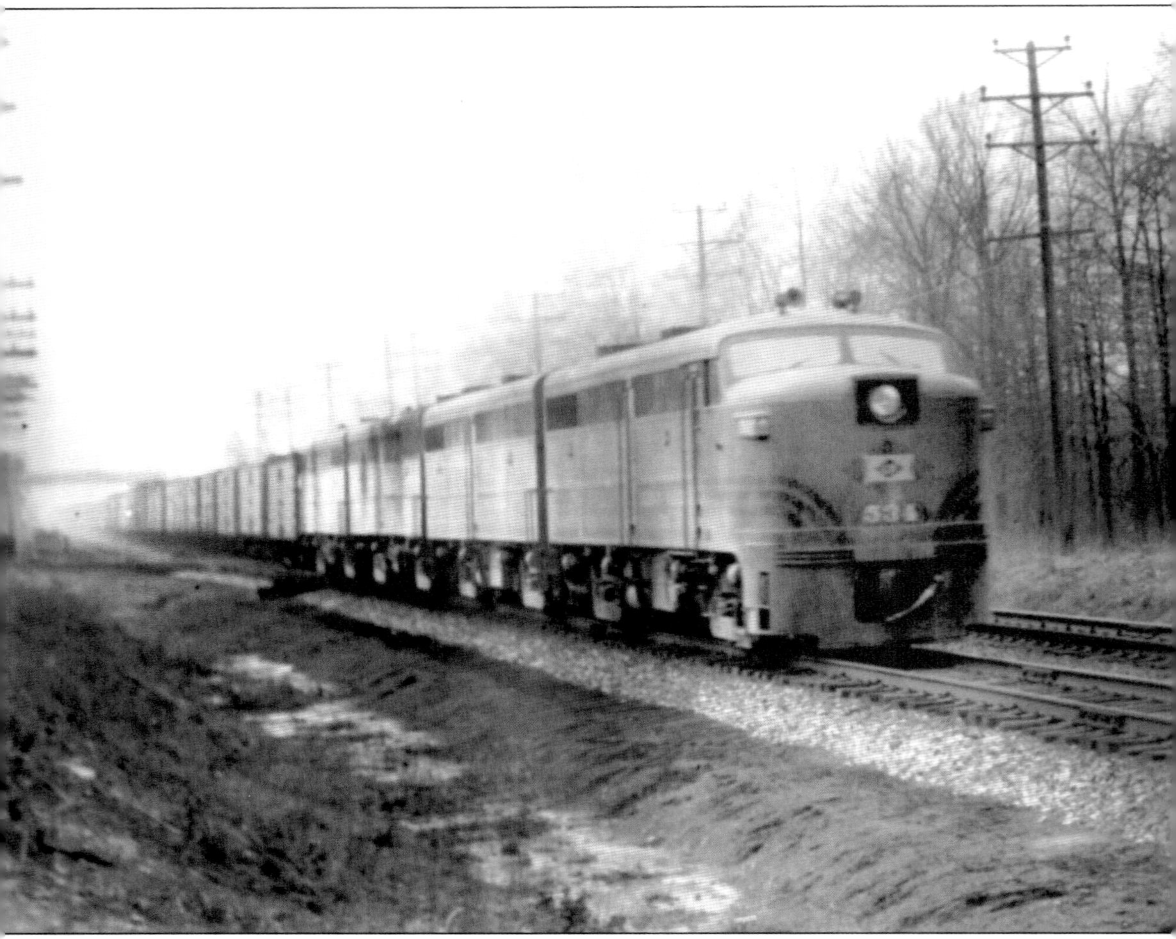

FA-1 diesel locomotive No. 534 leads a matched A-B-B-A set eastbound through Clark in this view from the 1950s. Just above the second and third cars in the train can be seen the steeple of the Clark train station, which was located near the Central Avenue bridge on the north side of the tracks. When the railroad was built through here in 1890, Clark was then known as Picton and was so referred to in railroad employee timetables until at least the early 1940s. The switch leading to the left just under the last diesel unit is the Bloodgood branch, which was originally built to reach the Taylor and Bloodgood Felt Mill and later served the plants of Hyatt Roller Bearing and United States Gypsum (USG). Today the branch sees sporadic service to the USG plant, the only remaining customer on the branch after the Hyatt plant was closed in 1987. (Courtesy of William Caloroso/ Cal's Classics.)

tember 24, 1950 September 24, 1

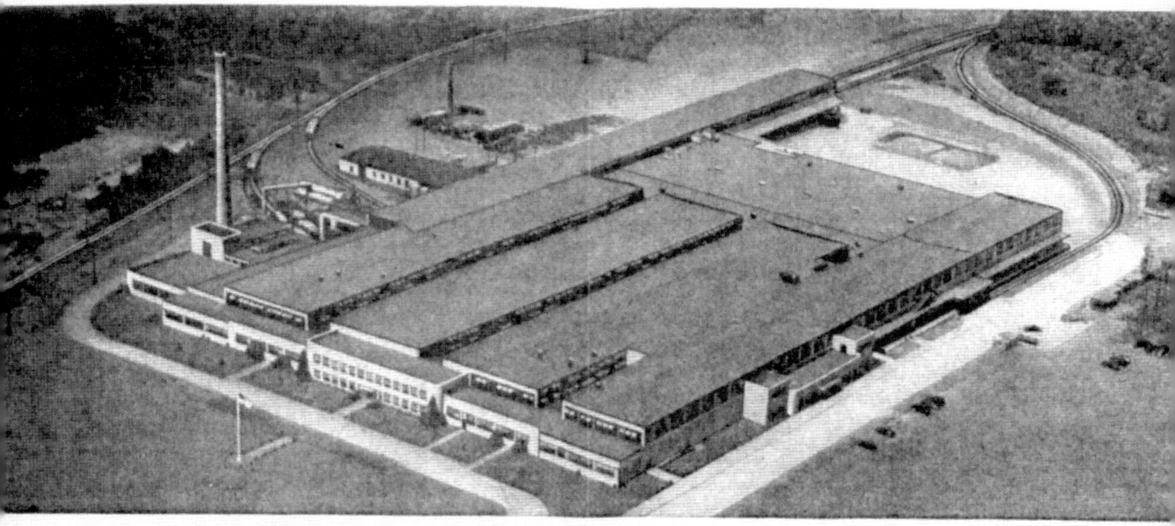

Hyatt Bearings Division—General Motors Corporation
Clark Township, N. J.

THE Clark Township plant of the Hyatt Bearings Division of General Motors Corporation is located on an eighty-four acre site served by Lehigh Valley Railroad. It is completely modern in design and equipment, occupying 427,000 square feet of floor space for the manufacture of precision roller bearings used in automotive, agricultural and industrial applications, as well as roller bearing journal boxes for railroad locomotives and passenger cars.

There are other desirable industrial sites available along the Lehigh Valley Railroad. Manufacturers and distributors seeking information regarding plant or warehouse locations will receive prompt and efficient attention by communicating with:

E. F. NEAGLE, General Development Agent
LEHIGH VALLEY RAILROAD
143 Liberty Street, New York 6, N. Y. Phone BArclay 7-5400

The LVRR liked to use the inside gatefold of its public timetables to inform the public about important new services or improvements to the railroad like passenger train services or even brand-new tugboats. Even customers along the railroad, both old and new alike, were no exception. In this advertisement, seen here taken from the September 1950 timetable, an artist's rendering of the Hyatt Roller Bearing plant can be seen. Built in 1938, the plant was a subsidiary of General Motors and produced automotive roller bearings. After sitting abandoned during most of the 1990s, today the property has been safely remediated with tons of clean, new soil, and in its place, the Hyatt Hills Golf Complex was built in 2002, which includes a nine-hole golf course, a driving range, and two miniature golf courses. (Courtesy of Ralph A. Heiss.)

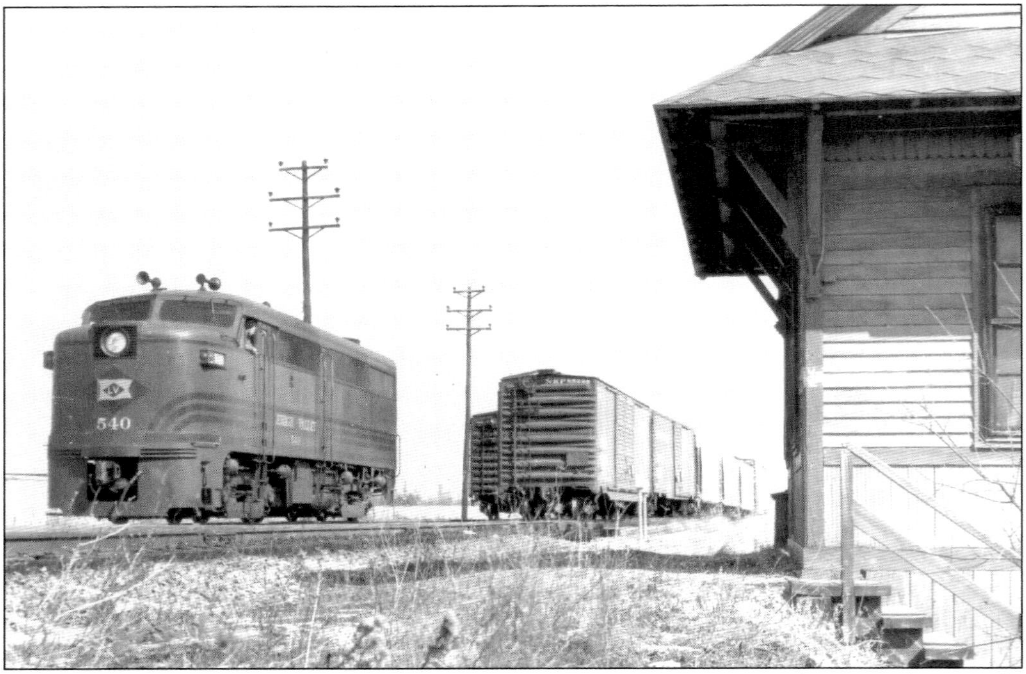

At Cranford, FA-1 No. 540 is seen switching at Staten Island Junction in this 1963 photograph. This is where the Baltimore and Ohio Railroad's Staten Island Rapid Transit Railway subsidiary from St. George, Staten Island, interchanged with the LVRR. This was also the location of the connection to the CNJ main line, built in 1888 when the Roselle and South Plainfield Railway was constructed by the LVRR as it built toward Jersey City. (Photograph by Don Walworth.)

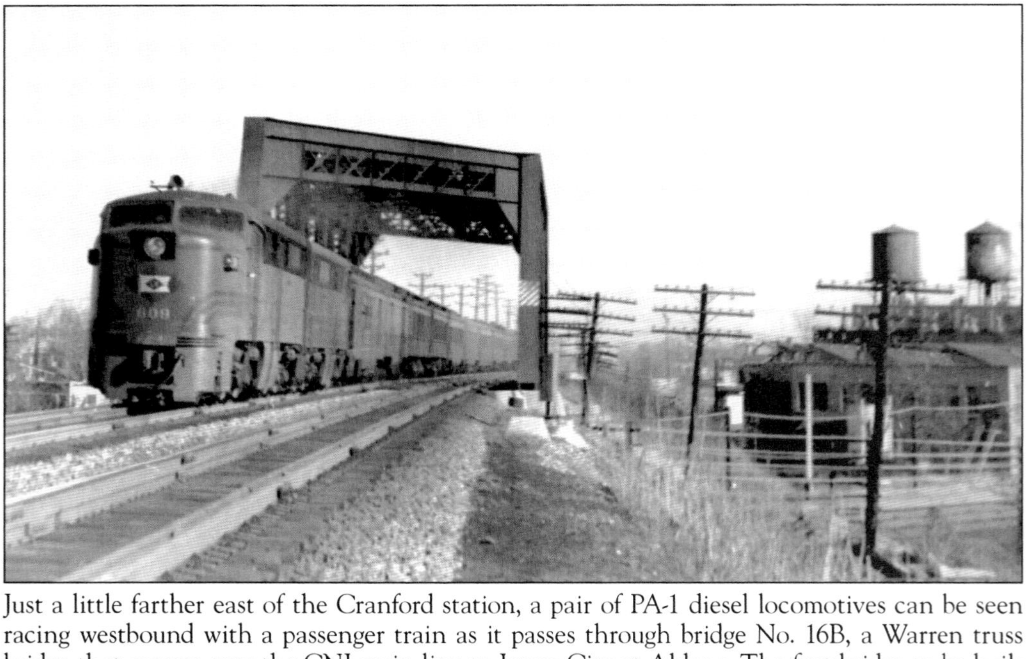

Just a little farther east of the Cranford station, a pair of PA-1 diesel locomotives can be seen racing westbound with a passenger train as it passes through bridge No. 16B, a Warren truss bridge that crosses over the CNJ main line to Jersey City at Aldene. The first bridge to be built here was constructed by the Newark and Roselle Railway in 1890 as the LVRR built eastward toward Newark. (Courtesy of William Caloroso/Cal's Classics.)

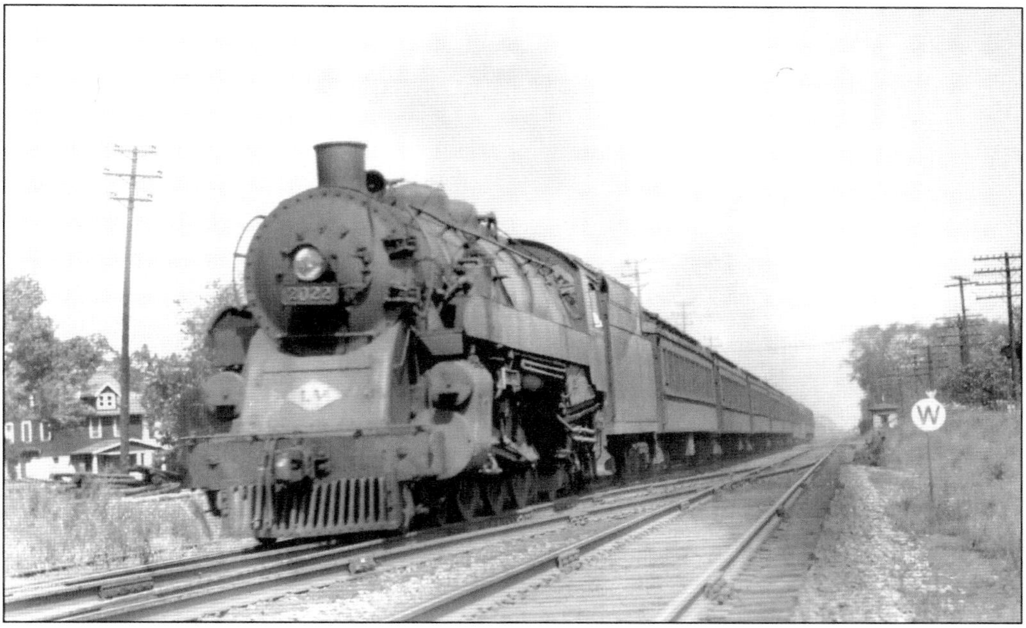

Steam locomotive No. 2022 races westbound with the *Asa Packer* as it crosses the Chestnut Street grade crossing in Roselle Park. Today this scene is very different, as the tracks in this location were placed on a fill during a grade-elimination project built in conjunction with the consolidation of the CNJ commuter service over the LVRR main line between Aldene and Newark in 1967. (Courtesy of Gene Collora.)

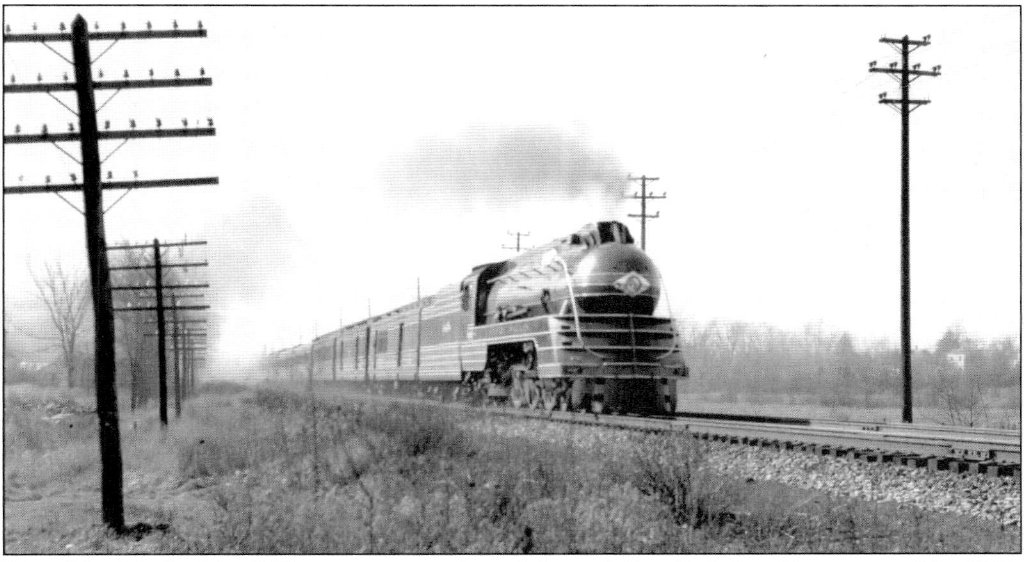

Train No. 28, the *John Wilkes*, steams westbound through Roselle behind locomotive No. 2102, just west of the passenger station at Chestnut Street. The Roselle Park station is just ahead and to the left of the train in this undated photograph. (Photograph by George Votava, courtesy of Joel Rosenbaum/Tom Gallo.)

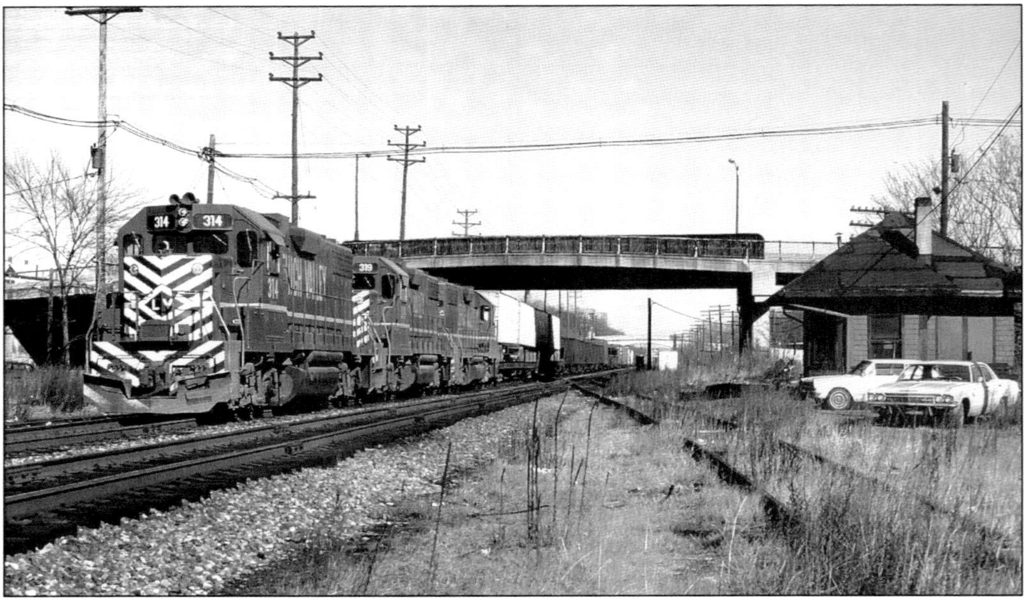

At Hillside, train NE-1 heads east behind three GP38-2 locomotives, led by No. 314 on February 2, 1975. The Irvington branch connected to the main line here via a wye. In 1915, the railroad operated a token commuter service on the branch between the station seen here and Clinton Avenue in Irvington. However, the more convenient public service streetcar service and the LVRR's own desire to schedule the service to be as inconvenient as possible to the public good caused the service to be unprofitable, and it was discontinued within six months. (Photograph by Richard Taylor.)

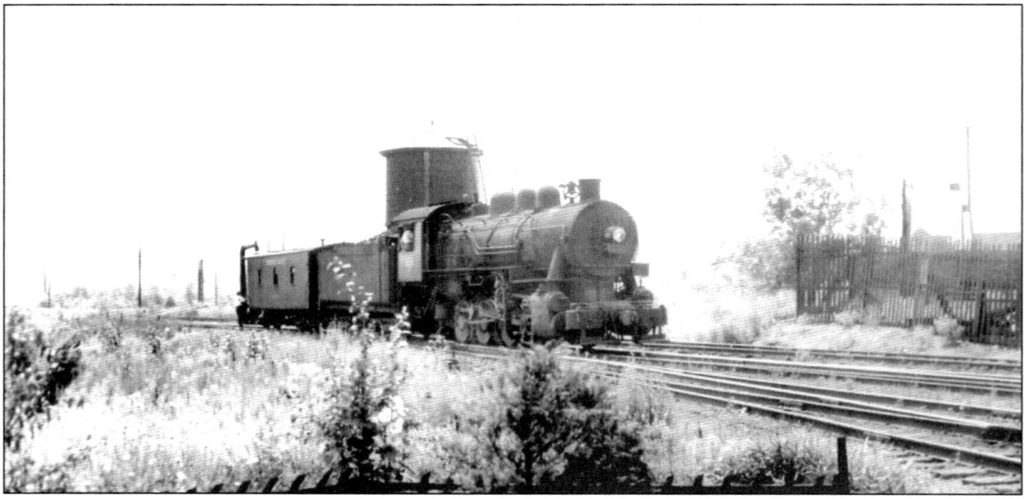

In this photograph, an unidentified 0-8-0 and its transfer caboose work the Irvington branch around 1945. Completed in 1905, the branch ran 2.9 miles, not including sidings. Although the area around Hillside and Irvington was heavily populated even in 1945, there was still a lot of open space than compared to today. The railroad helped to make the Hillside/Irvington area, known as "the Farm" by railroad men, in the early 1900s attractive to large industries. (Courtesy of Robert F. Guthlein/Theodore F. Gleichmann Jr.)

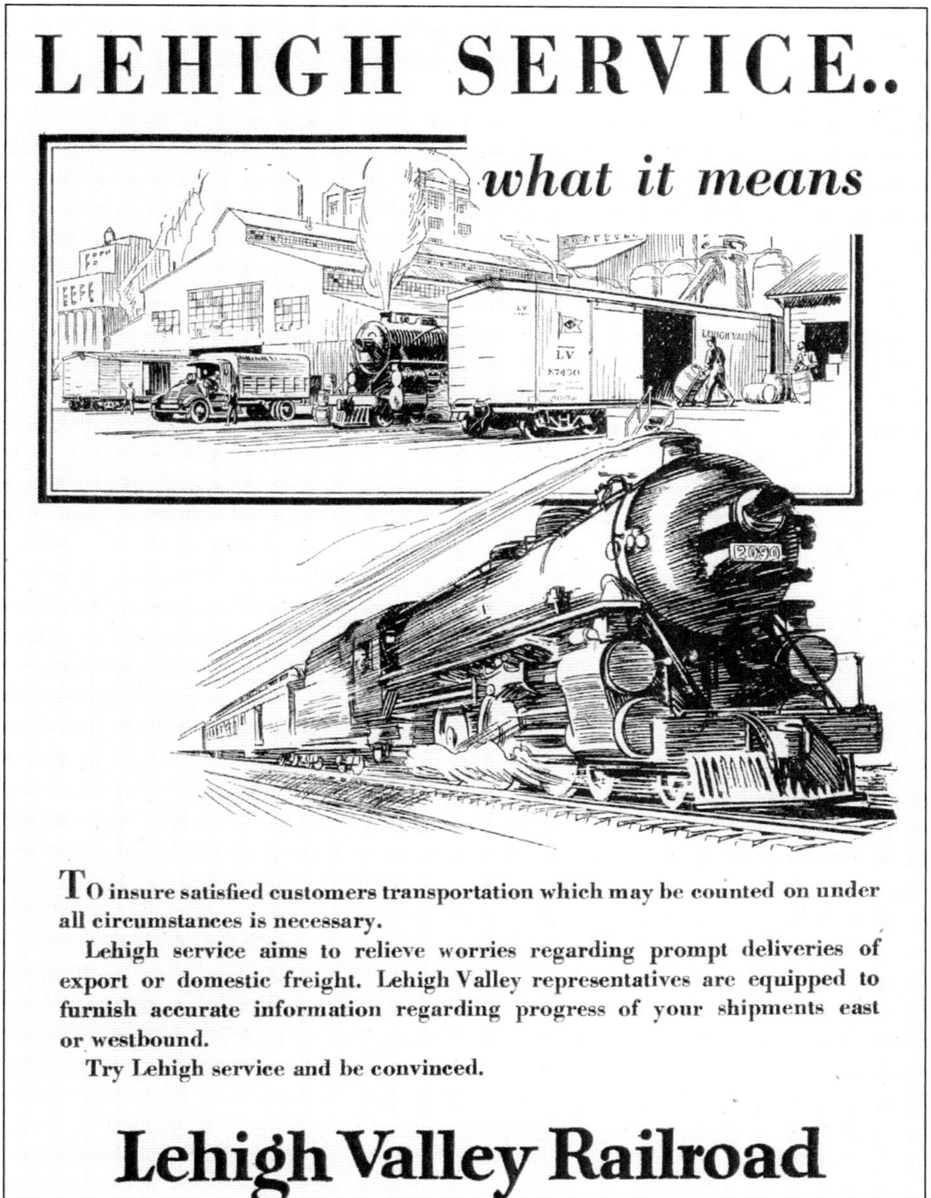

Just as in its timetables, the LVRR would also take out advertising space in trade publications like *Railway Age* to showcase particular companies that were located on the railroad, so as to convince prospective customers that the LVRR was the best railroad to do business with. In a supersaturated railroad market such as the New Jersey–New York metropolitan area, any advantage was an important one, and in the 1950s, railroads like the CNJ and LVRR bought large parcels of land to develop as industrial parks on land that was not considered suitable for much else. This 1929 advertisement really goes all out to prove to the customer that the LVRR is the last word in service and dependability. Unfortunately for the railroad, the industries it tried so hard to woo to build along its tracks would end up moving out of the state starting in the 1960s, contributing to the railroad's already declining revenues. (Courtesy of Ralph A. Heiss.)

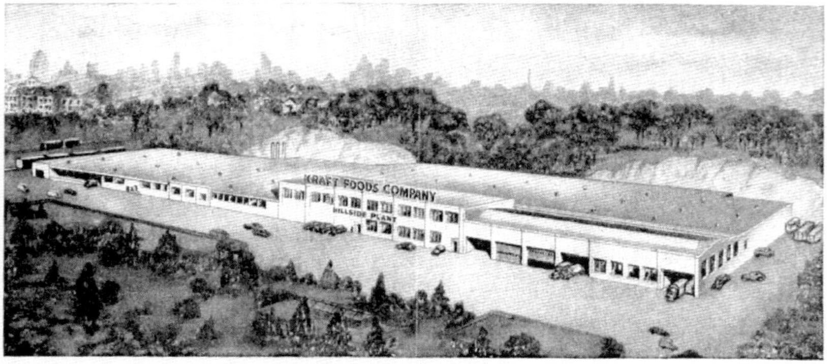

Kraft Foods Company,
Hillside, N. J.

THIS newly completed building, served exclusively by Lehigh Valley Railroad, covers six acres and contains 270,000 square feet of floor area. It is served by private side tracks with spotting capacity for thirty cars. Designed for production of Kraft Foods' various products this modern building represents the latest addition to Kraft Food Company's ever expanding production program throughout the United States.

This site is thirteen miles from New York City, immediately adjacent to Newark and has numerous improved thoroughfares in close proximity, providing an excellent location for a manufacturing plant or warehouse.

Lehigh Valley Railroad's Industrial Department has other desirable sites available to meet all requirements.

Write, telephone or wire:

E. F. NEAGLE, General Development Agent
LEHIGH VALLEY RAILROAD
143 Liberty Street, New York 6, N. Y. Phone BArclay 7-5400

In another timetable advertisement of a large industry located along the railroad, and this time taken from the June 1950 public timetable, the LVRR took advantage of using a popular household brand name, in this case Kraft Foods, by showcasing its manufacturing plant that was located along the Irvington branch in Hillside. (Courtesy of Ralph A. Heiss.)

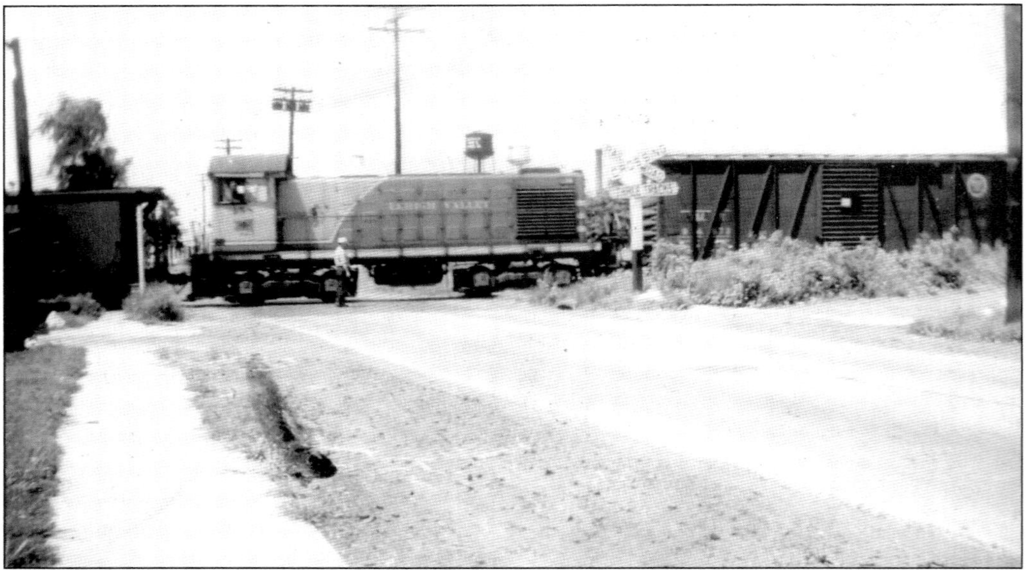

In this undated but rare photograph, diesel switcher No. 158, an S-2 model built by ALCO at Schenectady, New York, in 1945, crosses Nye Avenue in Irvington. The attractive "prewar" paint scheme on the locomotive was conceived by graphic designers at ALCO and was shared with at least one other railroad, the Copper Range Railroad in Michigan. (Courtesy of Ralph A. Heiss.)

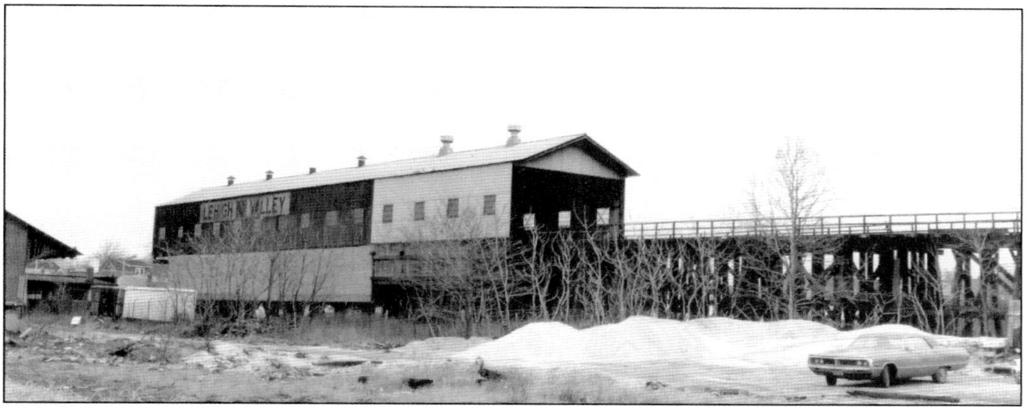

Even after coal had long since ceased to be king on the LVRR, the massive coal dock at the Clinton Avenue yard remained long after it had outlived its usefulness in this December 1971 photograph. Coal docks like these were common in almost every city along the railroad, serving distributors that delivered to the public at a time when coal stoves were still commonplace in every home and public building. (Courtesy of Bob's Photos.)

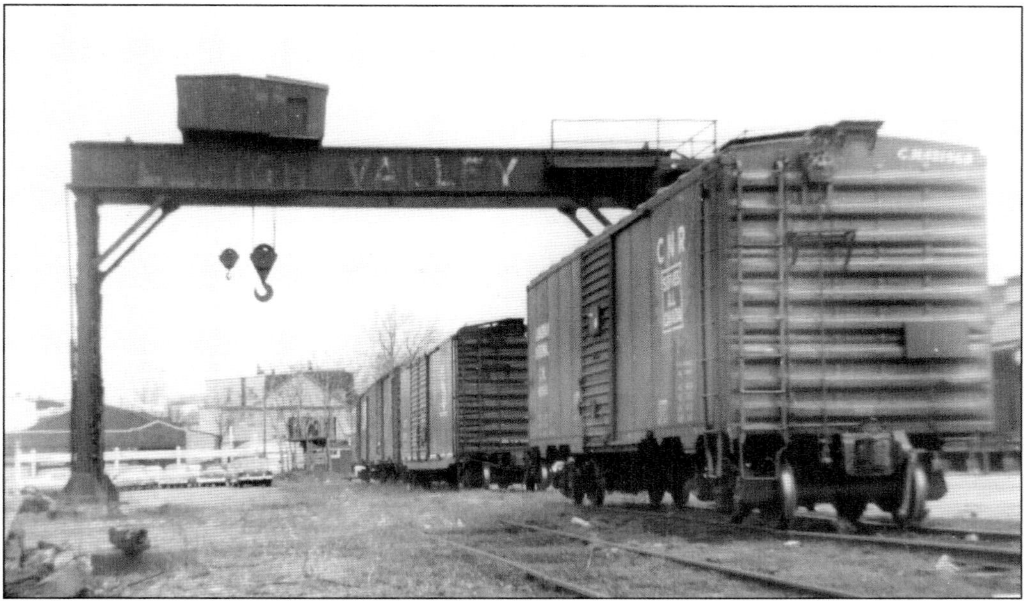

Most local fright yards had an overhead gantry crane to load and unload flatcars and gondolas, and the Clinton Avenue yard was no exception. In this photograph from the early 1960s, the yard still seems to be doing a little bit of business, although the crane looks like it has seen better days. (Courtesy of H. G. MacDonald.)

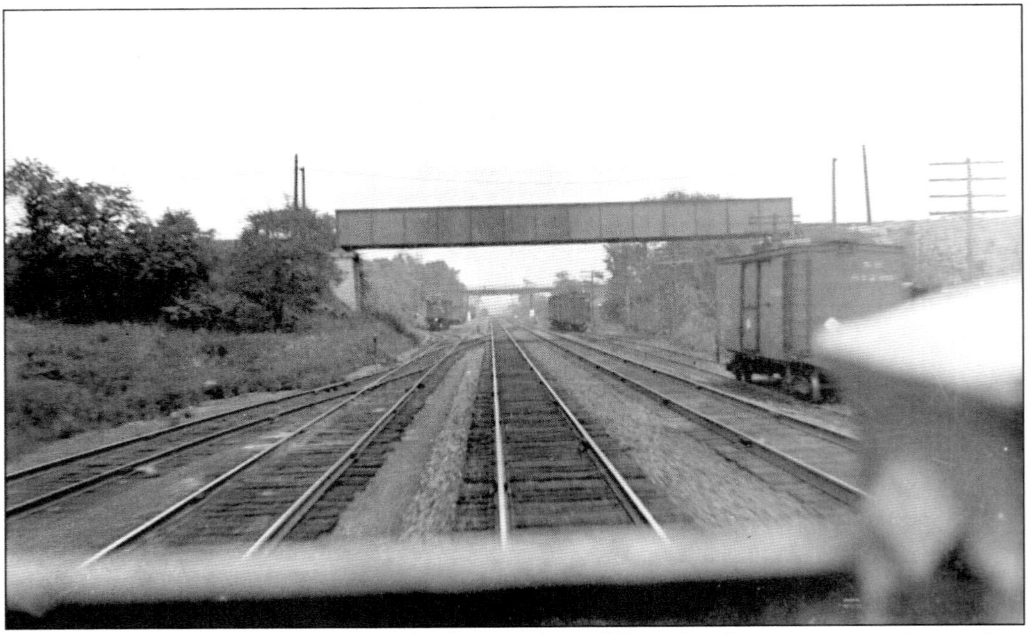

Now back on the main line, this view looking eastbound from the observation car of a speeding westbound train shows the overhead bridge of the public service union line between Bound Brook and Newark and beyond that the Weequahic Park Drive bridge. Today the trolley bridge over the main line is gone, but the section built over U.S. Route 22 still remains 60-plus years after the line was abandoned. (Courtesy of Richard Taylor.)

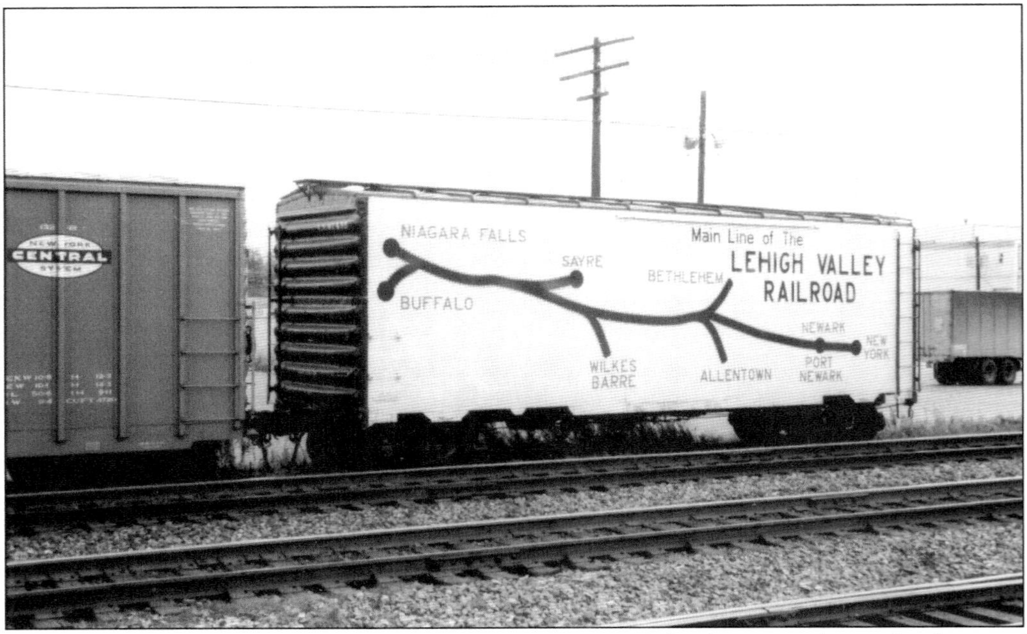

As another way to promote the railroad, the LVRR painted this boxcar with a stylized map of the railroad on one side to show the public just where the railroad went and how it could get its freight there. Although the map took some liberties of the route of the railroad by placing certain cities on branches, it made for a much more interesting map. It is seen here sitting along U.S. Route 22 in Hillside. (Courtesy of Richard Taylor.)

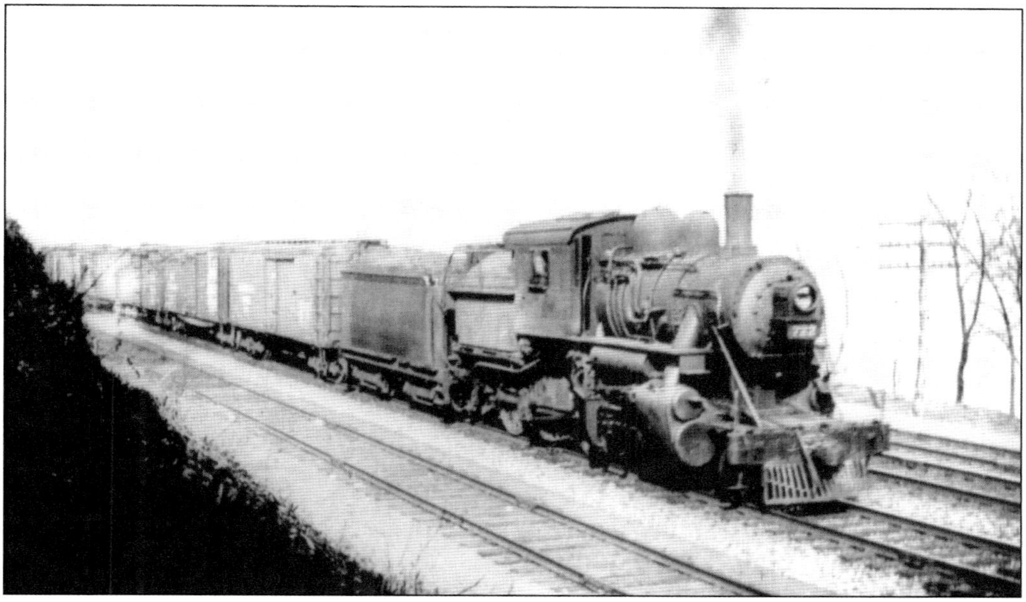

In this undated photograph looking east, 4-6-0 No. 722 can be seen with a local freight across from Weequahic Park on the border of Hillside and Newark. The town of Hillside, once known as Lyons Farms and then later as West Elizabeth, eventually acquired the name it is most well known for today in 1913. (Courtesy of Theodore F. Gleichmann Jr.)

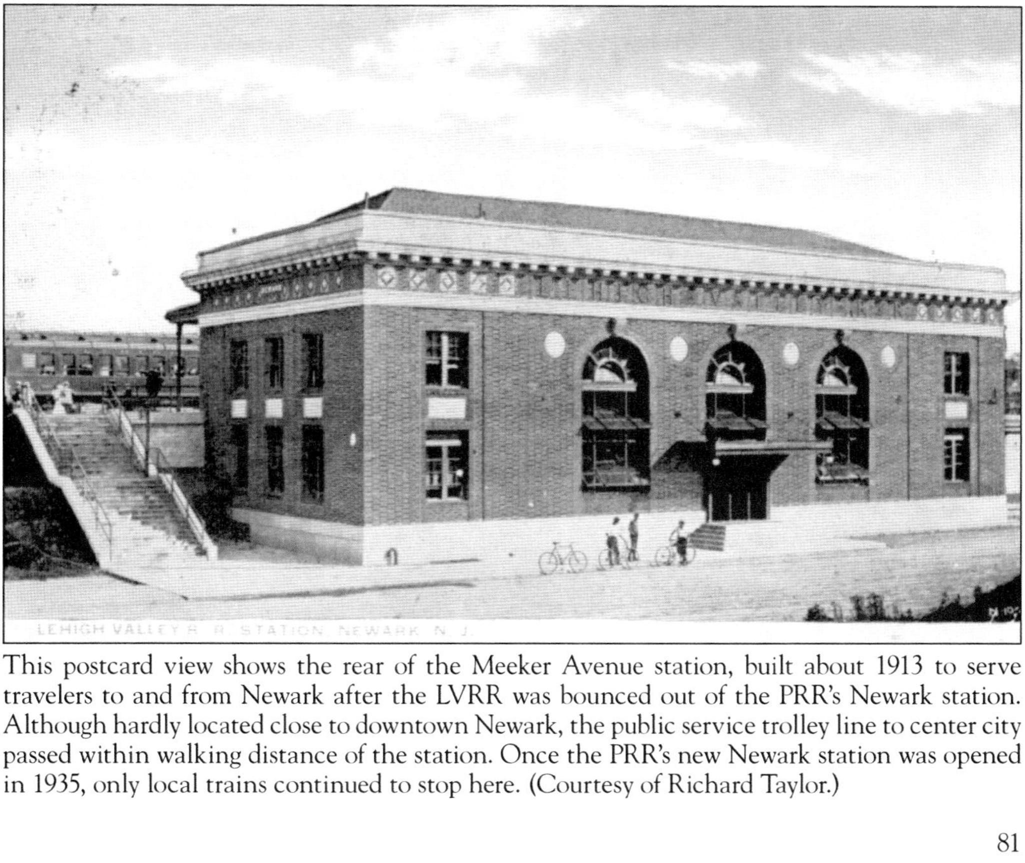

This postcard view shows the rear of the Meeker Avenue station, built about 1913 to serve travelers to and from Newark after the LVRR was bounced out of the PRR's Newark station. Although hardly located close to downtown Newark, the public service trolley line to center city passed within walking distance of the station. Once the PRR's new Newark station was opened in 1935, only local trains continued to stop here. (Courtesy of Richard Taylor.)

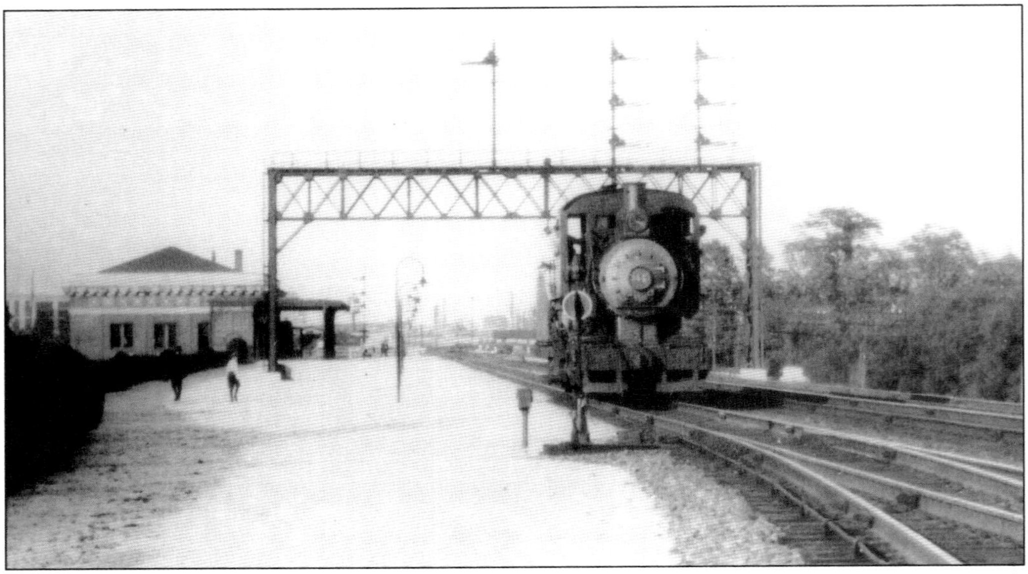

This c. 1920 photograph shows a small 0-6-0 switcher with its engineer looking out the cab for his signal to enter the Newark interlocking. Looking eastward along the railroad, the Meeker Avenue station can be seen to the left. The station was unique with its high level of ornamentation and brick construction. Perhaps the figures walking along the tracks were early railfans of that era. (Courtesy of Theodore F. Gleichmann/Railroad Museum of Pennsylvania.)

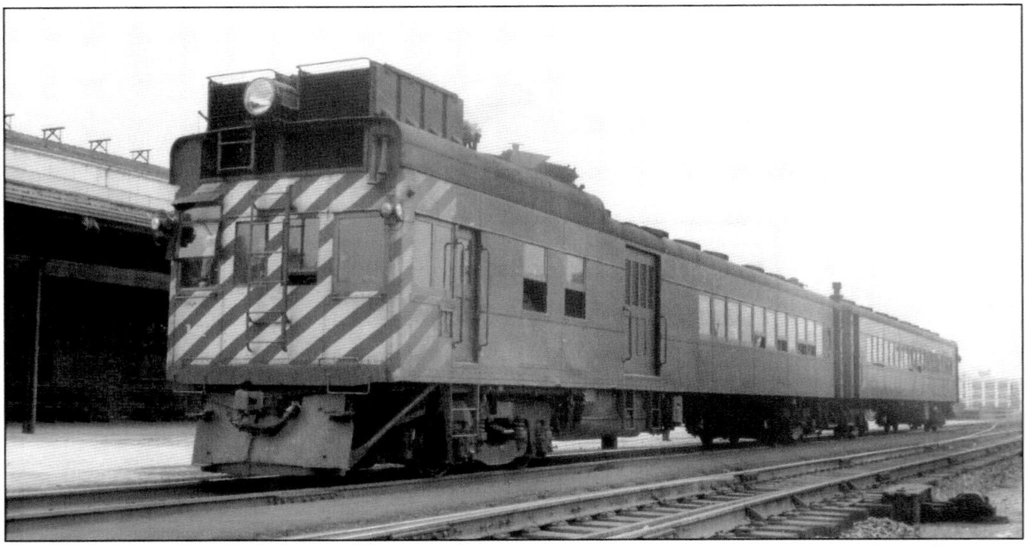

Getting ready to depart Meeker Avenue on July 3, 1937, is No. 67, a Saturday-only Jersey City-to-Flemington Junction local train. Gas-electric motor car No. 17 and its trailer car were both built by Osgood-Bradley in 1929. No. 17 could hold 51 passengers and had a baggage compartment and was scrapped in 1951. (Photograph by George Votava, courtesy of Joel Rosenbaum/Tom Gallo.)

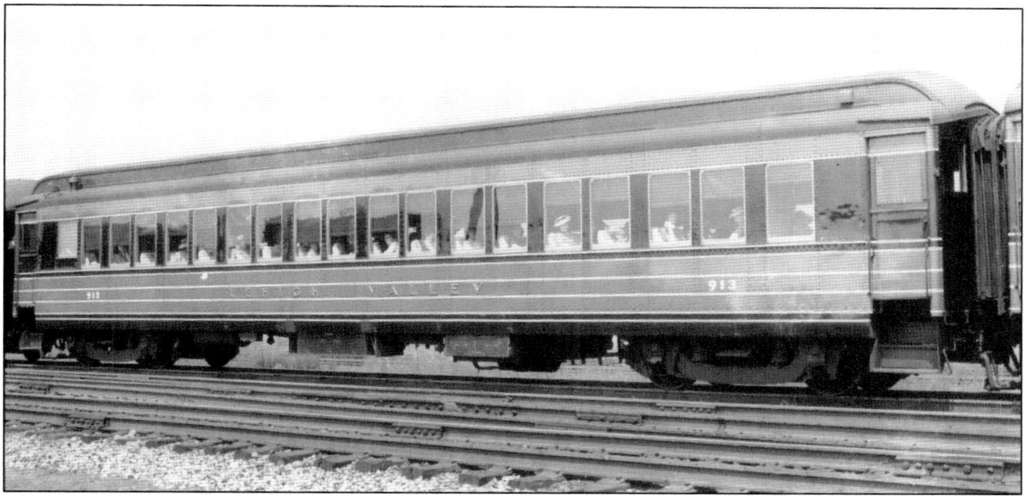

In the day when passenger train travel was a special affair and called for wearing one's best outfit, this July 4, 1939, photograph is full of smartly dressed ladies and gentlemen ready to leave for a holiday trip from the Meeker Avenue station. The car seen here was refurbished for use on the *John Wilkes* in a red, black, and white paint scheme. (Photograph by George Votava, courtesy of Joel Rosenbaum/Tom Gallo.)

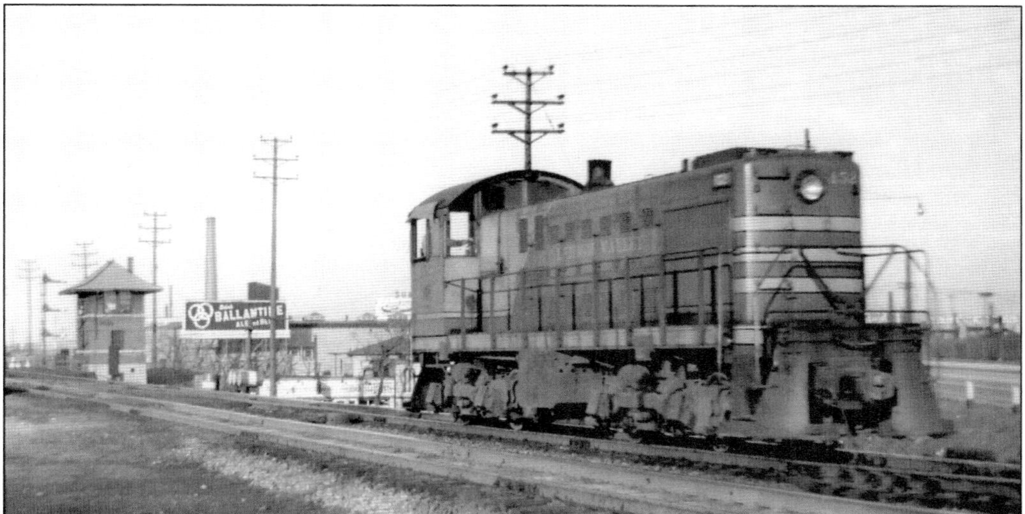

A dirty but well-maintained ALCO S-2 diesel switching locomotive rolls east toward NK Tower in this late-1940s view. NK Tower governed the entrance to the LVRR's Parkview Yard in Newark and the connecting track to the PRR at Hunter Tower via West Newark Junction for all main line passenger trains. Of interest is the classic Ballantine Ale billboard calling to thirsty drivers on parallel U.S. Route 22. (Courtesy of Gene Collora.)

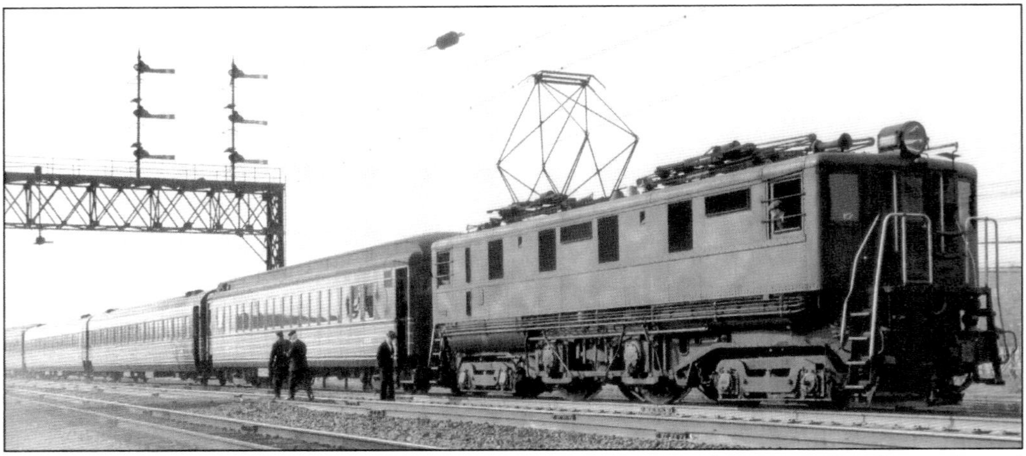

It appears that some railroad officials are making an inspection of train No. 28, the eastbound *John Wilkes* at West Newark Junction, and will soon be ready to roll toward South Newark Junction at Hunter Tower on the PRR main line, about a mile away. Passenger trains would swap their steam or diesel locomotives here to a PRR electric locomotive like the classic GG-1 or, as seen here, an O-1a class electric. (Photograph by George Votava, courtesy of Joel Rosenbaum/Tom Gallo.)

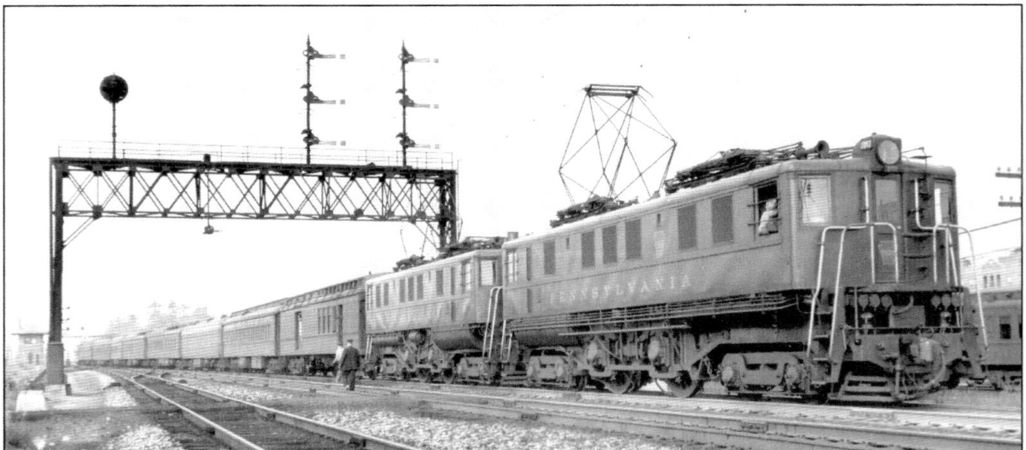

In this photograph, train No. 4, the eastbound *Maple Leaf*, gets ready to depart West Newark Junction on July 4, 1939, behind a pair of two PRR O-1c electrics with a 10-car train. The *Maple Leaf* was due to arrive at New York's Penn Station at 8:15 that morning. (Photograph by George Votava, courtesy of Joel Rosenbaum/Tom Gallo.)

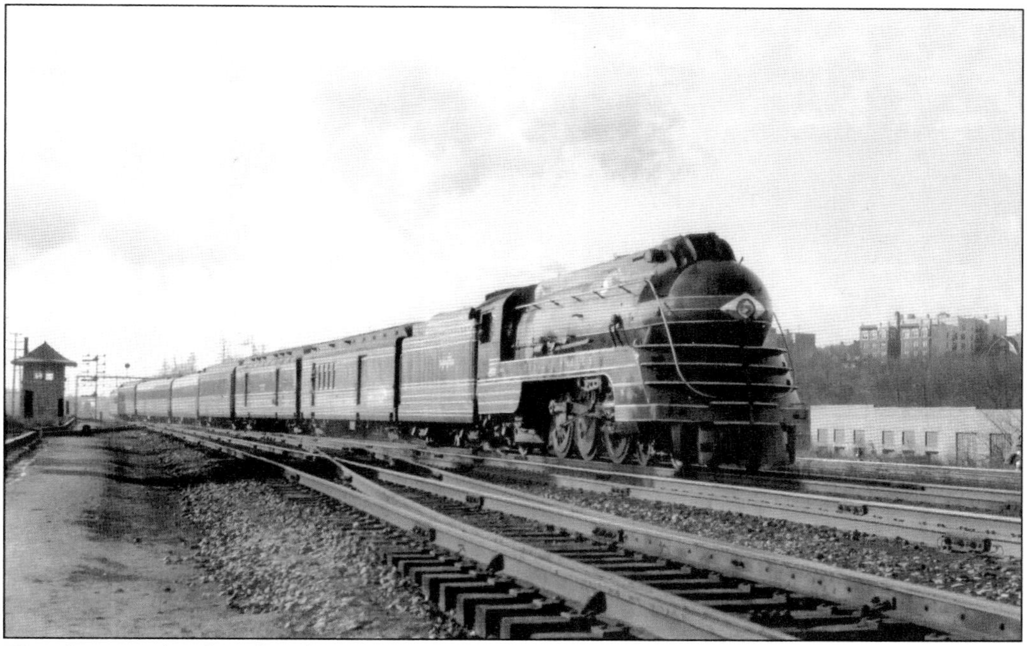

The photographer has the pleasure to be front and center for the arrival of train No. 28 behind steam locomotive No. 2101 pulling the *John Wilkes* as it passes NK Tower for its quick stop to swap its Otto Kuhler–designed steam locomotive for a PRR electric locomotive, two days before Christmas 1939. (Photograph by George Votava, courtesy of Joel Rosenbaum/Tom Gallo.)

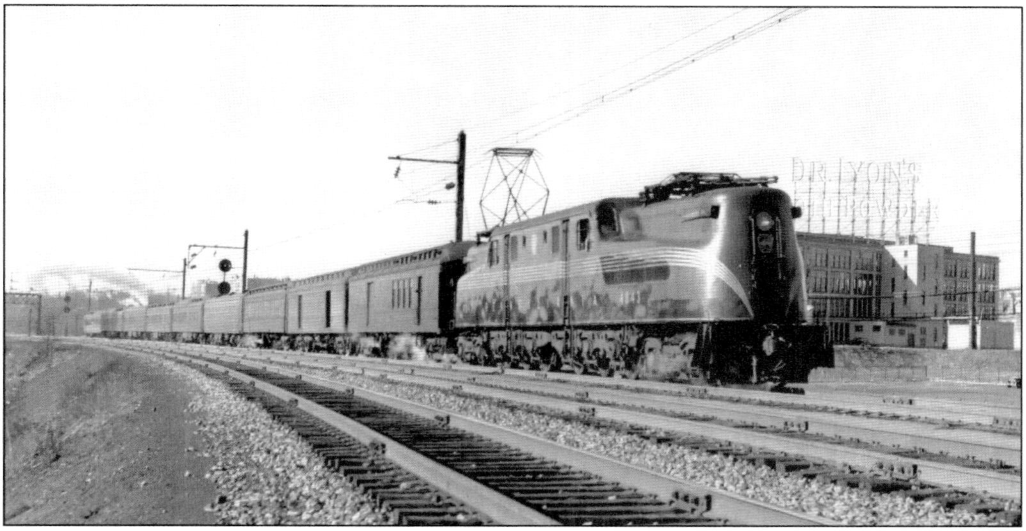

PRR GG-1 electric No. 4843 takes charge of this unidentified train bound for New York's Penn Station as it rolls down the connection toward the PRR main line at Hunter Tower from the inbound LVRR crew on the same December day in 1939. Rising up above the seventh car in the train can been seen the smoke and steam from locomotive No. 2101. (Photograph by George Votava, courtesy of Joel Rosenbaum/Tom Gallo.)

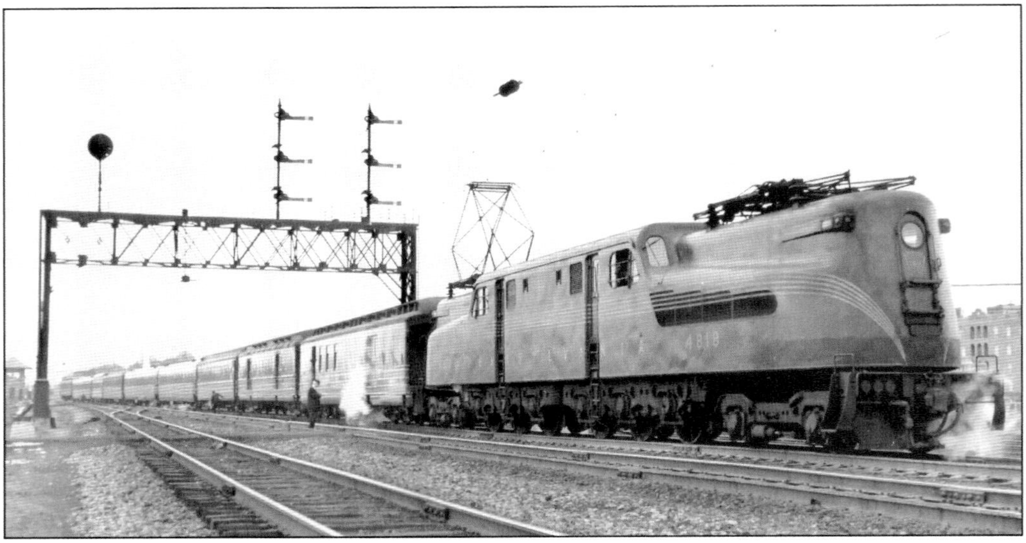

Resplendent in its classic Brunswick green pin-striped paint scheme, PRR GG-1 No. 4818 has train No. 28, the *John Wilkes*, all coupled up and ready to depart West Newark Junction for the run into New York on December 10, 1939. After the passengers are off-loaded at Penn Station, the train will be serviced at the Sunnyside yards in Long Island City, Queens, before returning west for another run to Pittston, Pennsylvania. (Photograph by George Votava, courtesy of Joel Rosenbaum/Tom Gallo.)

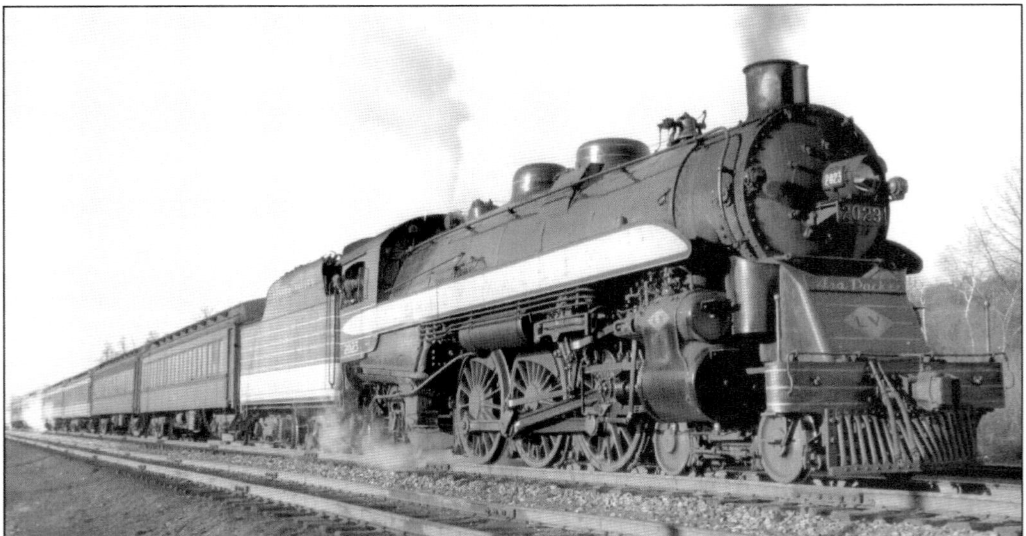

As one prepares to leave West Newark Junction and visit Oak Island Yard and a few miles farther east reach the Hudson River at Jersey City, a final look at the eastbound *Asa Packer* is seen here as it arrives behind locomotive No. 2023 on December 23, 1939. (Photograph by George Votava, courtesy of Joel Rosenbaum/Tom Gallo.)

Four

Oak Island Yard to Jersey City

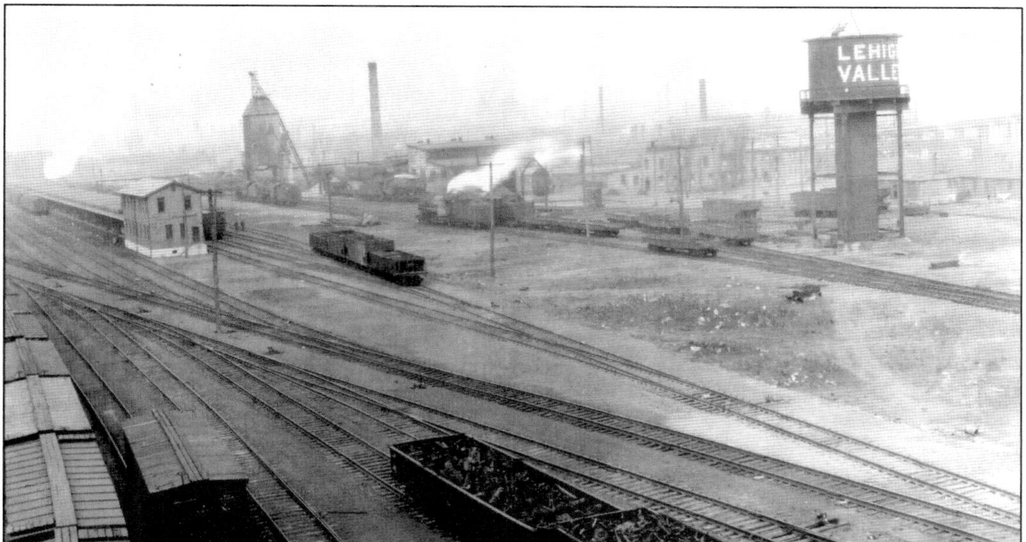

This 1931 view looking west provides a good overview of Oak Island Yard. The building to the left of the coaling tower is the LCL transfer station. This yard was the easternmost classification yard on the railroad, and all symbol freight trains either began or ended their journey here. (Courtesy of Bob's Photos.)

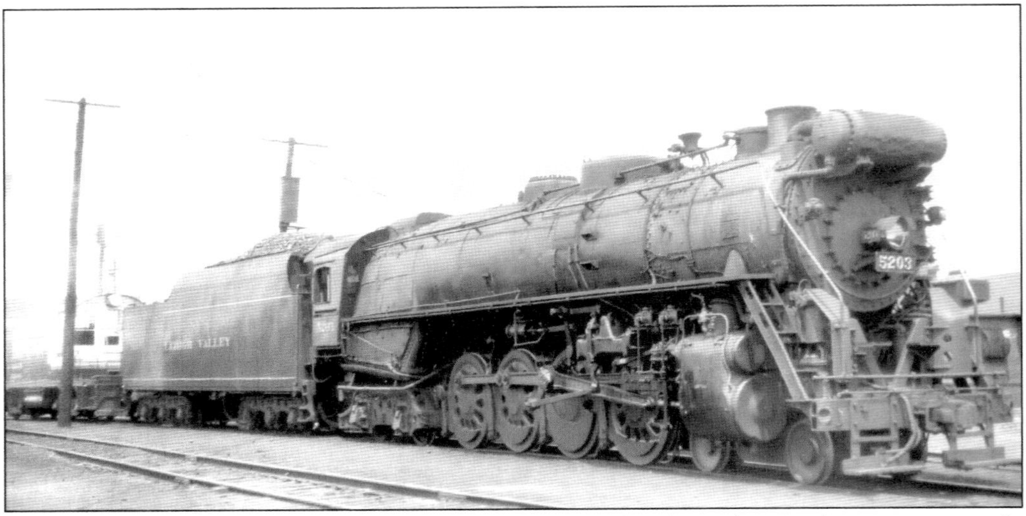

Here is T-2 class 4-8-4 No. 5203 coupled up to one of the diesel invaders. In this case, it is newly delivered EMD SW-1 diesel switching locomotive No. 115 seen here at the Oak Island engine facility. While the SW-1 would not replace this steam locomotive, its larger brethren would do so by 1951. (Photograph by John Brinckmann, courtesy of Joel Rosenbaum/Tom Gallo.)

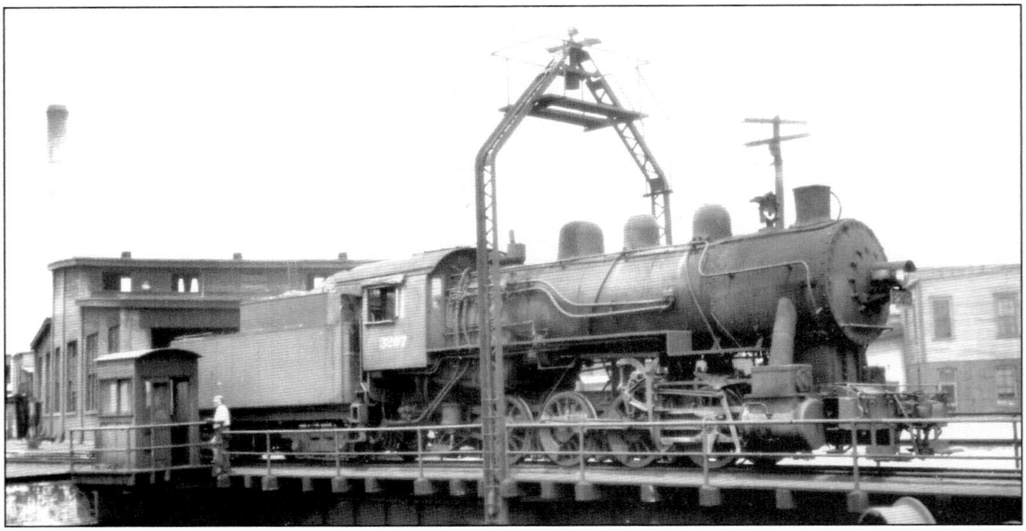

This 0-8-0 steam locomotive takes a spin on the Oak Island turntable in 1940. The engine is probably headed into the roundhouse for some light maintenance. No. 3207 was another locomotive on the LVRR's large roster of home-built locomotives, having been built in the mid-1920s. (Photograph by O. H. Borsum, courtesy of M. D. McCarter.)

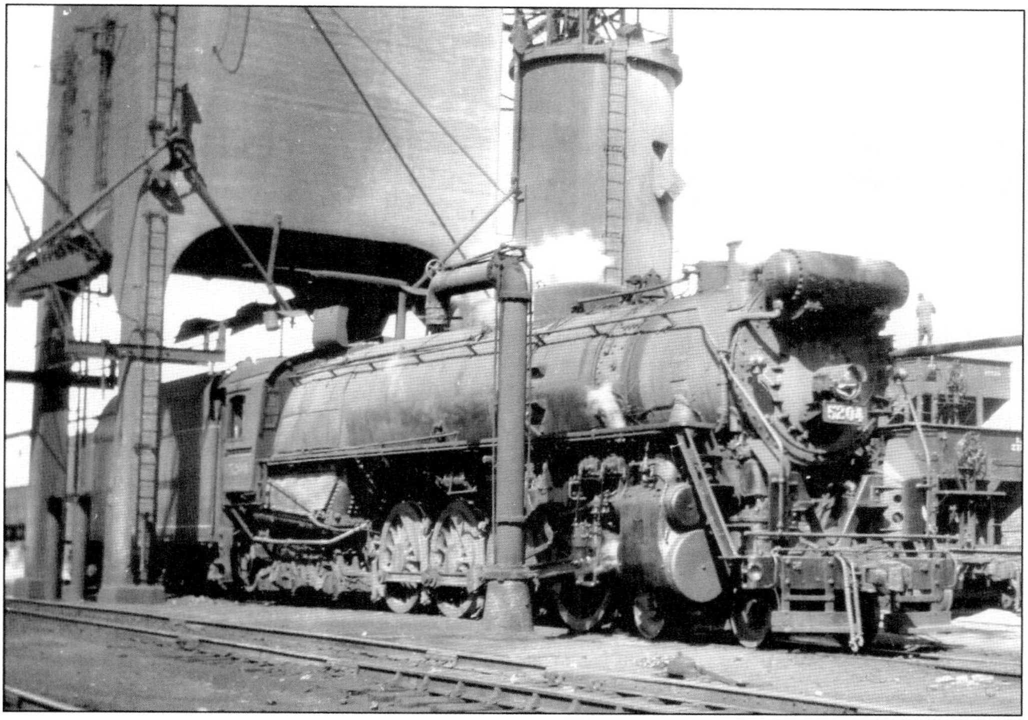

One of the first 4-8-4 Wyoming-type steam locomotives of the T-2 class, delivered to the railroad in 1932 as No. 5204, sits under the coaling tower at Oak Island on this fine day around 1940. The coal hoppers to the right of the locomotive kept the coaling tower full of "food" for these hungry locomotives. (Photograph by O. H. Borsum, courtesy of M. D. McCarter.)

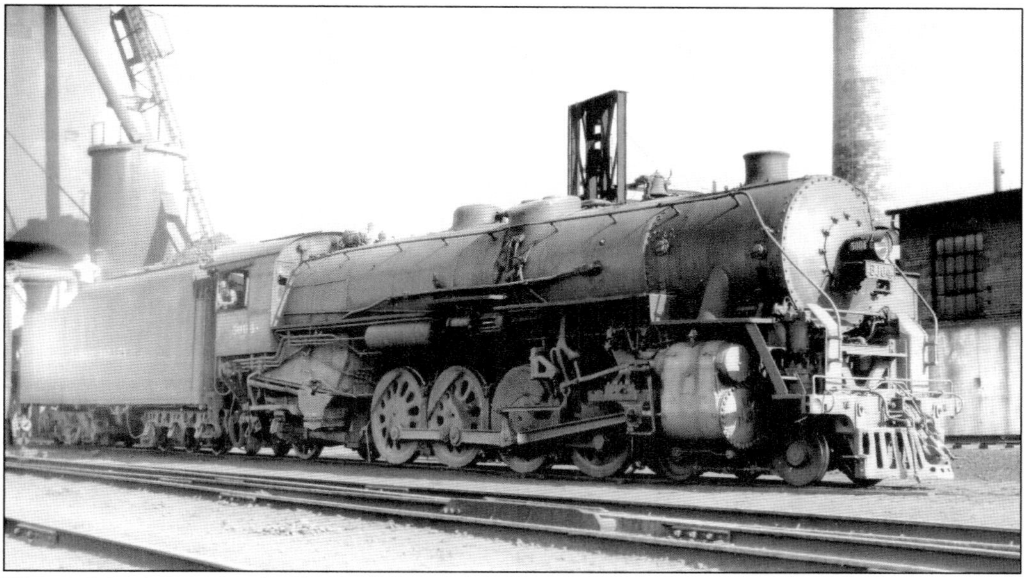

The LVRR also rostered a fleet of six S-1 class Seneca-type 4-8-2 steam locomotives that were built by ALCO in 1929. In 1939, the LVRR rebuilt the entire class into the S-2 class, with new driving wheels, tenders, and cylinders and a host of other improvements. No. 5004 gets a tender full of water in this 1947 photograph. (Photograph by R. P. Morris, courtesy of Jack deRosset/ Frank T. Reilly.)

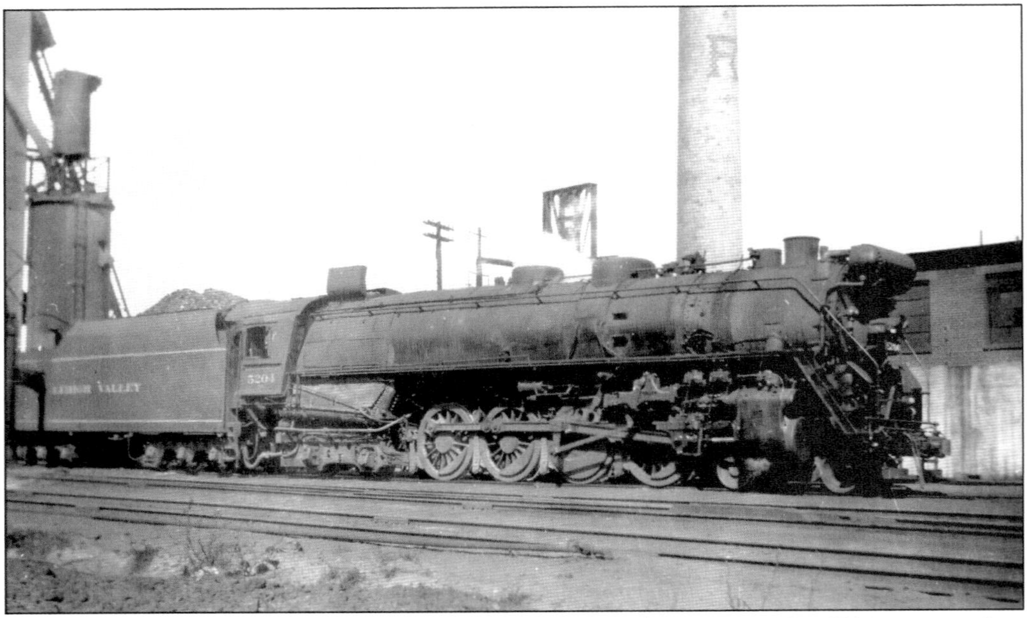

Here is a photograph of the 4-8-4 Wyoming-type steam locomotive No. 5204 again, taken sometime in the 1940s with a full tender of coal and water and ready for another trip west from Oak Island Yard on any one of the four symbol freights scheduled to go west to Buffalo or Suspension Bridge. (Photograph by O. H. Borsum, courtesy of M. D. McCarter.)

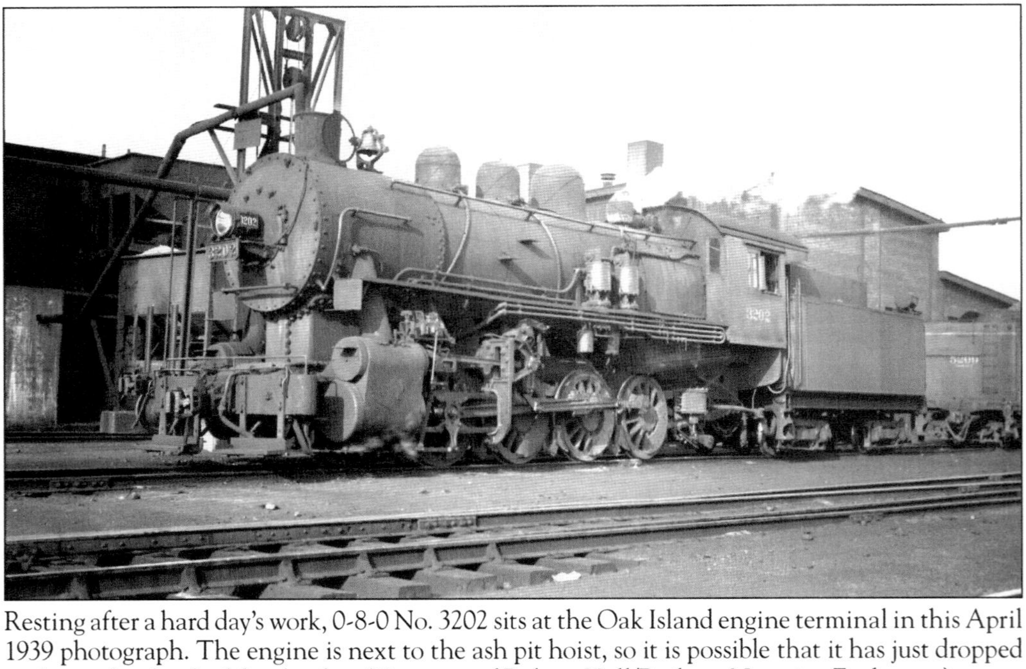

Resting after a hard day's work, 0-8-0 No. 3202 sits at the Oak Island engine terminal in this April 1939 photograph. The engine is next to the ash pit hoist, so it is possible that it has just dropped its fire and is finished for the day. (Courtesy of Robert Hall/Railway Negative Exchange.)

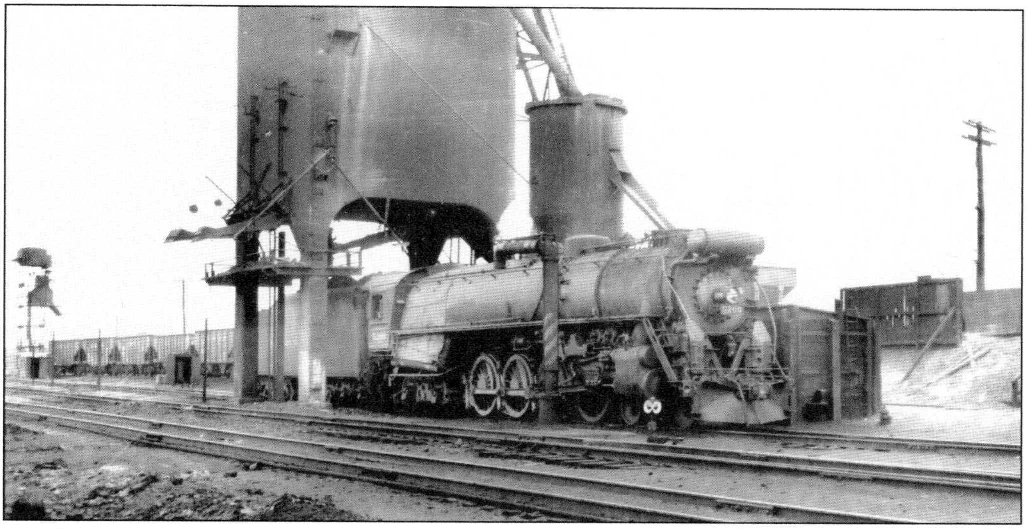

LVRR locomotive No. 5200, the first of the T-2 class 4-8-4 Wyomings built in 1931, sits under the Oak Island coaling tower in this *c.* 1945 photograph. By 1953, the final locomotives of the T-2 class, the T-2bs, were being sent to scrap, barely nine years old and still in good shape. (Courtesy of Robert F. Guthlein/Theodore F. Gleichmann Jr.)

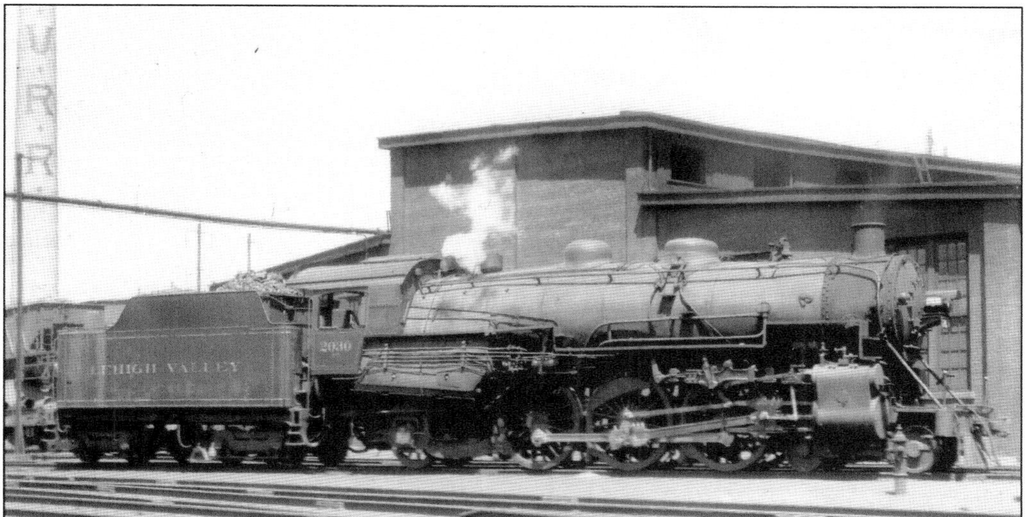

No. 2030, a 4-6-2 Pacific-type steam locomotive, sits in front of the roundhouse ready for its next job in this undated photograph. This K-3 class steam locomotive was of the same type that was also used on the *Asa Packer*. (Photograph by R. P. Morris, courtesy of Jack deRosset/Frank T. Reilly.)

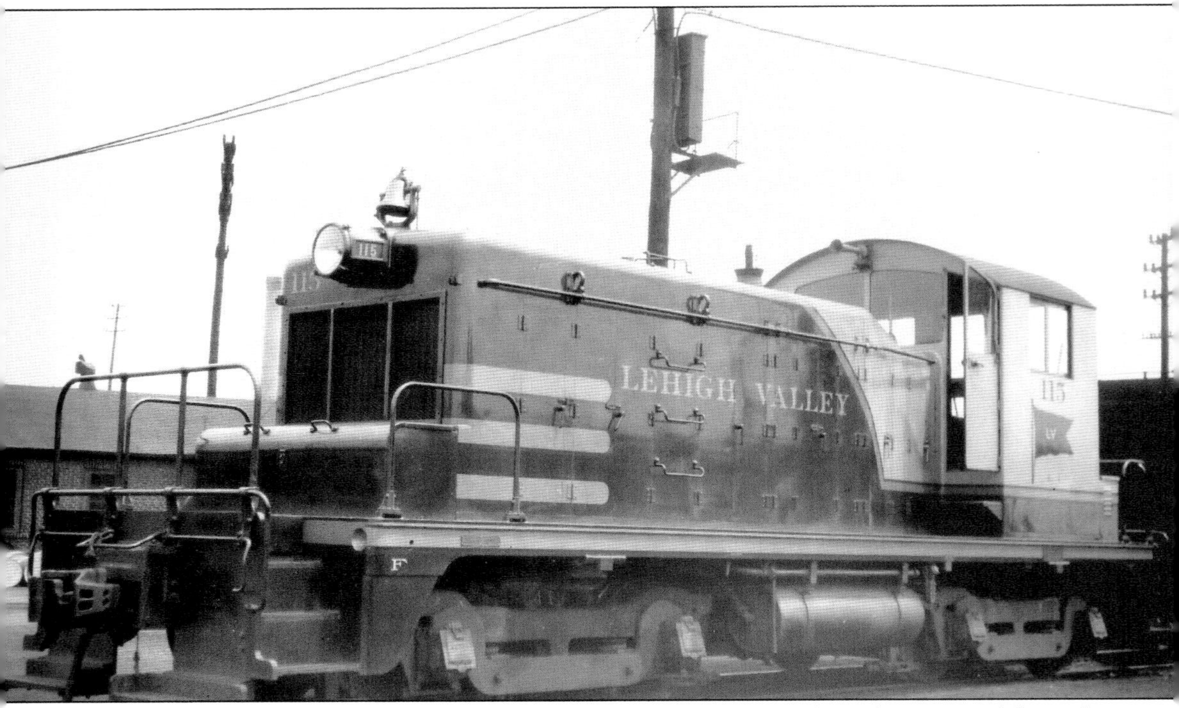

EMD SW-1 No. 115 was the second diesel to be assigned this number when it was delivered in 1940. Before the SW-1 was delivered to the LVRR, the first engine No. 115 and sister locomotive No. 116 were renumbered to No. 75 and No. 76, respectively. This was common on the LVRR, with seven of the original pioneer diesel locomotives requiring renumbering as newer and larger locomotives took those number slots in the roster and then again in later years when the PRR leased a number of engines to the LVRR to replace the ailing locomotive fleet. (Photograph by John Brinckmann, courtesy of Joel Rosenbaum/Tom Gallo.)

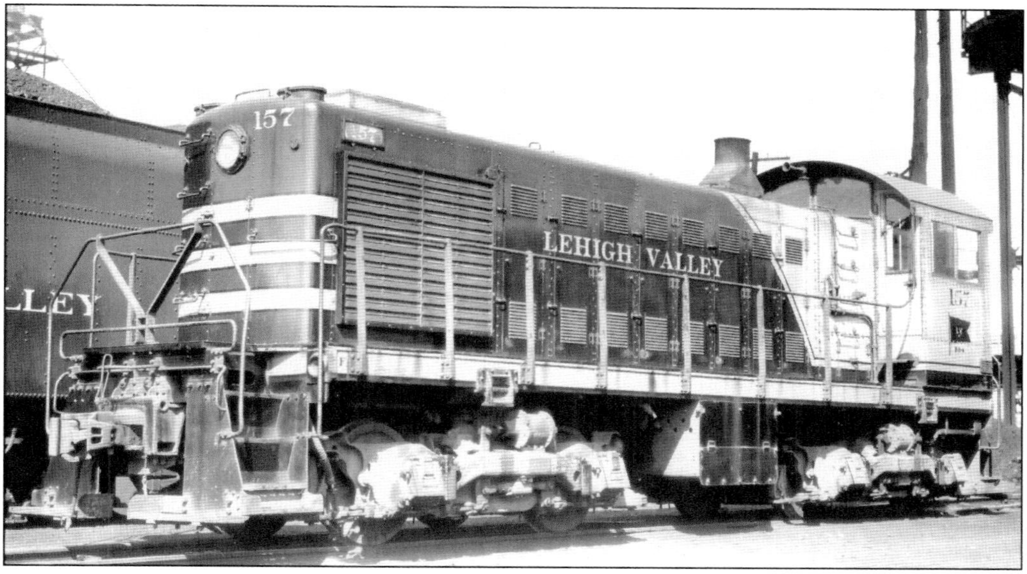

As the 1930s wore on, the diesels began to take over, especially where the economics of switching locomotives were realized. ALCO S-2 No. 157 was delivered in the middle of World War II in 1944, at a time when ALCO was forced by the U.S. government to produce only small switching locomotives, whereas the competing EMD of General Motors was allowed to construct larger locomotives for main line use. (Courtesy of Richard Chapin.)

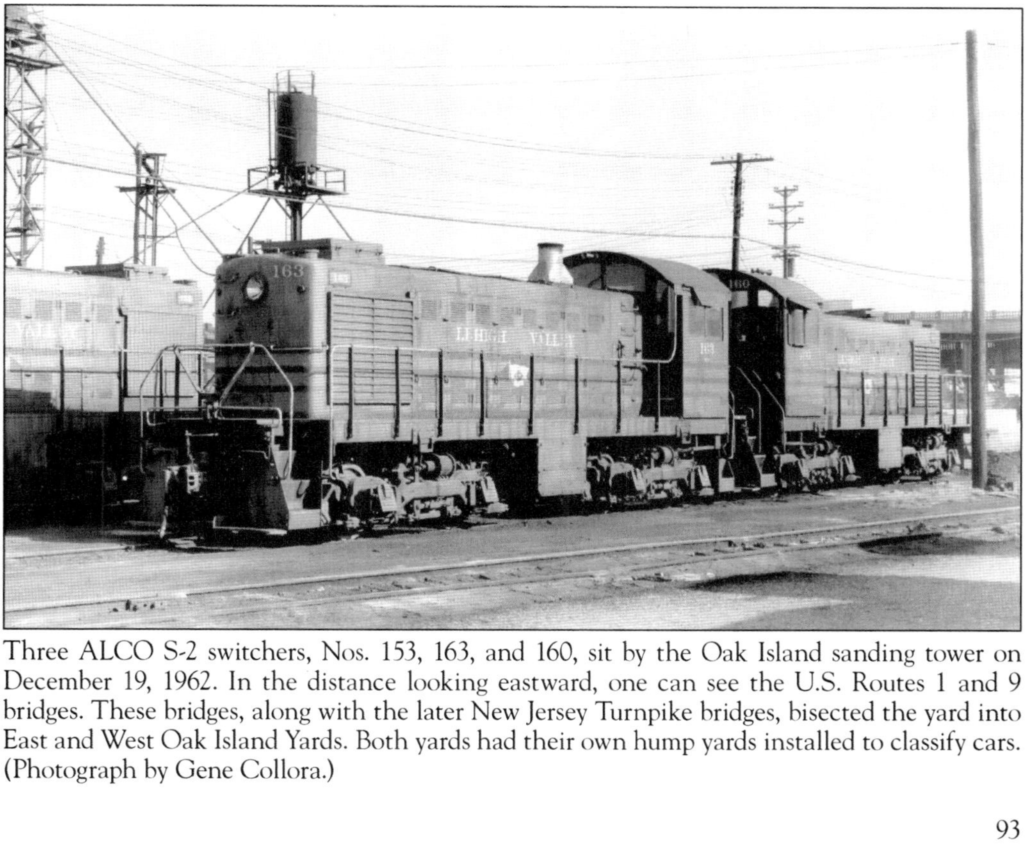

Three ALCO S-2 switchers, Nos. 153, 163, and 160, sit by the Oak Island sanding tower on December 19, 1962. In the distance looking eastward, one can see the U.S. Routes 1 and 9 bridges. These bridges, along with the later New Jersey Turnpike bridges, bisected the yard into East and West Oak Island Yards. Both yards had their own hump yards installed to classify cars. (Photograph by Gene Collora.)

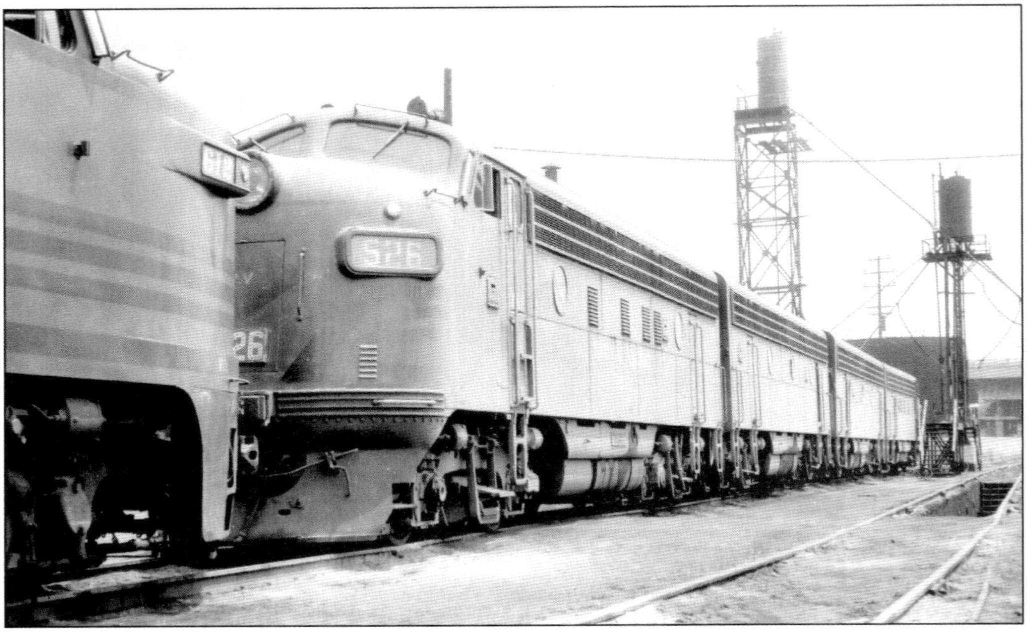

Here is a photograph of for what in later years was a rare A-B-B-A set of EMD F units led by F-3 No. 526, sitting nose to nose with ALCO PA-1 No. 612 at the same location sometime in the early 1960s. Both of these locomotive models that so gloriously ushered in the era of the diesel locomotive on the LVRR would find themselves as trade-in fodder for newer diesels in the mid-1960s, as first generation gave way to the second. The C-420, RS-11, and C-628 models from ALCO would have to keep the railroad running until the new EMD GP-38 and General Electric (GE) U-23B locomotives came along in the 1970s. (Photograph by Don Walworth.)

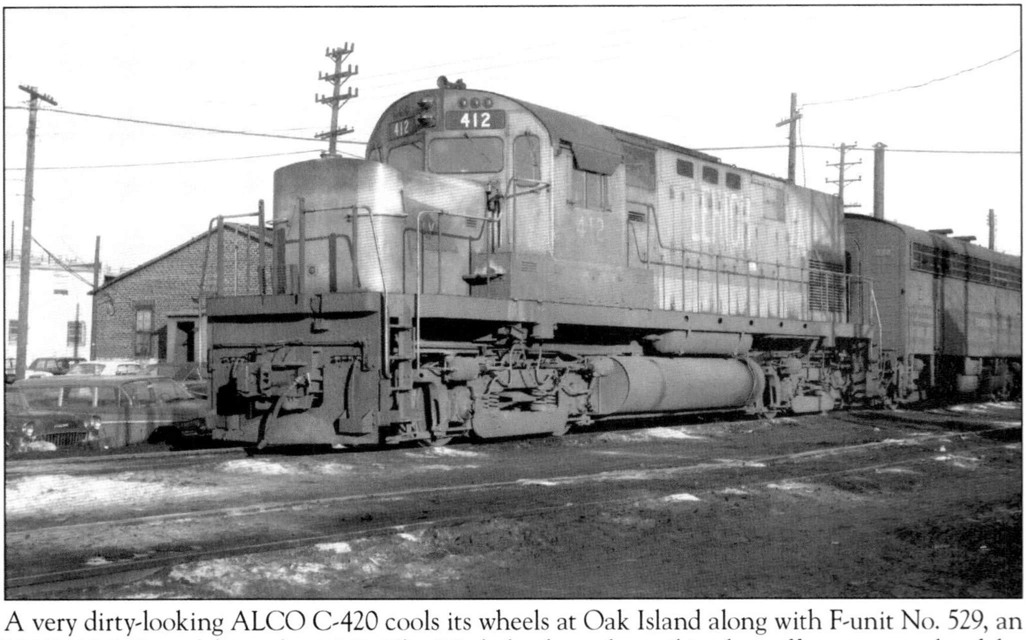

A very dirty-looking ALCO C-420 cools its wheels at Oak Island along with F-unit No. 529, an EMD F-3 A-B set delivered in 1948. The F-3s helped put the nail in the coffin, so to speak, of the steam locomotive fleet, and engines like the C-420 helped do the same to the first-generation diesels like the F-3. (Photograph by Jim Claflin, courtesy of Craig Zeni.)

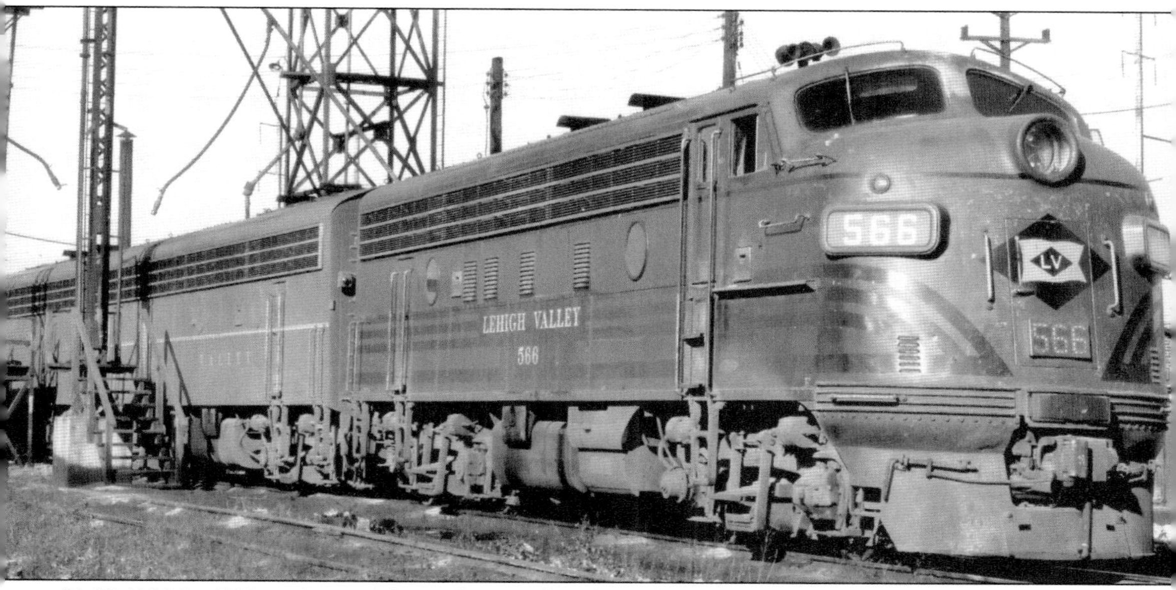

EMD F-7 No. 566 in the as-delivered Cornell red and black pin-striped scheme coupled to an unidentified sister locomotive painted in the PRR-inspired Tuscan red and yellow stripe scheme sits at the Oak Island engine facility. No. 566 was later traded in on an order of EMD GP-38AC diesels in 1971. (Photograph by Don Walworth.)

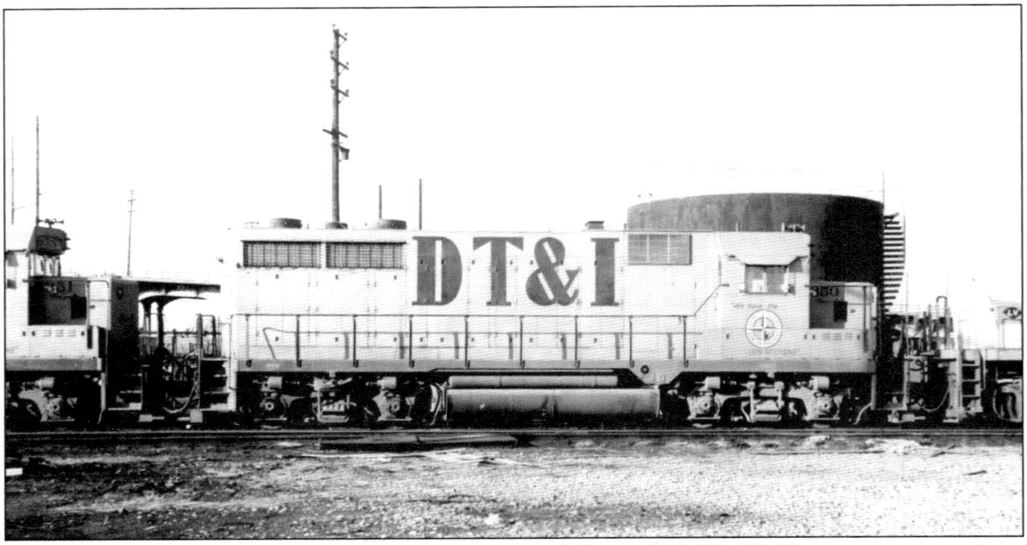

In 1965, three Detroit, Toledo and Ironton Railroad (DT&I) EMD GP-35s were sent east from Michigan to the LVRR for evaluation of the model, and in turn the LVRR sent three of its ALCO C-420s in exchange. However, the diesels ended up not in service on the DT&I but rather on a DT&I subsidiary, the Ann Arbor Railroad (AA), which was more familiar with the operation and maintenance of ALCO diesels than EMD-friendly DT&I. This power swap was facilitated by the PRR, which controlled both the DT&I/AA and LVRR in the 1960s. Nos. 351 and 350 are seen here sitting at the Oak Island engine facilities at 91 Bay Avenue. (Photograph by Richard Taylor.)

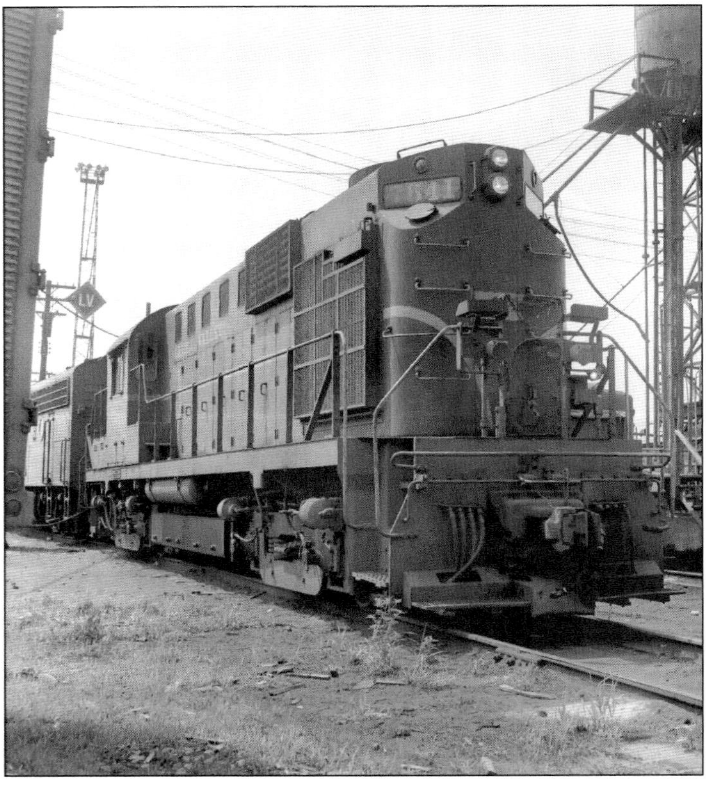

ALCO road switcher RS-11 No. 7641 gets another load of "seashore" (sand) for traction on the rails at Oak Island in July 1967. Locomotive No. 7641 was originally PRR RS-11 No. 8641 and was leased along with six of its sisters to the cash-strapped LVRR in the 1960s. (Photograph by Jim Claflin, courtesy of Craig Zeni.)

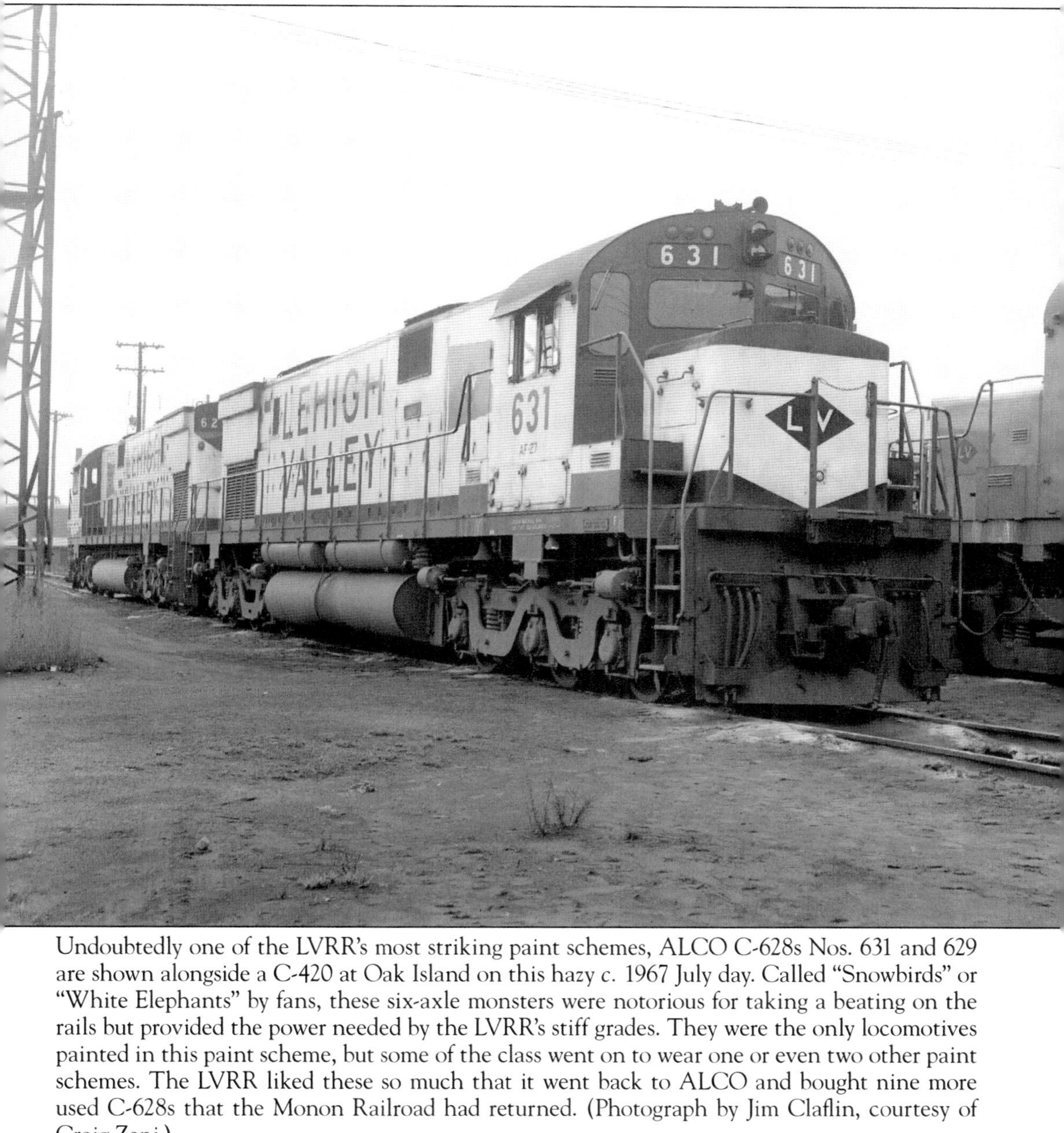

Undoubtedly one of the LVRR's most striking paint schemes, ALCO C-628s Nos. 631 and 629 are shown alongside a C-420 at Oak Island on this hazy c. 1967 July day. Called "Snowbirds" or "White Elephants" by fans, these six-axle monsters were notorious for taking a beating on the rails but provided the power needed by the LVRR's stiff grades. They were the only locomotives painted in this paint scheme, but some of the class went on to wear one or even two other paint schemes. The LVRR liked these so much that it went back to ALCO and bought nine more used C-628s that the Monon Railroad had returned. (Photograph by Jim Claflin, courtesy of Craig Zeni.)

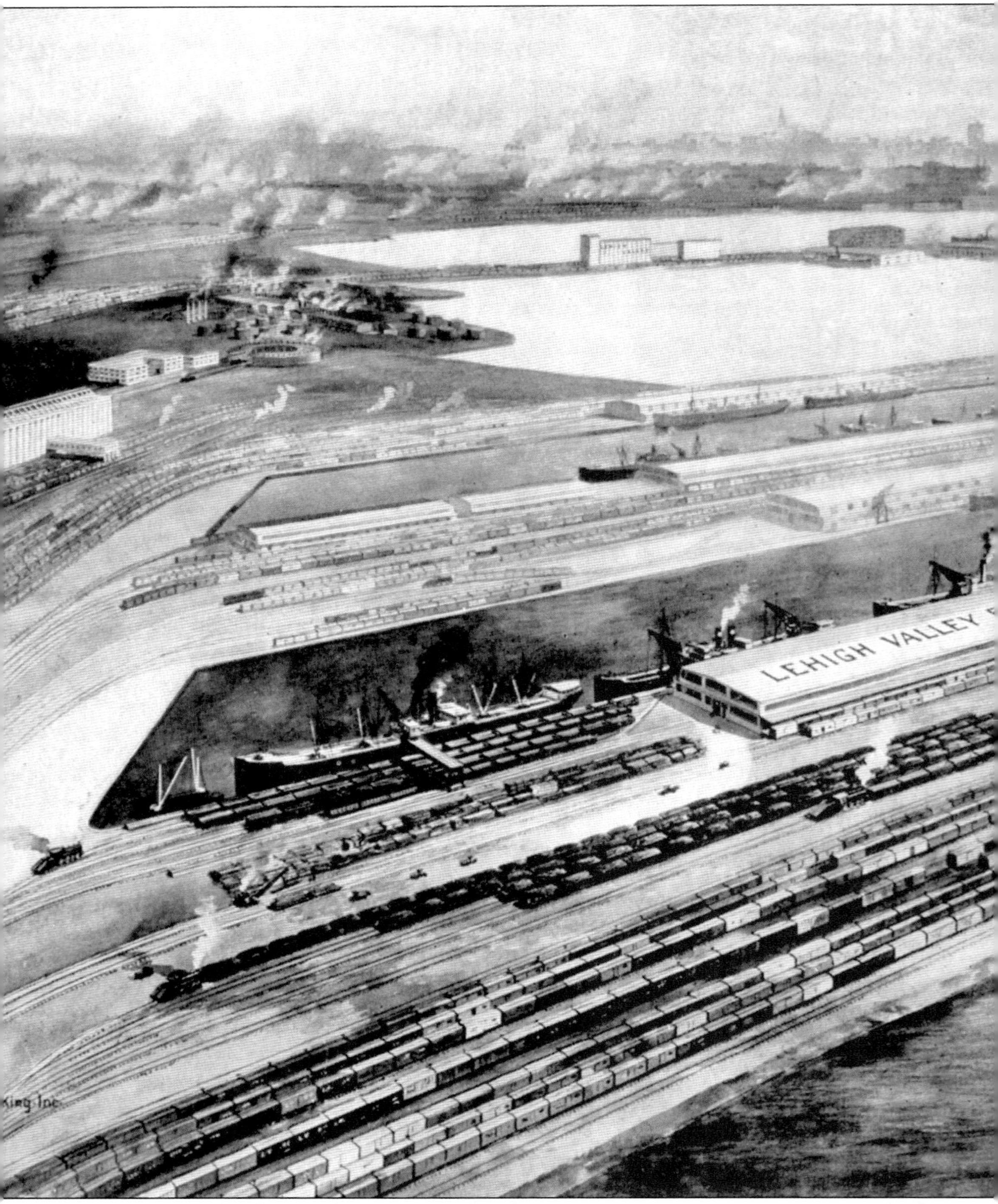

Leaving Oak Island, Newark Bay is crossed and one arrives in Jersey City to encounter the first of the LVRR's Jersey City properties, the Claremont terminal. Constructed in 1923 just north of the PRR's huge Greenville yard, the Claremont terminal was actually the last property built to serve New York Harbor. In this artist's rendering, one can see the expansive dreams of its designers and the relation of its location to the rest of New York Harbor. The LVRR built this

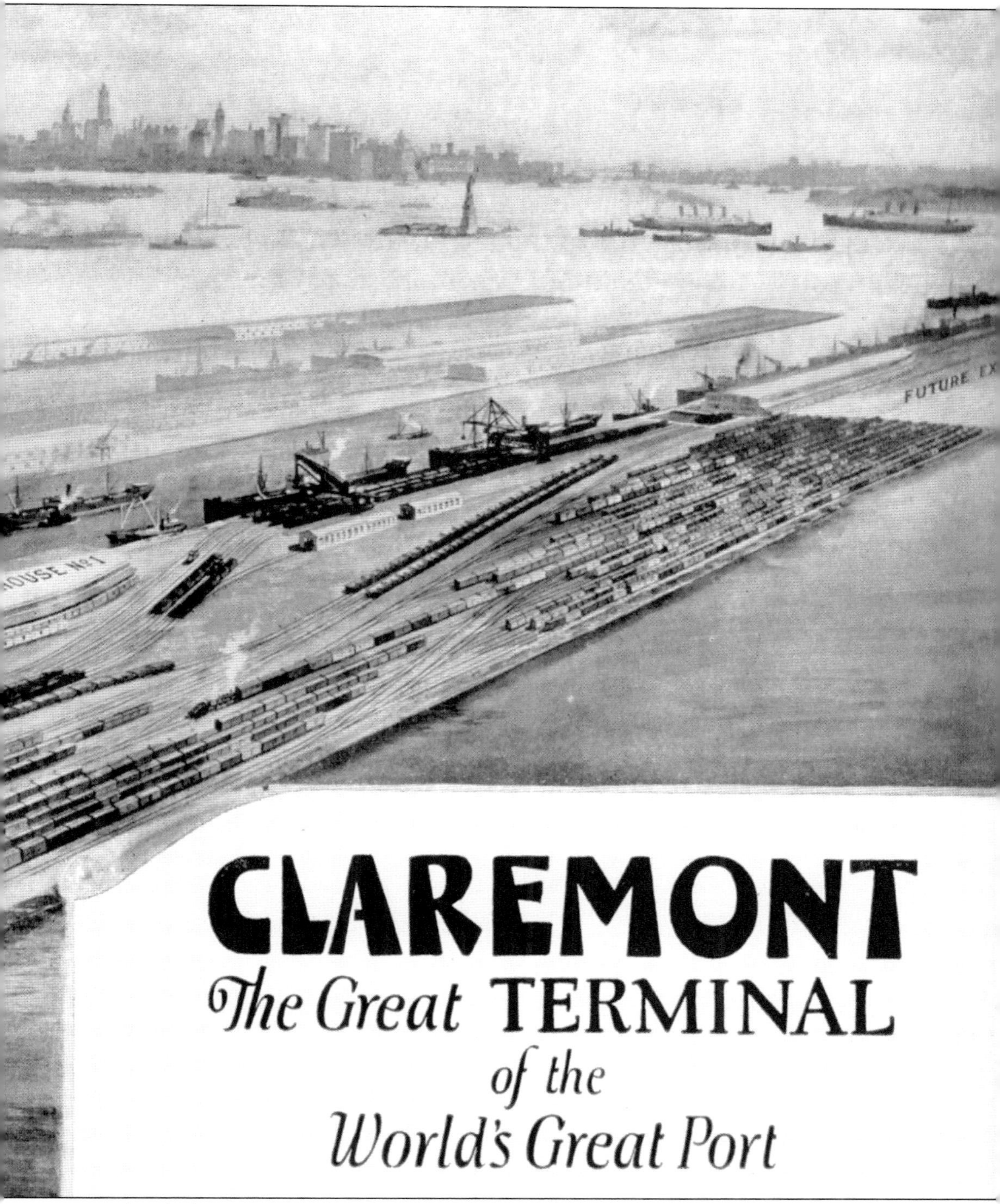

terminal with the idea of serving oceangoing ships that could dock portside and transfer freight more efficiently than the standard lightering procedure so common in New York Harbor. Even though ore freighters did dock here to unload at Claremont's Hulett ore unloaders, it never really lived up to the expansive dreams of its builders. (Courtesy of Ralph A. Heiss.)

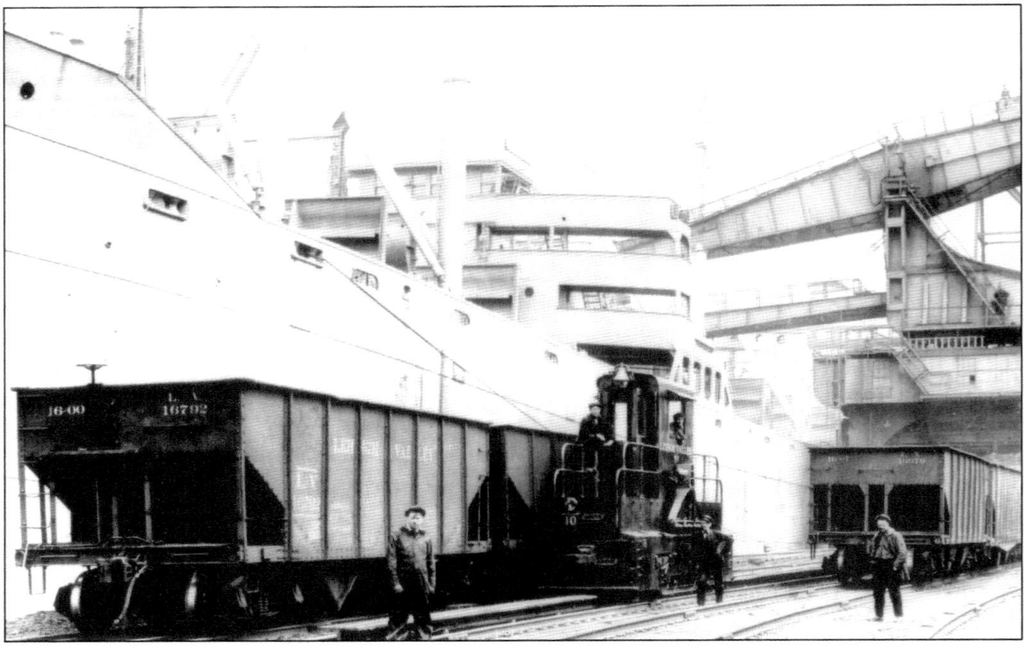

This 1925 photograph is a close-up of the huge Hulett ore unloaders, built by Bethlehem Steel to move ore from ships coming from Central America to the mills at Bethlehem, Pennsylvania. The workers here pose in front of one of the five small electric locomotives that ran on narrow-gauge track and picked up their power from a third rail. A pusher arm would engage the hopper car ends to move them for loading. (Courtesy of Theodore F. Gleichmann Jr.)

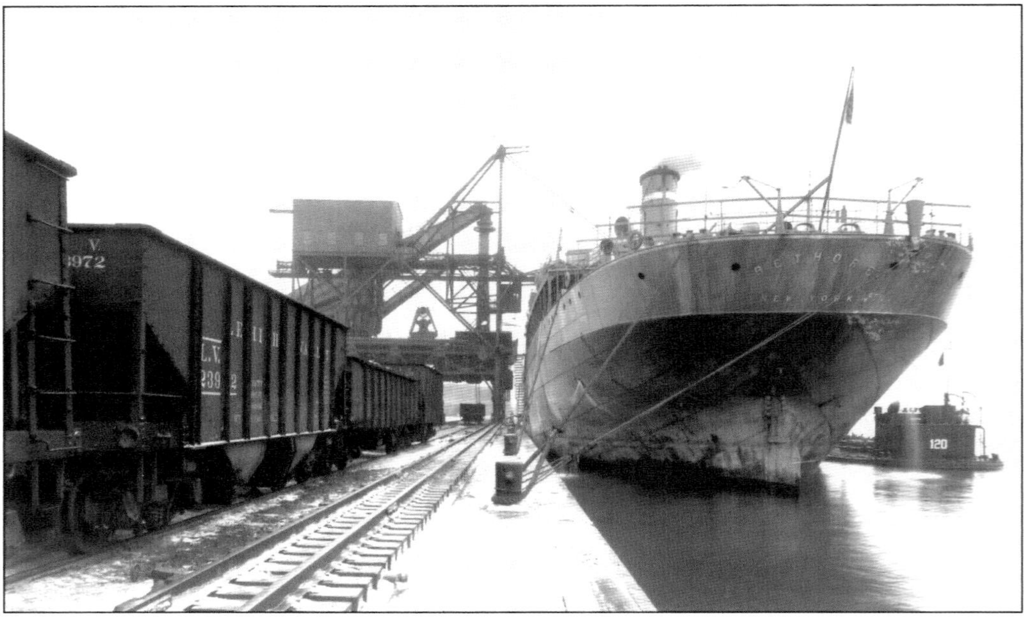

In this photograph from 1923, the ore freighter *Bethore* is seen here as its iron ore from the Bethlehem Steel–owned iron ore open-pit mines in Chile gets unloaded into the awaiting hoppers. The LVRR did not have specialized ore hoppers like railroads in the upper Midwest, so it used coal hoppers to move the ore. Note the fuel tender barge to the starboard side of the *Bethore*. (Courtesy of Bob's Photos.)

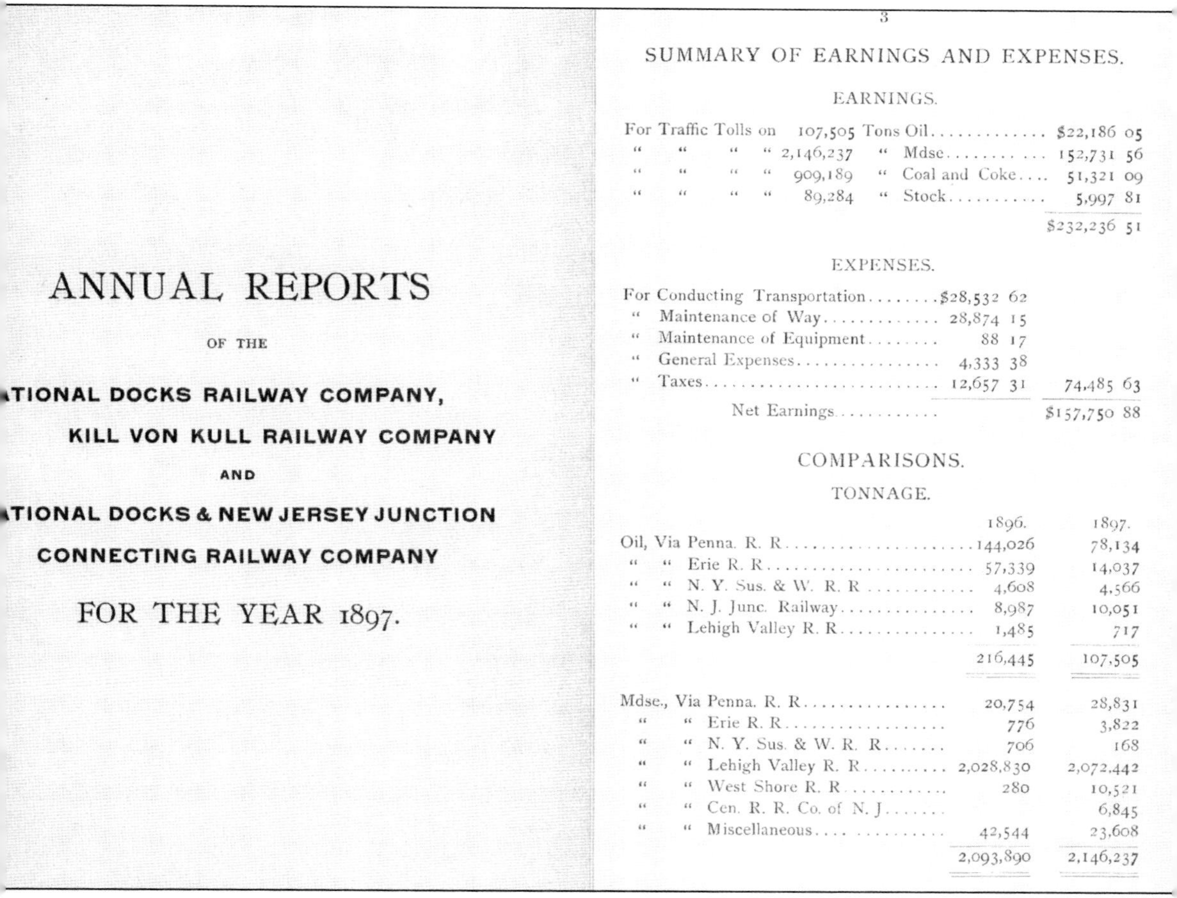

ANNUAL REPORTS

OF THE

[NA]TIONAL DOCKS RAILWAY COMPANY,

KILL VON KULL RAILWAY COMPANY

AND

[NA]TIONAL DOCKS & NEW JERSEY JUNCTION CONNECTING RAILWAY COMPANY

FOR THE YEAR 1897.

3

SUMMARY OF EARNINGS AND EXPENSES.

EARNINGS.

For Traffic Tolls on	107,505	Tons Oil	$22,186 05
" " " "	2,146,237	" Mdse	152,731 56
" " " "	909,189	" Coal and Coke	51,321 09
" " " "	89,284	" Stock	5,997 81
			$232,236 51

EXPENSES.

For Conducting Transportation	$28,532 62	
" Maintenance of Way	28,874 15	
" Maintenance of Equipment	88 17	
" General Expenses	4,333 38	
" Taxes	12,657 31	74,485 63
Net Earnings		$157,750 88

COMPARISONS.

TONNAGE.

	1896.	1897.
Oil, Via Penna. R. R	144,026	78,134
" " Erie R. R	57,339	14,037
" " N. Y. Sus. & W. R. R	4,608	4,566
" " N. J. Junc. Railway	8,987	10,051
" " Lehigh Valley R. R	1,485	717
	216,445	107,505
Mdse., Via Penna. R. R	20,754	28,831
" " Erie R. R	776	3,822
" " N. Y. Sus. & W. R. R	706	168
" " Lehigh Valley R. R	2,028,830	2,072,442
" " West Shore R. R	280	10,521
" " Cen. R. R. Co. of N. J		6,845
" " Miscellaneous	42,544	23,608
	2,093,890	2,146,237

This 1897 National Docks Railway (NDR) annual report shows not only the three distinct companies that made up the core of the NDR but also the railroads that benefited from the NDR's existence. After the LVRR gained control of the NDR in 1898 and merged the component companies into the NDR, the line continued to be an important connecting line for the CNJ, PRR, and NYC, as part of a consolidated beltline serving the waterfront, stretching from Weehawken to Bayonne. Today the section of the NDR from the Greenville section of Jersey City north to just past New Jersey Junction (where the LVRR and NYC properties met each other), where the old Erie Railroad tunnel under Bergen Hill is located, is still used by Norfolk Southern Railroad and Conrail Shared Assets to move trains between the ex-LVRR Oak Island and the ex-Erie Lackawanna Croxton Yards. (Courtesy of Ralph A. Heiss.)

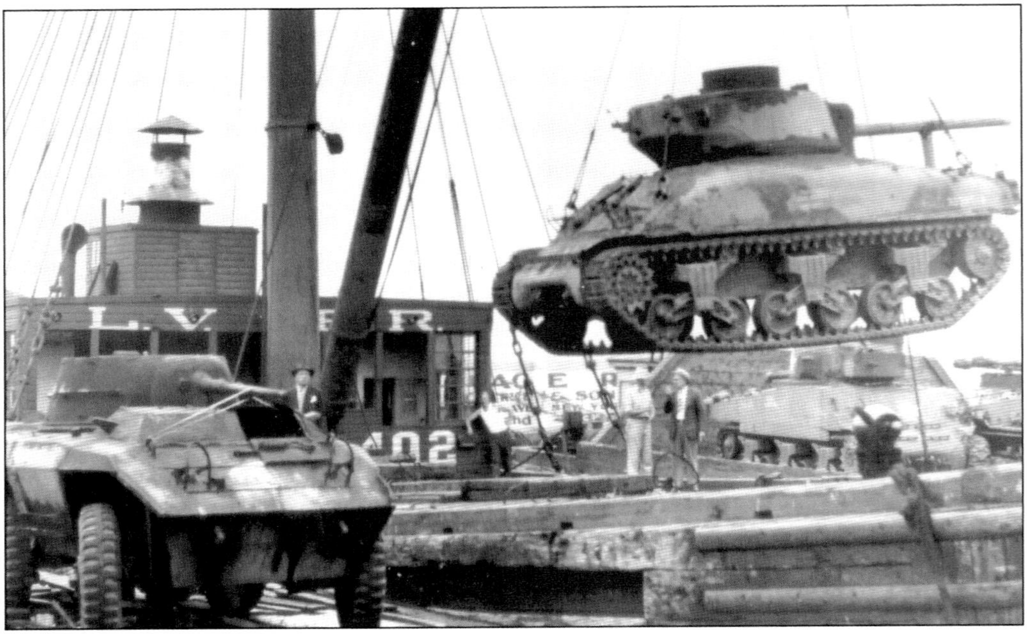

The marine department of the LVRR had many specialized pieces of equipment to move freight around the harbor. In this photograph, steam derrick lighter No. 402, which had a capacity to lift 30 tons, lifts a Sherman tank returning from the European theater in 1946 onto the dock at the Claremont terminal. Note the lack of hard hats, in what would today be cited for breaking many OSHA safety rules! (Courtesy of Robert J. Lewis.)

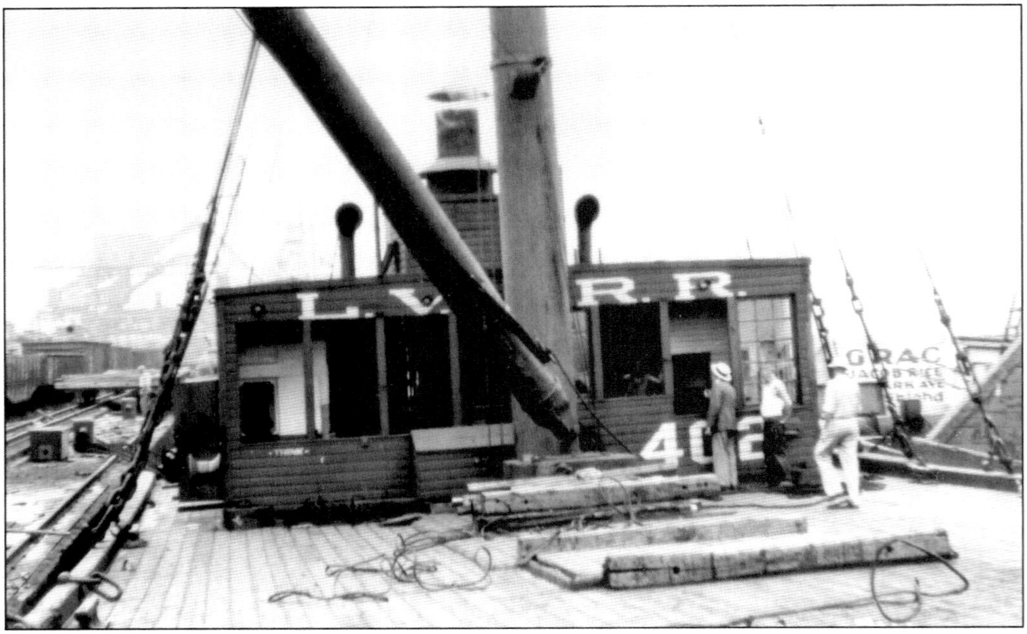

Here is another view of No. 402 as it swings around for another load. In the background can be seen the ore unloaders out near the end of the pier at the Claremont terminal. Craft like No. 402 would eventually outlive their usefulness, and many others like it found a final resting place rotting away in the many hidden inlets surrounding Staten Island in the 1970s and 1980s. (Courtesy of Robert J. Lewis.)

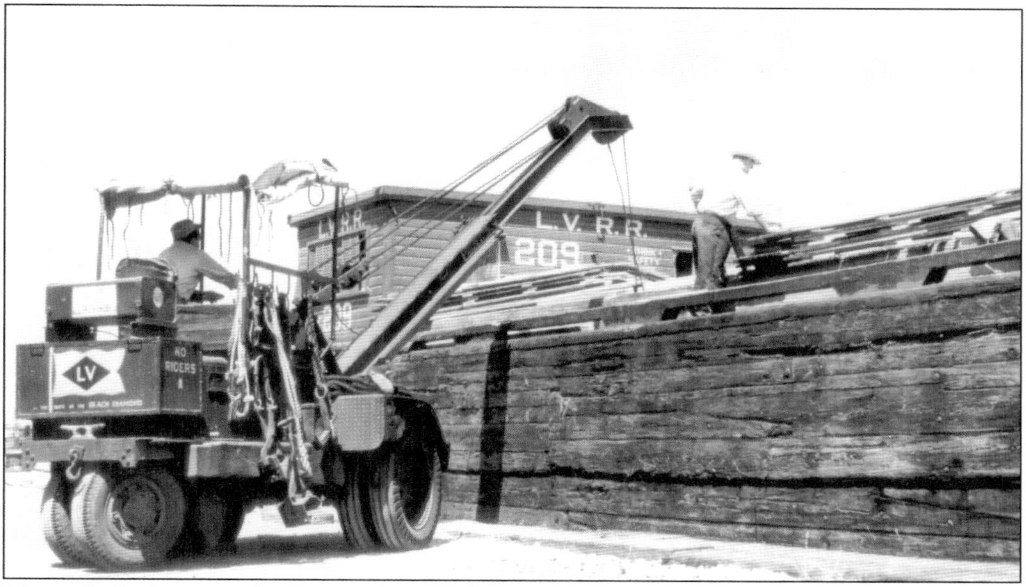

This nifty little piece of equipment is seen loading scow No. 209 in 1946. Note the slogan "the Route of the Black Diamond" on the back of the crane. Scow No. 209 was an unpropelled barge that served as the flatcar of the marine department and could be loaded with any large bulky items that needed to be moved via the "water beltline" of New York Harbor. (Courtesy of Robert J. Lewis.)

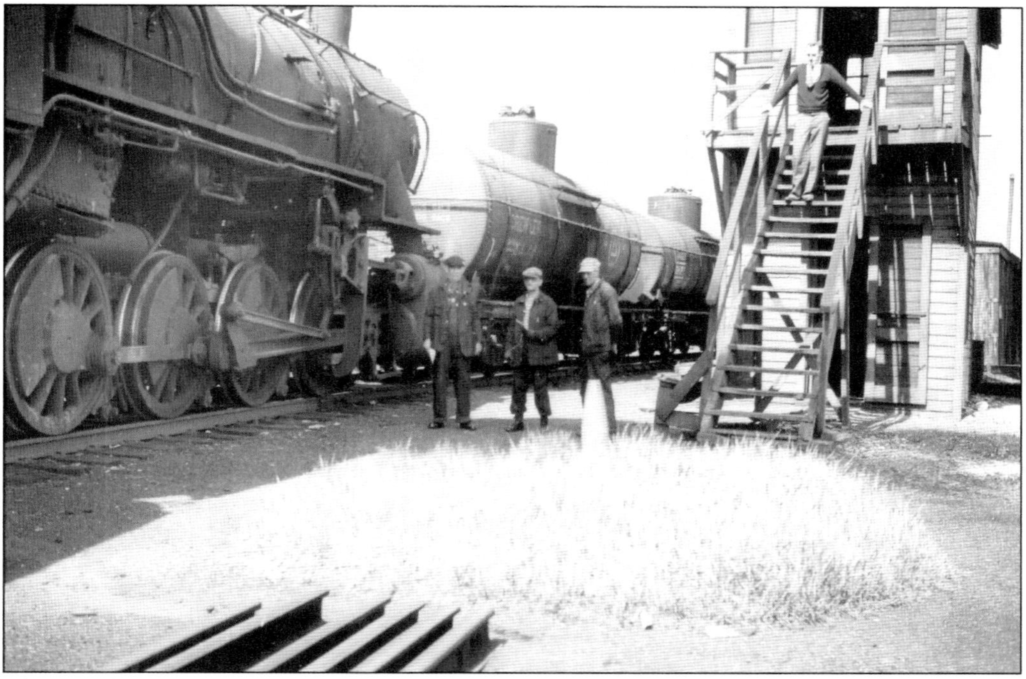
The switching crew of this local at Standard Oil's Eagle Works, adjacent to the National Docks on Black Tom, takes a minute to have a photograph taken for prosperity, sometime in the 1930s. The shoreline from here south to Constable Hook in Bayonne was mostly tank farms, and in the 1880s, both Standard Oil and Tidewater Oil built the first pipelines to tank farms and refineries in Bayonne. (Photograph by Wayne Brumbaugh, courtesy of Bob's Photos.)

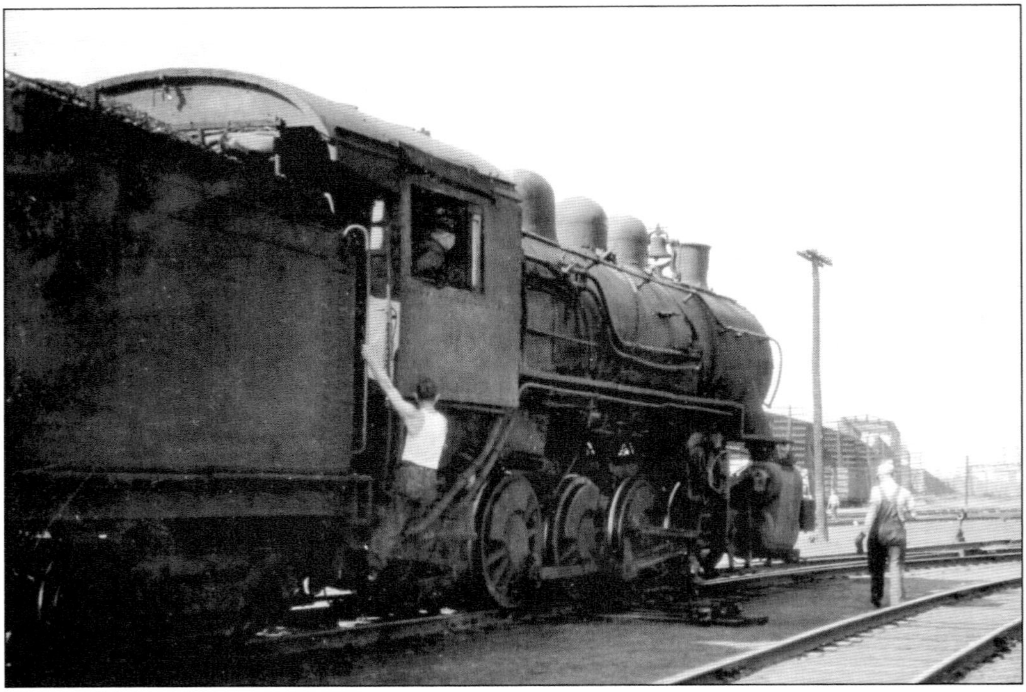

This unidentified locomotive switches around East Claremont Yard on what appears to be a warm day, as evidenced by the crew's choice of dress. The signal bridge in the distance guards the main line of the CNJ leading to its huge waterfront yards. The lines of the CNJ and LVRR crisscrossed each other in this part of Jersey City, making it sometimes very difficult to tell just who owned what. (Photograph by Wayne Brumbaugh, courtesy of Bob's Photos.)

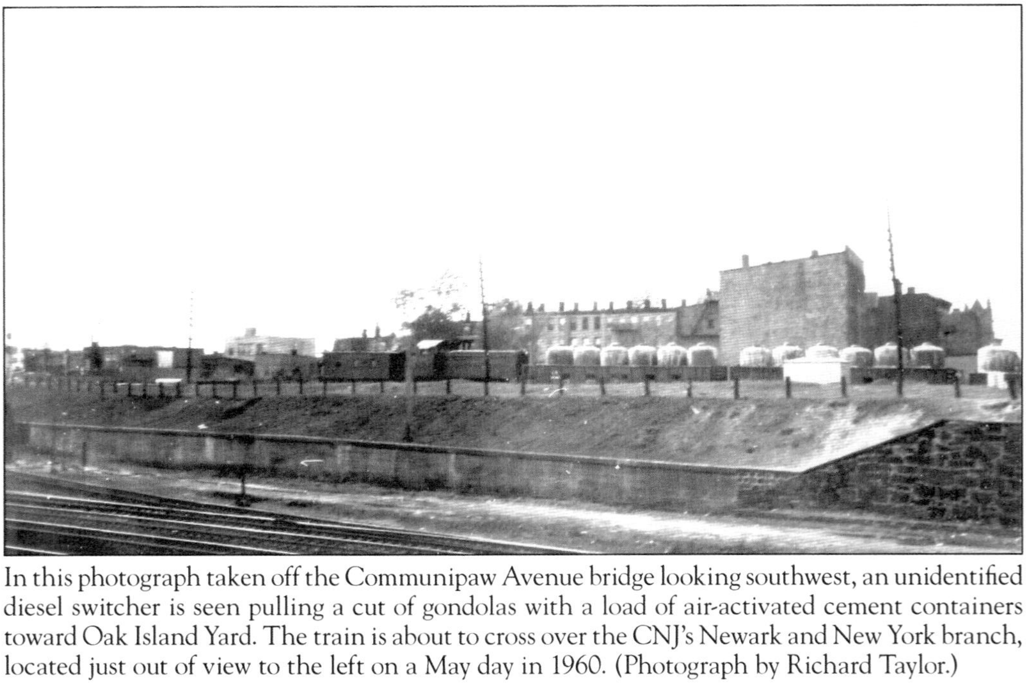

In this photograph taken off the Communipaw Avenue bridge looking southwest, an unidentified diesel switcher is seen pulling a cut of gondolas with a load of air-activated cement containers toward Oak Island Yard. The train is about to cross over the CNJ's Newark and New York branch, located just out of view to the left on a May day in 1960. (Photograph by Richard Taylor.)

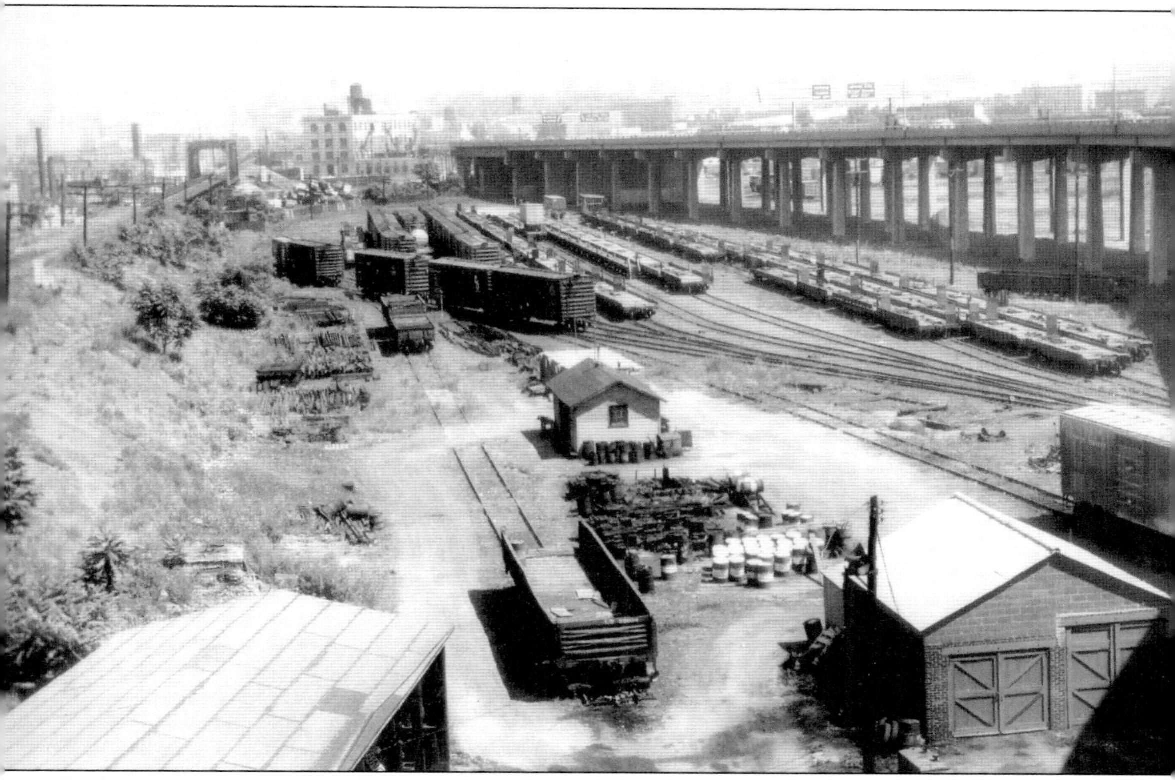

In this panoramic view of the west yard at Jersey City, one can see not only the Grand Street trailer-on-flatcar (TOFC) facility for piggyback traffic that opened in 1954 but also the New Jersey Turnpike Newark Bay Extension, built in 1956. The highway paralleled the LVRR main line all the way from Newark, which only helped draw more freight off the railroad and into trucks on the highway once completed. The piggyback yard for the LVRR's TOFC service was plagued by vandalism and thievery in the 1960s, causing the LVRR to move it to Oak Island Yard and relative safety. This photograph dates to around 1960 and looks north along the National Docks branch. (Courtesy of Ralph A. Heiss.)

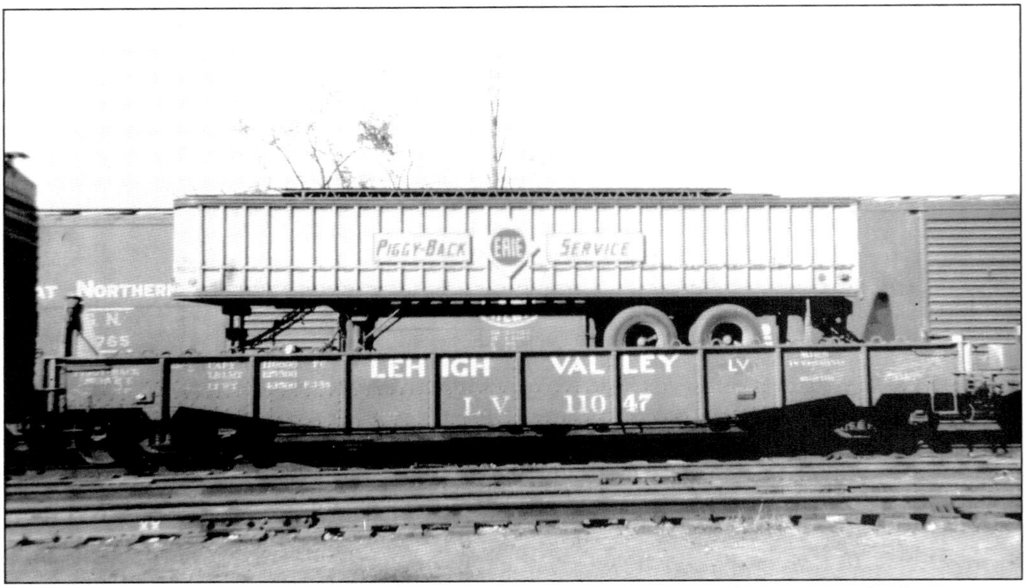

Like most railroads, when the LVRR began its TOFC service, very few purpose-built cars were available to handle the truck trailers, so railroads like the DL&W and LVRR were forced to build piggyback flatcars from old hopper car and gondola frames. This early LVRR car was rebuilt from a 40-foot gondola car in the 1950s. (Courtesy of Bob's Photos.)

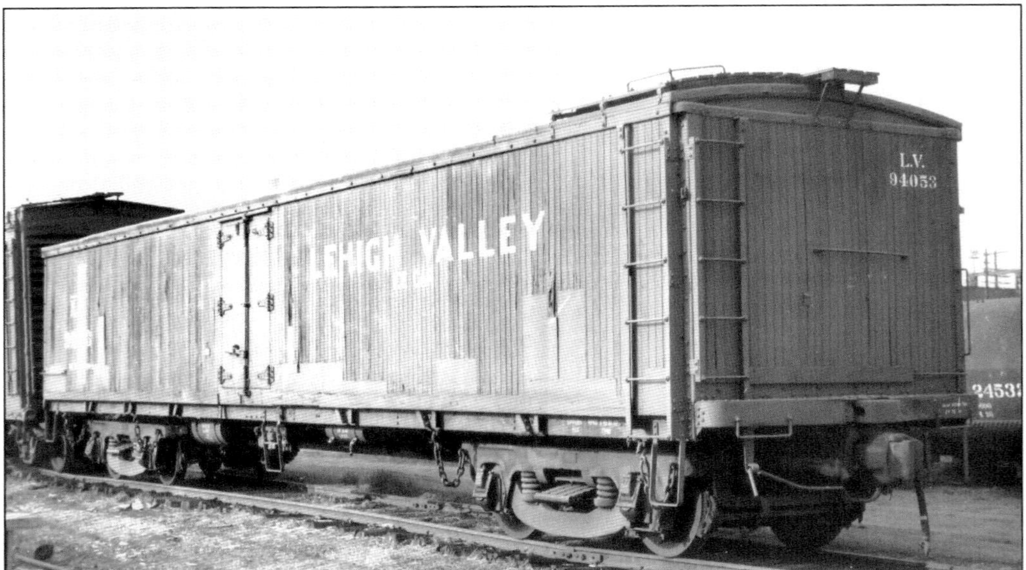

Until 1948, No. 37, the *Big Milk*, hauled milk brought down from New York State creameries from Sayre, Pennsylvania, on a fast schedule to a platform located long the Morris Canal in Jersey City on the Edgewater branch. The milk car seen here was by this time running in company ice service, and the cars would service icing platforms like the ones located in Jersey City and Manchester, New York. (Courtesy of Chuck Yungkurth/Rail Data Services.)

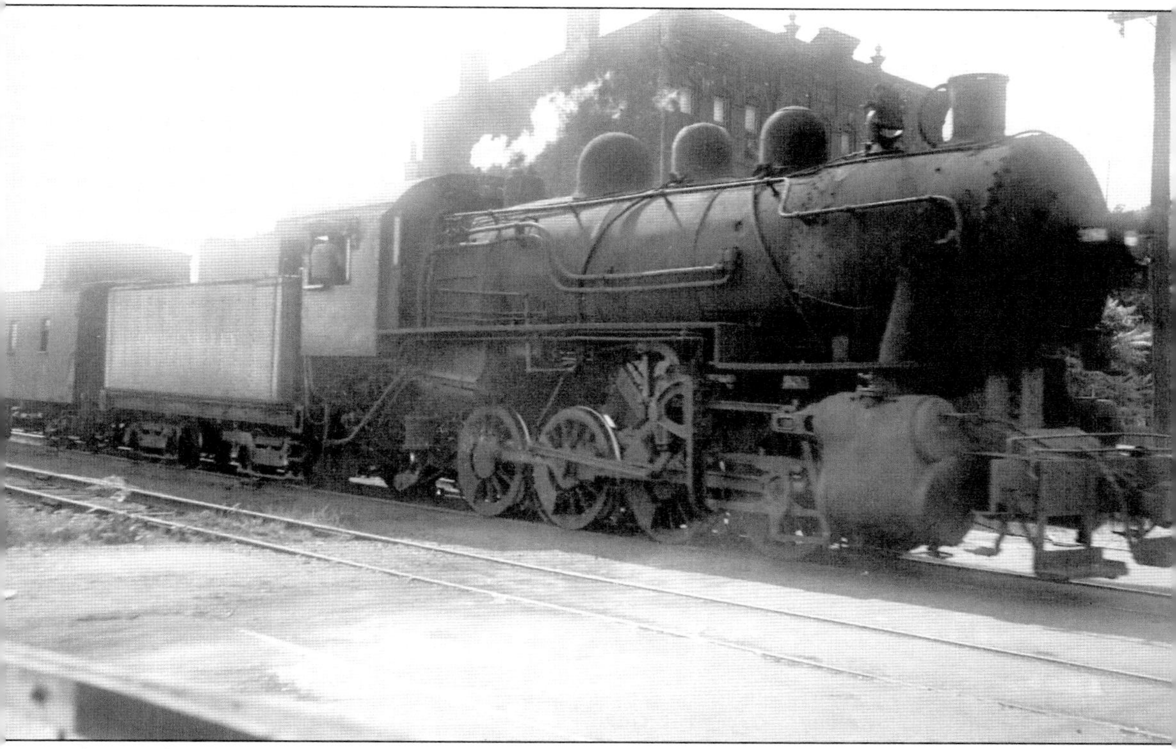

This unidentified 0-8-0 is seen here switching the local industries along the Edgewater branch in Jersey City on this August day in 1939. The Edgewater branch was a industrial branch built alongside the towpath of the Morris Canal. It was chartered in 1890 as the Edgewater Railway Company and merged into the parent railroad the following year. It was built solely to take advantage of the property owned by the Morris Canal. The branch served a large coal dealer and other assorted industries but was important for being the terminus of train No. 37, the *Big Milk*. (Photograph by C. J. Crawford, courtesy of Ralph A. Heiss.)

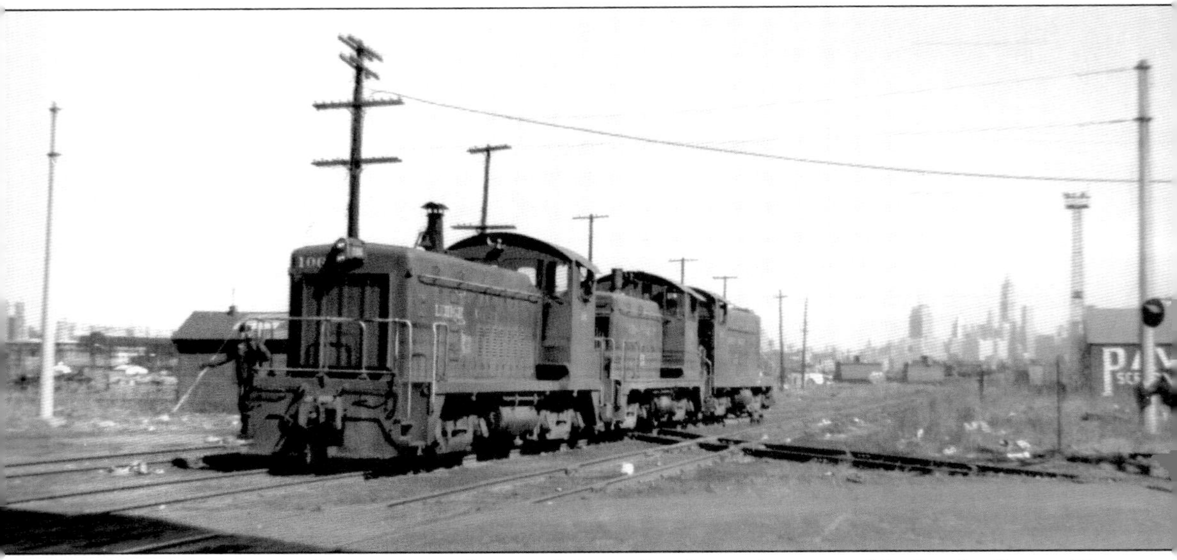

Here the photographer catches a brace of three diesel switchers, possibly for the Jersey City pullout (LVRR speak for a yard transfer run between Oak Island Yard and Jersey City) later that day. EMD SW-900M No. 106 is seen here leading another EMD product and a lone BLW S-12 model switcher across the Johnston Avenue grade crossing. SW-900M No. 106 was originally a SW-type diesel locomotive delivered in the late 1930s and was rebuilt and upgraded by EMD in 1956 instead of buying a new diesel, while also dodging accounting rules by classing it and three other SWs as rebuilt instead of new. The shadow being cast in front of the locomotive is from the New Jersey Turnpike, and the diamond crossing under the locomotives is the at-grade crossing of the CNJ's Henderson Street branch. (Photograph by Robert Pennisi, courtesy of Railroad Avenue Enterprises.)

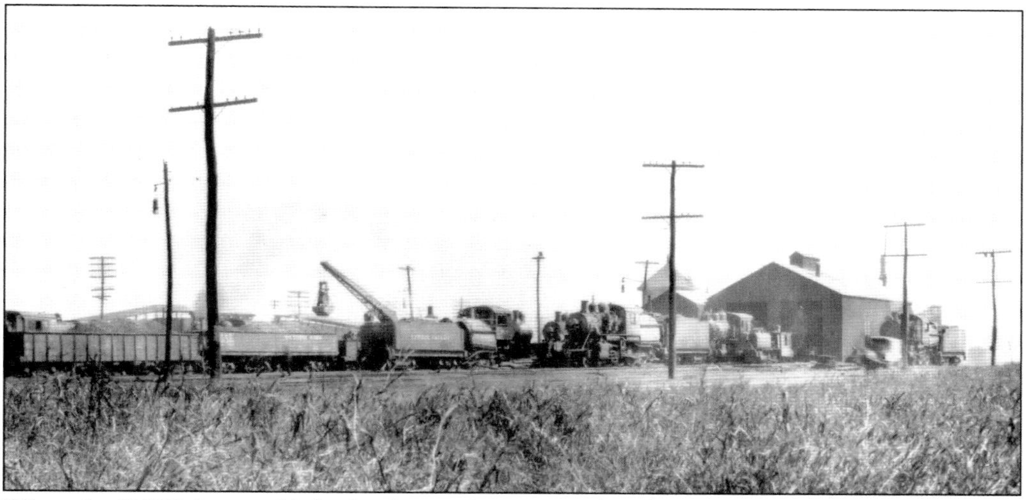

When the LVRR first established its Jersey City terminal in the late 1880s, it needed to establish an engine-servicing facility, so a modest complex complete with an engine house and water and coaling stations was located at the west end of the yard alongside Johnston Avenue. In this 1920 photograph looking east along Johnston Avenue, a horse and buggy can be made out speeding alongside the engine house. (Courtesy of Theodore F. Gleichmann/Railroad Museum of Pennsylvania.)

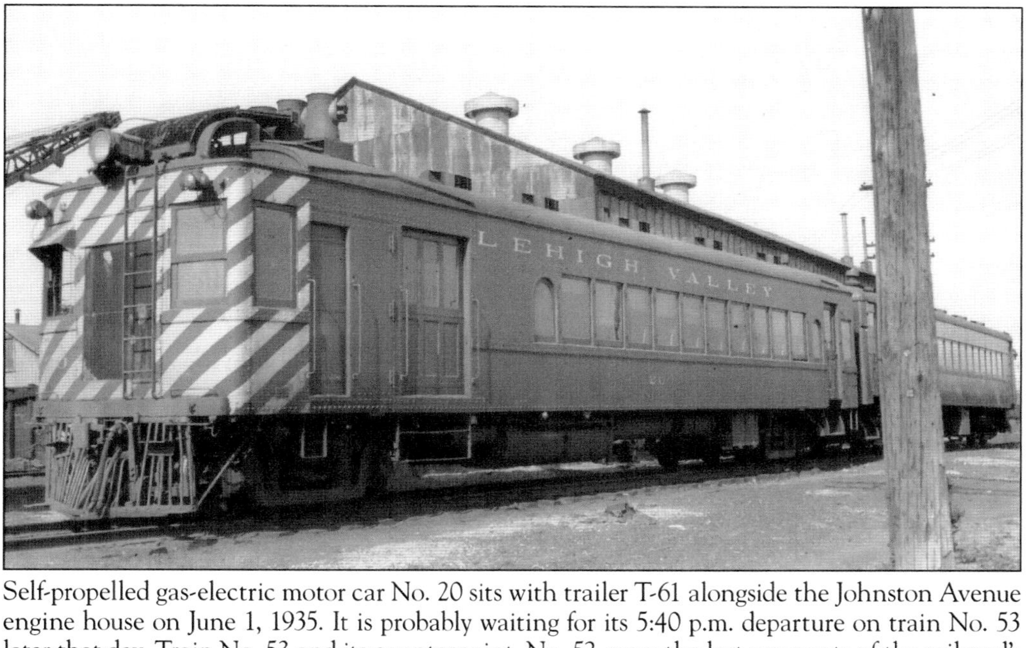

Self-propelled gas-electric motor car No. 20 sits with trailer T-61 alongside the Johnston Avenue engine house on June 1, 1935. It is probably waiting for its 5:40 p.m. departure on train No. 53 later that day. Train No. 53 and its counterpoint, No. 52, were the last remnants of the railroad's local passenger service, which finally ended in 1948. (Photograph by George Votava, courtesy of Joel Rosenbaum/Tom Gallo.)

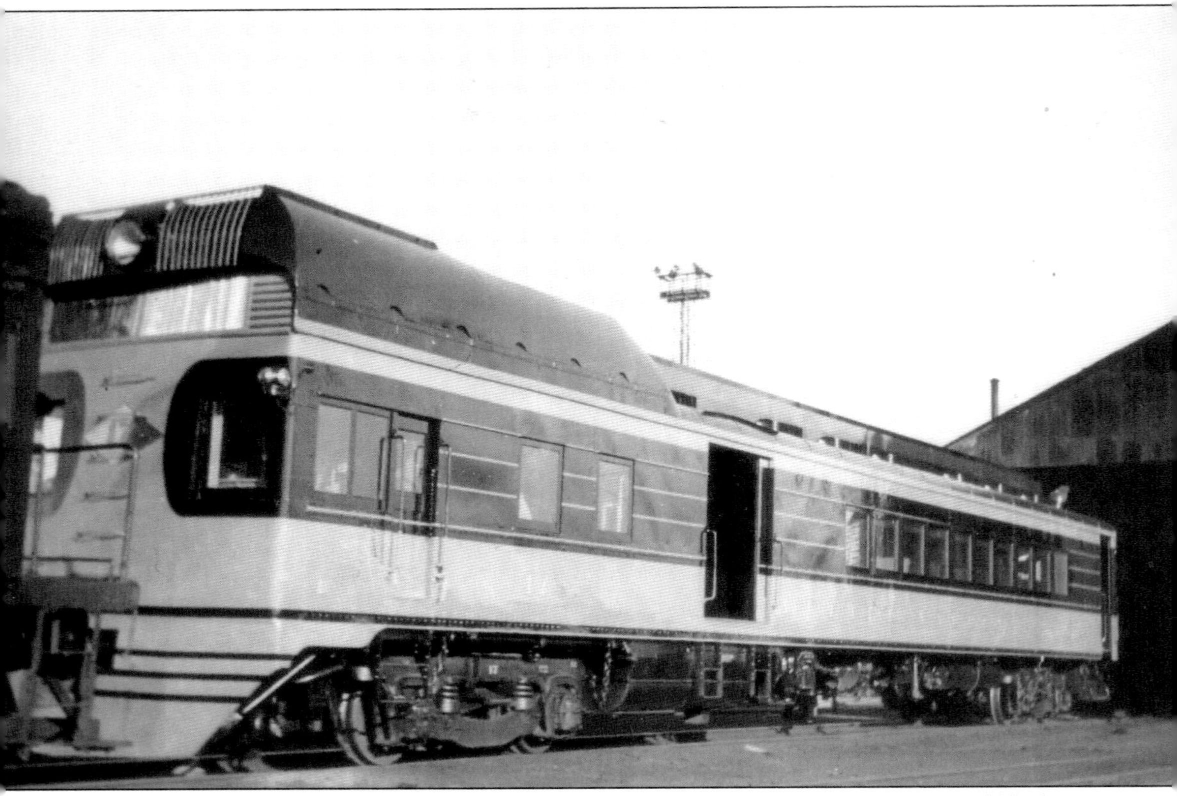

Looking as if it had just rolled out of the shop and resplendent in its new orange and black paint job, gas-electric motor car No. 17 sits outside the Jersey City engine house. The gas-electric was streamlined in 1938 by the famous industrial designer Otto Kuhler for use on train Nos. 25 and 26 that ran between Mauch Chunk, Pennsylvania, and New York (Newark). This new train was a bold effort by the LVRR management to revitalize the flagging passenger business and proved to be the catalyst for the *Asa Packer* express train in 1939. No. 17 later went on to wear a two-tone red and black paint job before being scrapped in 1951. (Courtesy of Ralph A. Heiss.)

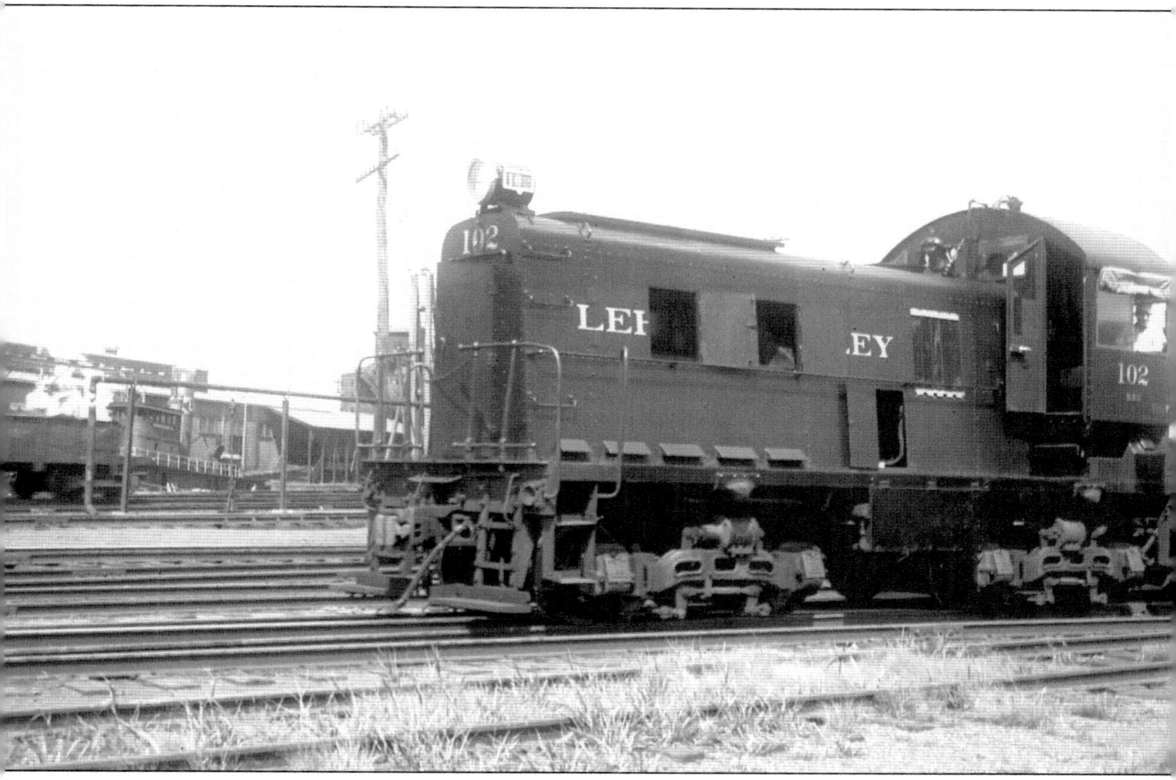

In the 1920s, many of the railroads serving New York Harbor were forced to dieselize their New York City area terminals in conjunction with smoke abatement laws, and the LVRR was no exception. Diesel No. 102, seen here, was built as demonstrator No. 300, a 300-horsepower locomotive built by ALCO. Apparently the railroad was impressed and the price was right, as the LVRR purchased it sometime in the early 1930s for use in and around New York Harbor. This particular locomotive model became the catalyst for the popular HH-series diesel locomotives from ALCO in the 1930s. (Photograph by C. J. Crawford, courtesy of Ralph A. Heiss.)

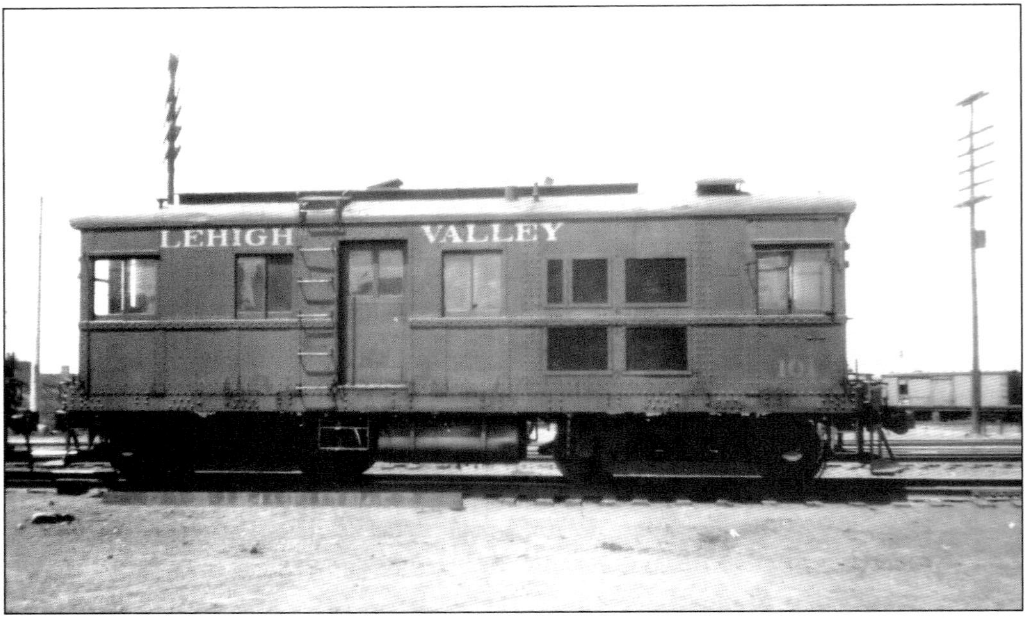

Another early diesel switching unit, No. 101, was another box cab, built by Brill and GE in 1927, and was delivered as locomotive No. 125. Seen here at Oak Island in 1935, this locomotive was assigned to the Bronx terminal yard and was probably here for some mechanical work. (Photograph by John Brinckmann, courtesy of Joel Rosenbaum/Tom Gallo.)

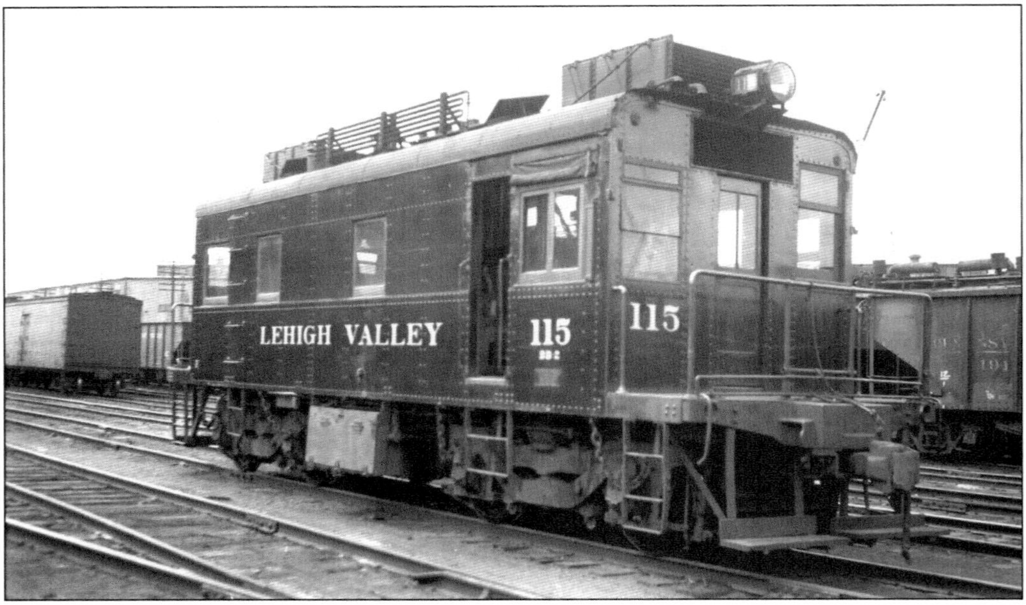

Pioneer diesel box cab No. 115 was a 60-ton locomotive built by the Electro-Motive Corporation (EMC) in 1930 and was also built as a demonstrator unit. It and sister diesel No. 116 remained active on the roster until the 1950s. (Photograph by C. J. Crawford, courtesy of Ralph A. Heiss.)

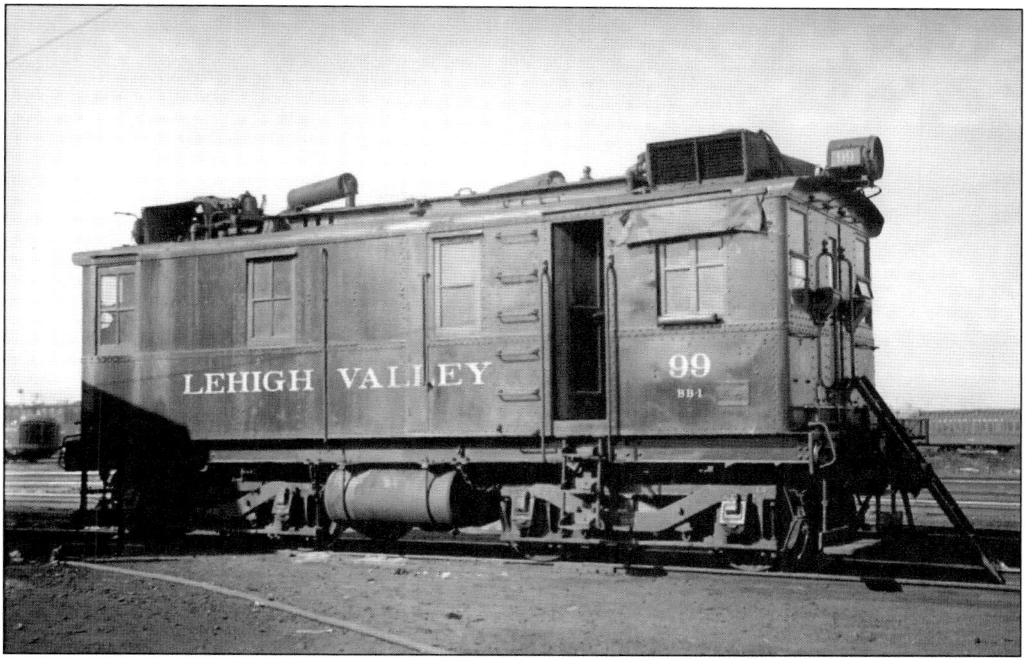

Continuing the look at the box cab locomotives of the LVRR, No. 99 and sister diesel No. 100 were the first two internal combustion locomotives bought by the railroad in 1926 from EMC. As with just about any of the early diesels, it could be found operating just about anywhere around the New York Harbor terminal area. (Courtesy of Richard Chapin.)

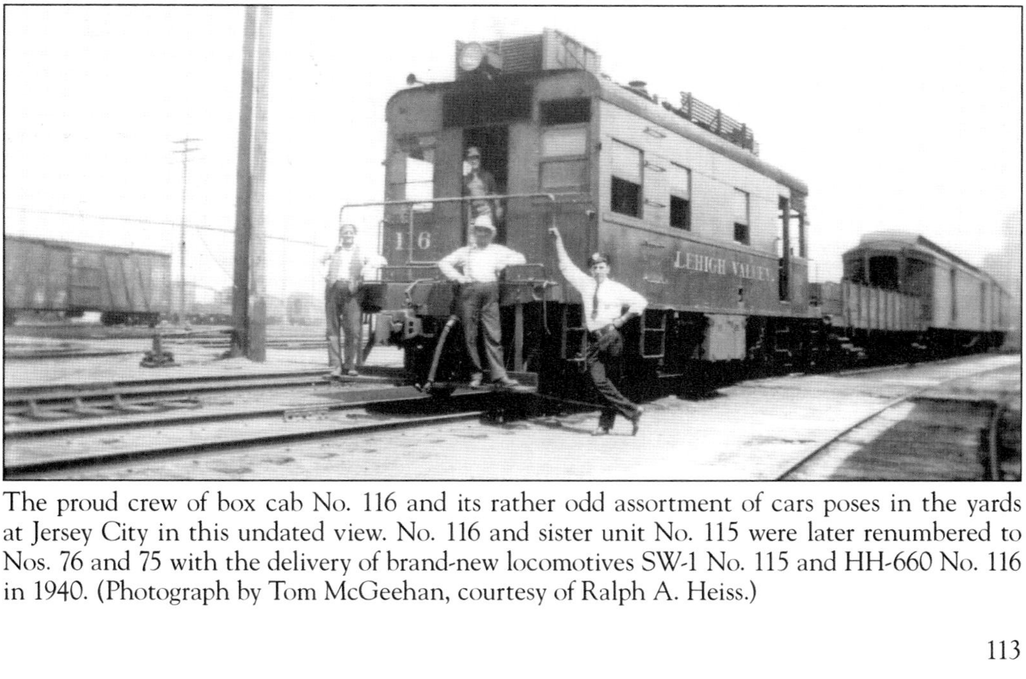

The proud crew of box cab No. 116 and its rather odd assortment of cars poses in the yards at Jersey City in this undated view. No. 116 and sister unit No. 115 were later renumbered to Nos. 76 and 75 with the delivery of brand-new locomotives SW-1 No. 115 and HH-660 No. 116 in 1940. (Photograph by Tom McGeehan, courtesy of Ralph A. Heiss.)

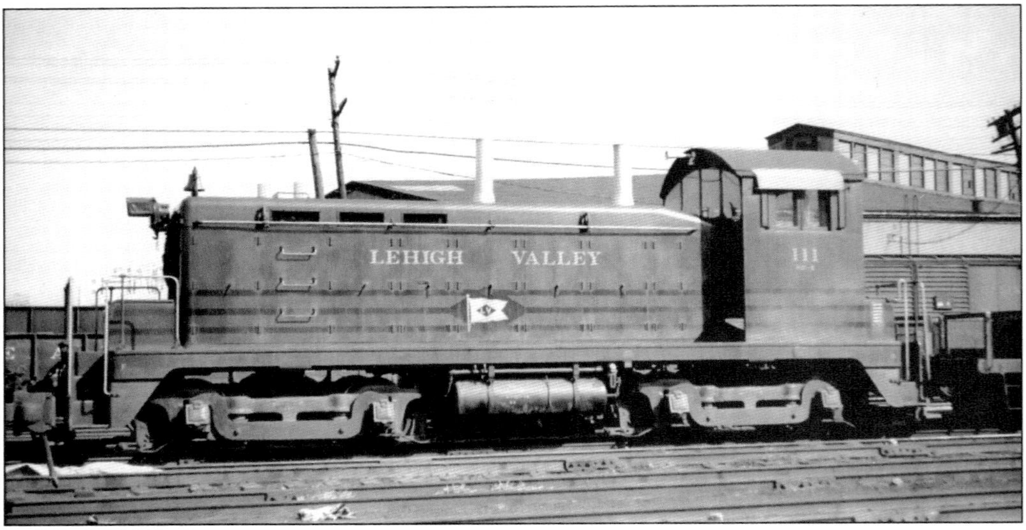

Seen here is No. 111, an SW model diesel built by EMC, as it works a cut of cars off the float bridges and past Pier C in this 1953 photograph. The earlier SW model is very similar to the later SW-1 model but can be distinguished by its tall exhaust stacks and three car body vents. (Courtesy of Gene Collora.)

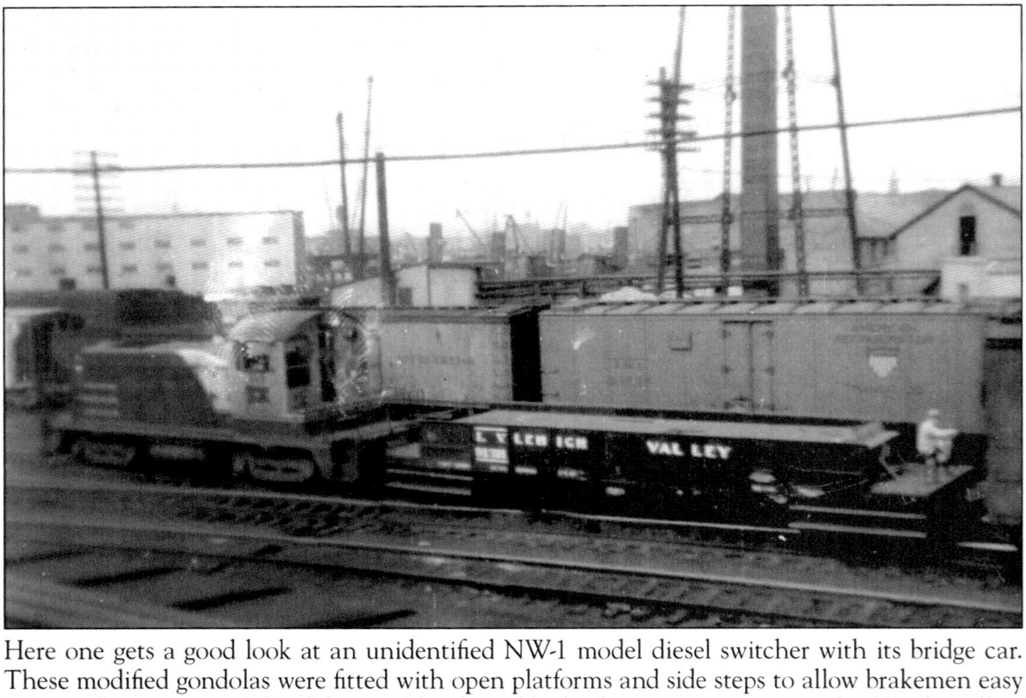

Here one gets a good look at an unidentified NW-1 model diesel switcher with its bridge car. These modified gondolas were fitted with open platforms and side steps to allow brakemen easy egress. The car was weighted down with a large block of concrete to give it a dead load to allow them to adjust the level of the float bridge when bridging a car float. (Courtesy of Tom Callan.)

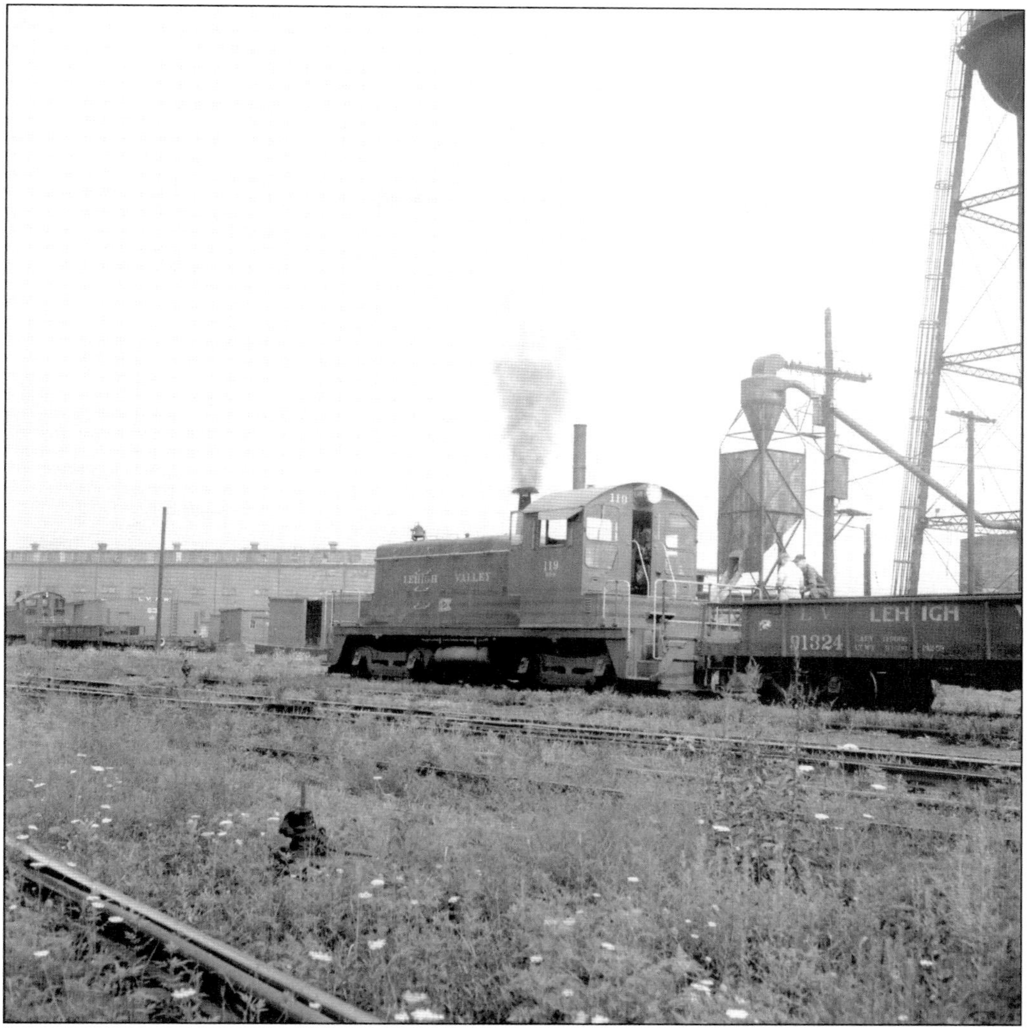

EMD SW-1 No. 119 is seen here with its idler gondola No. 91324 passing the water tower at the Washington Street yard office on July 25, 1965. The open gondolas must have provided a pleasant ride in good weather, but with no protection from the weather, it must have been miserable otherwise. The other part of Washington Street in downtown Jersey City was separated from this part of town by the Mill Creek Basin, known to locals as "the Gap," but the city required the right of way of the street to be maintained even though it was not a through street. Until 1953, there was a gentleman who had a small boat that would ferry passengers back and forth across the 500-foot-wide waterway, charging a nickel for his services. In the background, another SW with its bridge car (gondola) and some covered barges in the slip next to Pier G can be seen. (Photograph by Jim Claflin, courtesy of Craig Zeni.)

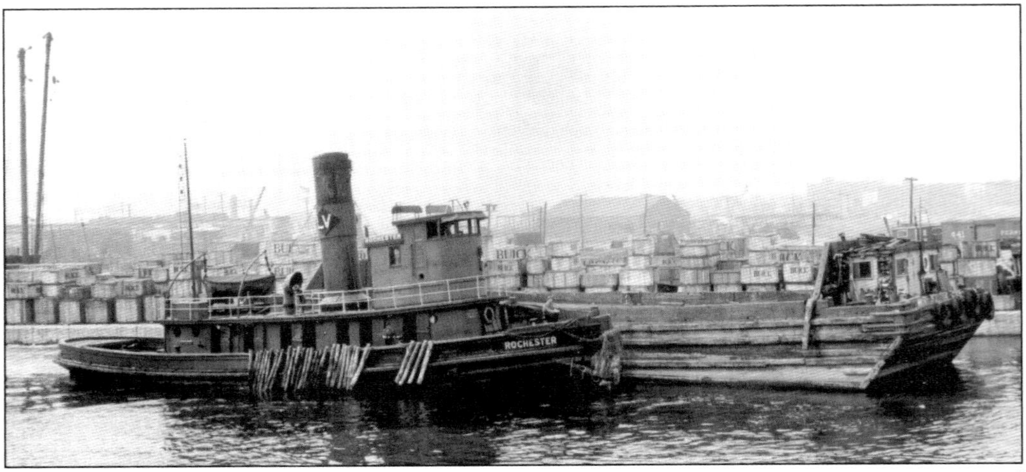

The steam tugboat *Rochester* is seen here moving a stone scow at Jersey City in 1946. During and after World War II, these scows were used to move scrap metal that was loaded off the south side of L Dock, and the tugboat is seen here moving out between I and L Docks, which is where the Buick crates are sitting awaiting movement to elsewhere. (Courtesy of Robert J. Lewis.)

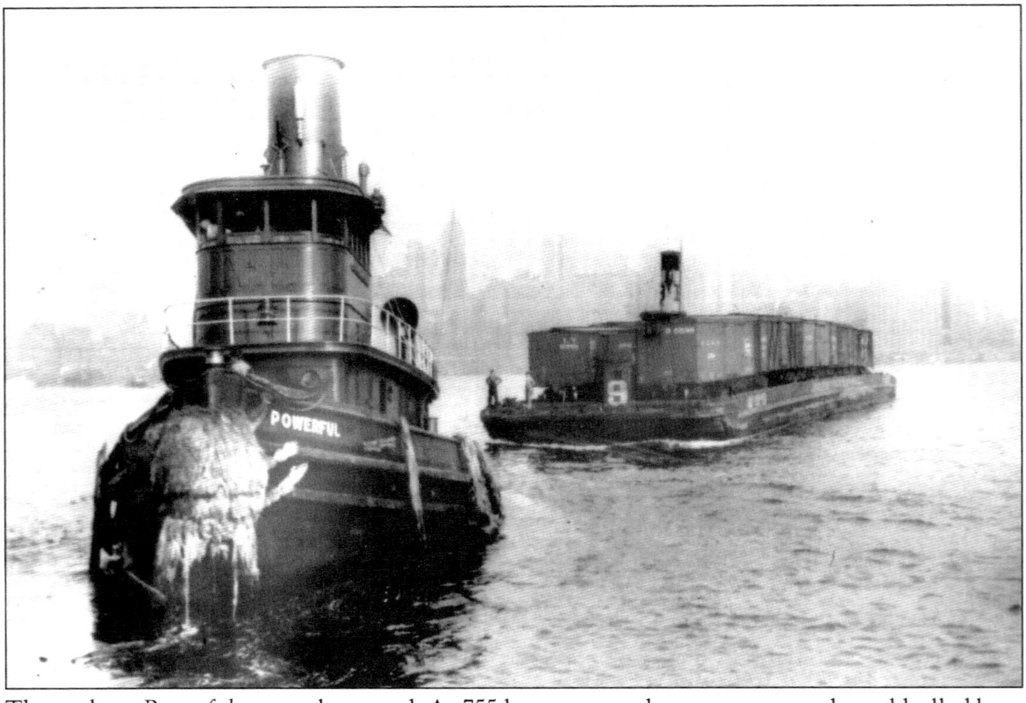

The tugboat *Powerful* was aptly named. At 755 horsepower, the steam-powered, steel-hulled boat was built in 1908 in Staten Island and served the railroad proudly until 1959. Seen here in 1911, the *Powerful* is backing away from the Jersey City float bridges with a Bush Terminal Company car float. (Courtesy of Theodore F. Gleichmann Jr.)

Bulk-Cement Handling in New York Harbor

FULLER-KINYON SYSTEM

Unloads Hopper Cars . . . Conveys to Barges . . . Unloads Barges

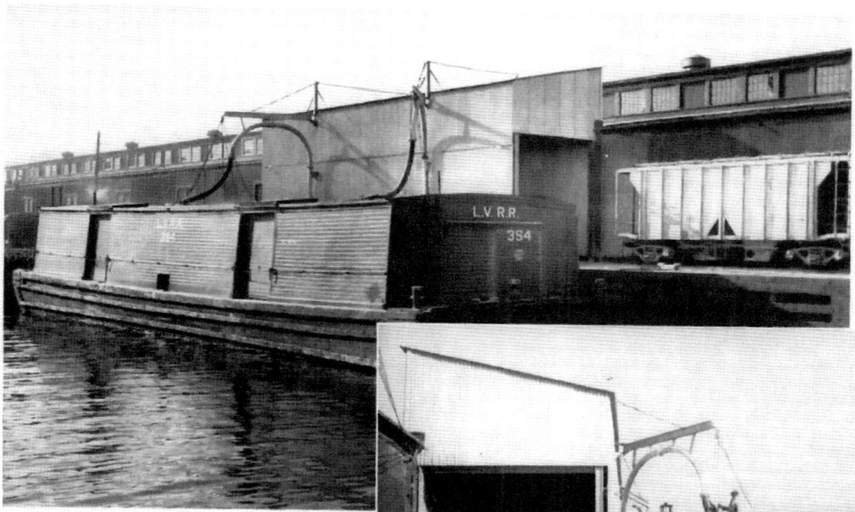

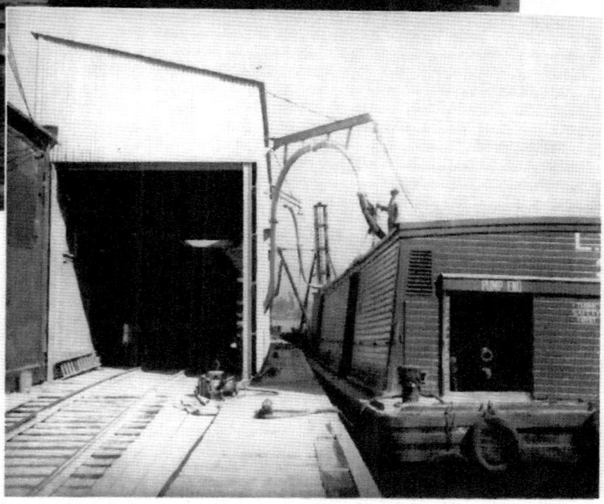

General overall views of Lehigh Valley Railroad Company's, Jersey City, N. J., terminal facilities for conveying cement from cars to barges. Details of operation are illustrated and described in this folder.

BULLETIN FK-27

FULLER COMPANY — Catasauqua, Pa.

GENERAL AMERICAN TRANSPORTATION CORPORATION SUBSIDIARY

Chicago · San Francisco · Los Angeles · Seattle · Birmingham

In 1957, the LVRR contracted the Fuller Company to build this dry bulk cement unloader on Pier B to allow covered hoppers to dump their loads and then have the cement blown into specially assigned covered barges for transshipment around the harbor. The Fuller-Kinyon pneumatic pumping system as installed was also able to unload barges as well, although the need to do so was questionable as most cement traffic was loaded outbound from the pier. The Fuller-Kinyon pneumatic pumping system is still in use today by companies who need to move dry bulk materials like cement and clay, having been first developed shortly after World War I. As one can imagine, the close proximity of water and cement is just asking for trouble, but apparently the LVRR was willing to risk the consequences on what was its largest on-line commodity. (Courtesy of Tom Fausser.)

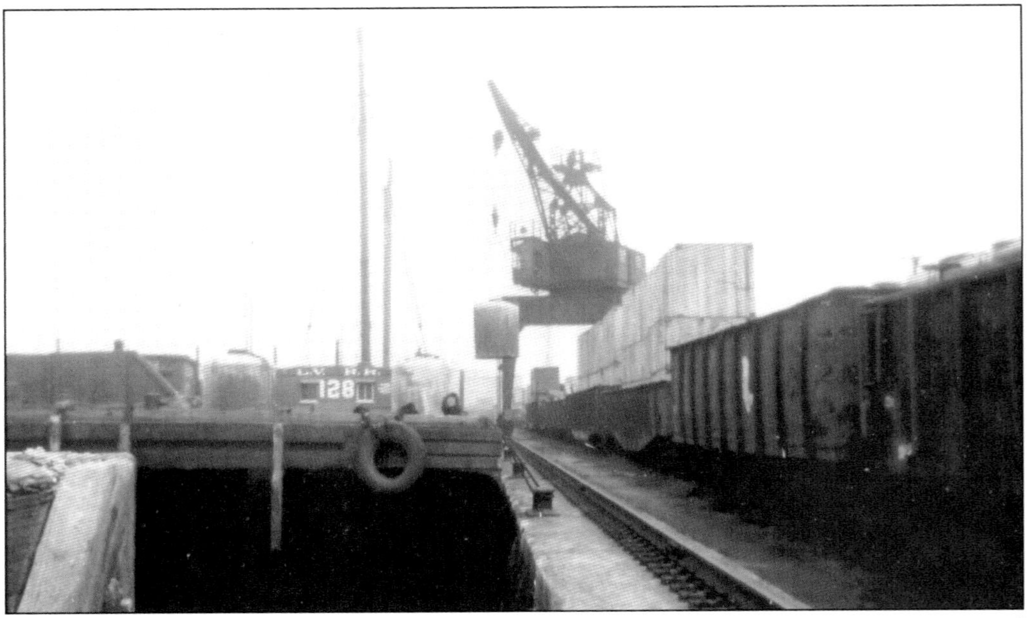

Before the widespread use of covered hoppers to haul cement, the DL&W, NYC, D&H, and LVRR used air-activated steel containers that used pressurized air to load and unload cement wherever it was required. The containers seen here being unloaded at the L crane could be removed from their specially modified gondolas or could be left inside the cars and be emptied without being removed if so desired. (Courtesy of Robert J. Lewis.)

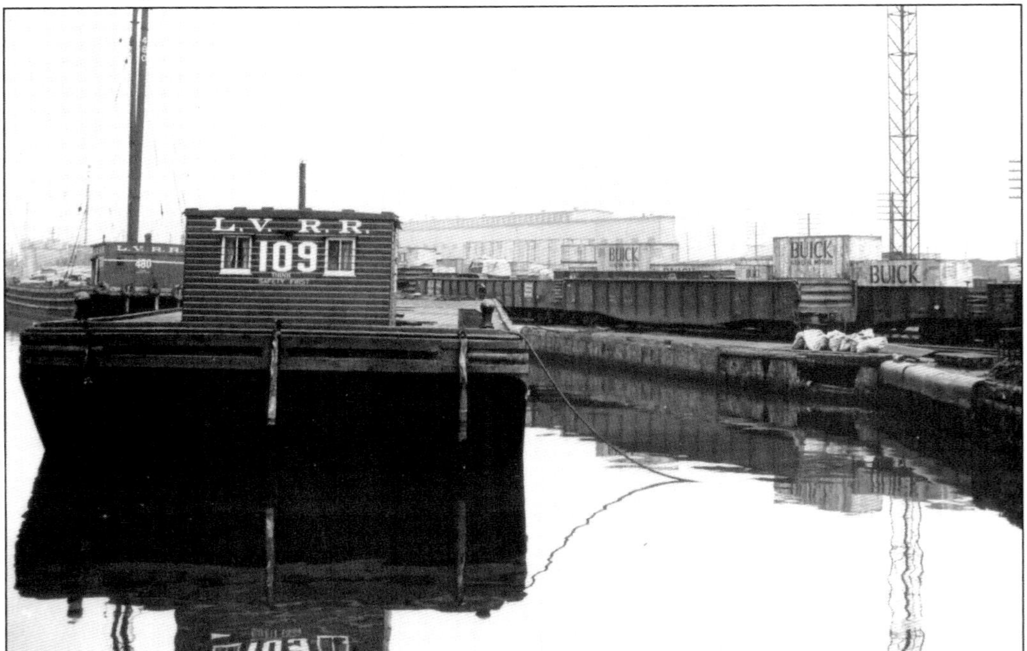

Open scow No. 109 sits quietly awaiting to be towed elsewhere to receive or deliver its next load around the harbor, as it reflects in the calm waters alongside Pier H in 1946. The gondolas in the background have probably brought their loads of crates from Buick east on train SJ-4 and are awaiting export or transshipment to New York City dealers. (Courtesy of Robert J. Lewis.)

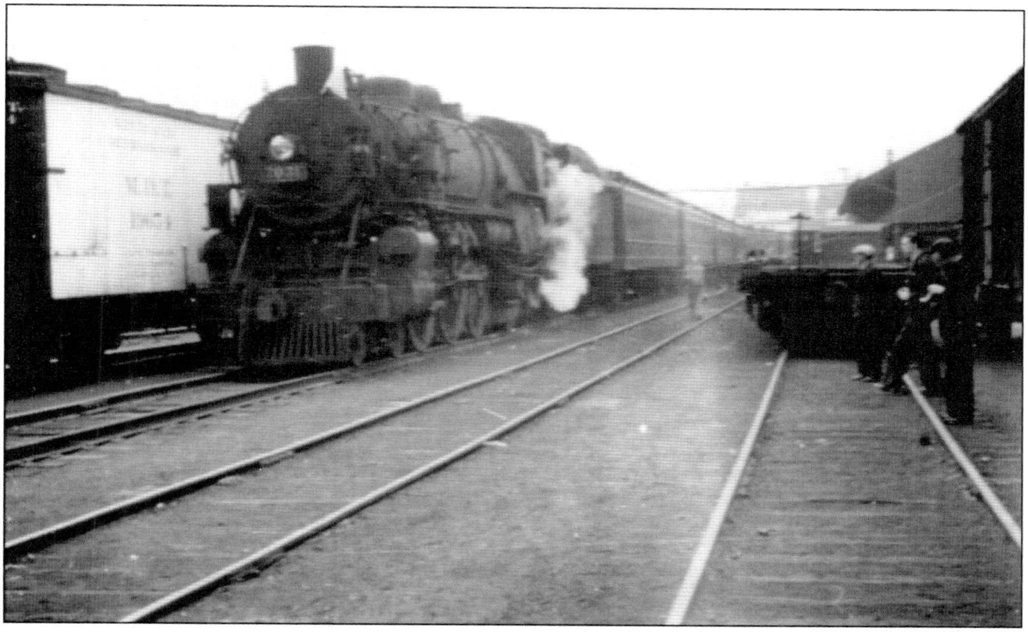

This rare photograph of a passenger train in the float yard at Jersey City is actually a fan trip chartered by the Railroad Enthusiasts in 1939 that went from Jersey City to Pen Argyl, Pennsylvania, on the Lehigh and New England Railroad and back. In the haze in the background, one can see the arches of the steel float bridges along the water's edge. (Photograph by G. Lester Whitfield, courtesy of Joel Rosenbaum/Tom Gallo.)

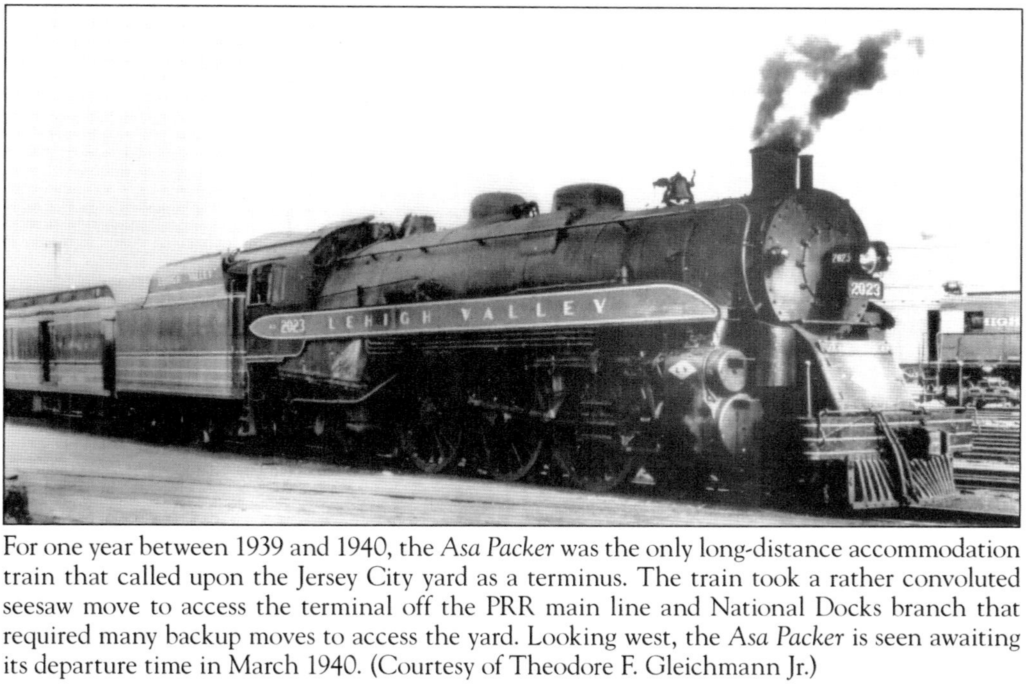

For one year between 1939 and 1940, the *Asa Packer* was the only long-distance accommodation train that called upon the Jersey City yard as a terminus. The train took a rather convoluted seesaw move to access the terminal off the PRR main line and National Docks branch that required many backup moves to access the yard. Looking west, the *Asa Packer* is seen awaiting its departure time in March 1940. (Courtesy of Theodore F. Gleichmann Jr.)

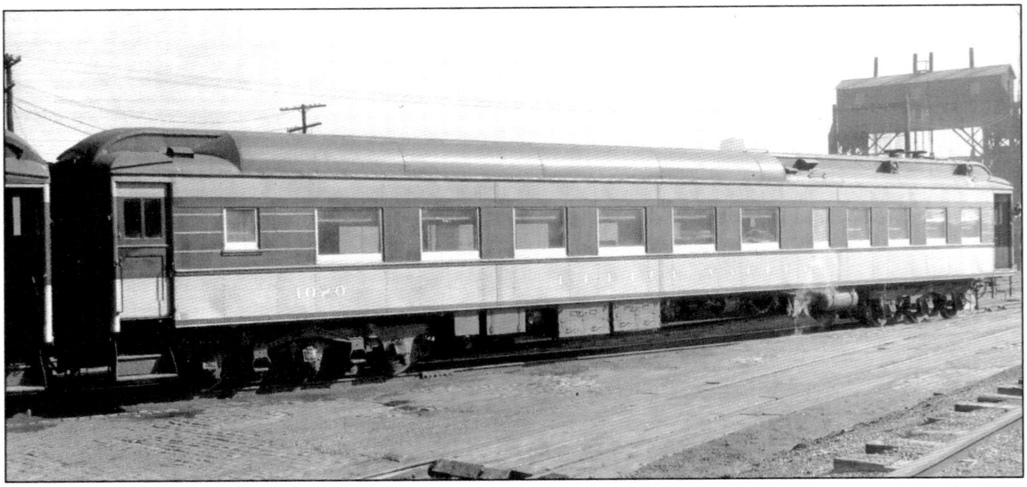

Parlor coach No. 1020 brings up the rear of the *Asa Packer* at Jersey City on a sunny March 1939 day. In the background, float bridge No. 1A marks the boundary between the LVRR and the other railroads serving New York City. Passengers wishing to travel to Gotham would need to cross the tracks and enter the CNJ's ferry terminal for a quick boat ride to New York. (Courtesy of Bob's Photos.)

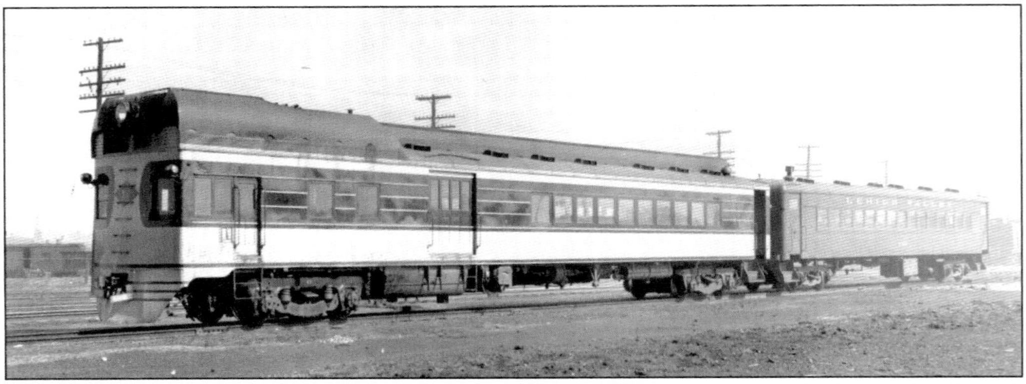

Gas-electric No. 17 visits Jersey City again, on the same day as parlor coach No. 1020 in March 1939. No. 17's trailer car, T-63, seems a poor match for such an elegant (if one can use such a term) gas electric, but it and many others of its kind provided quality service during the final years of the LVRR's local and regional passenger service. (Courtesy of Bob's Photos.)

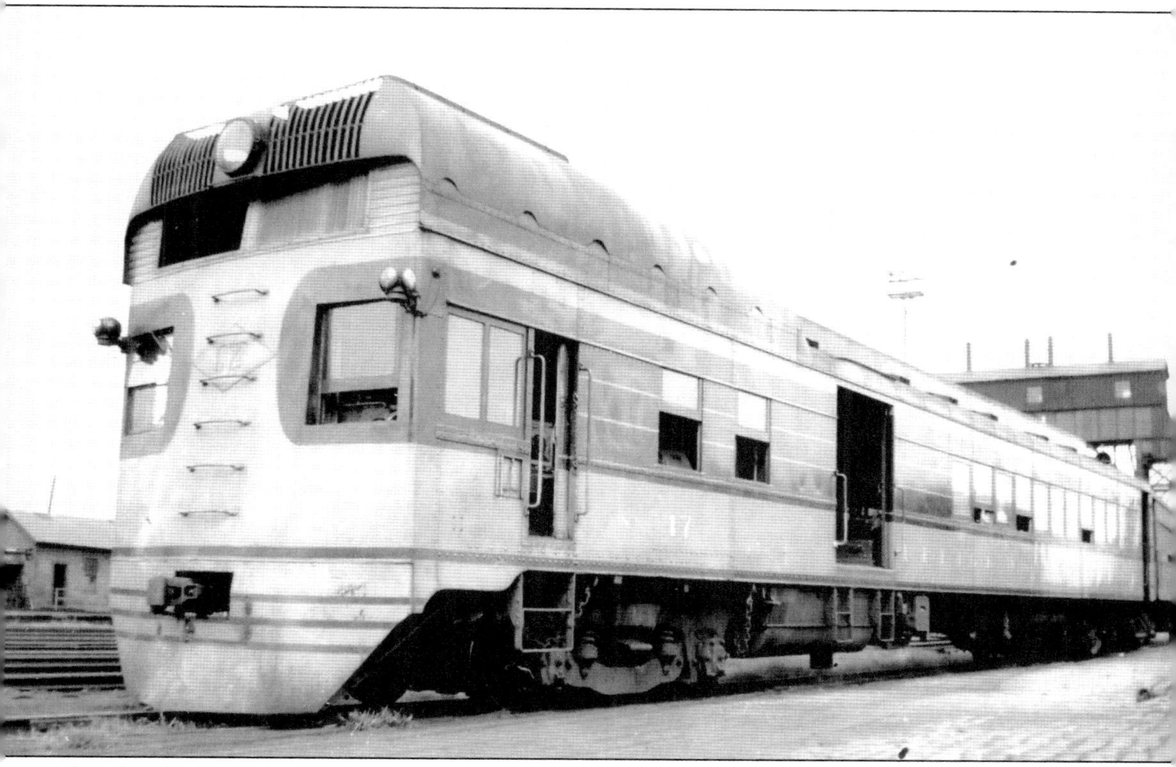

One last look at gas-electric motor car No. 17 on that same day in March 1939 shows it backed into the Local 7 track next to float bridge No. 1. All the tracks in the yard were identified by name, such as Upper 4, Bulkhead, and Old 2, to allow the crews to spot and locate cars in a particular location as per the yardmaster's instructions. The Local 7 track was the closest track to the CNJ's terminal, thus is where the train would be spotted. In the year since No. 17 was seen at the Jersey City engine house, it has taken on a bit of dirt and grime but is still wearing its regal streamlined body work and paint job. At this late date of 1939, No. 17 is probably in charge of taking train No. 53 west to Manville, although it only carried passengers as far as South Plainfield. All other local service had been dropped between 1937 and 1938 to Flemington and Easton. (Courtesy of Bob's Photos.)

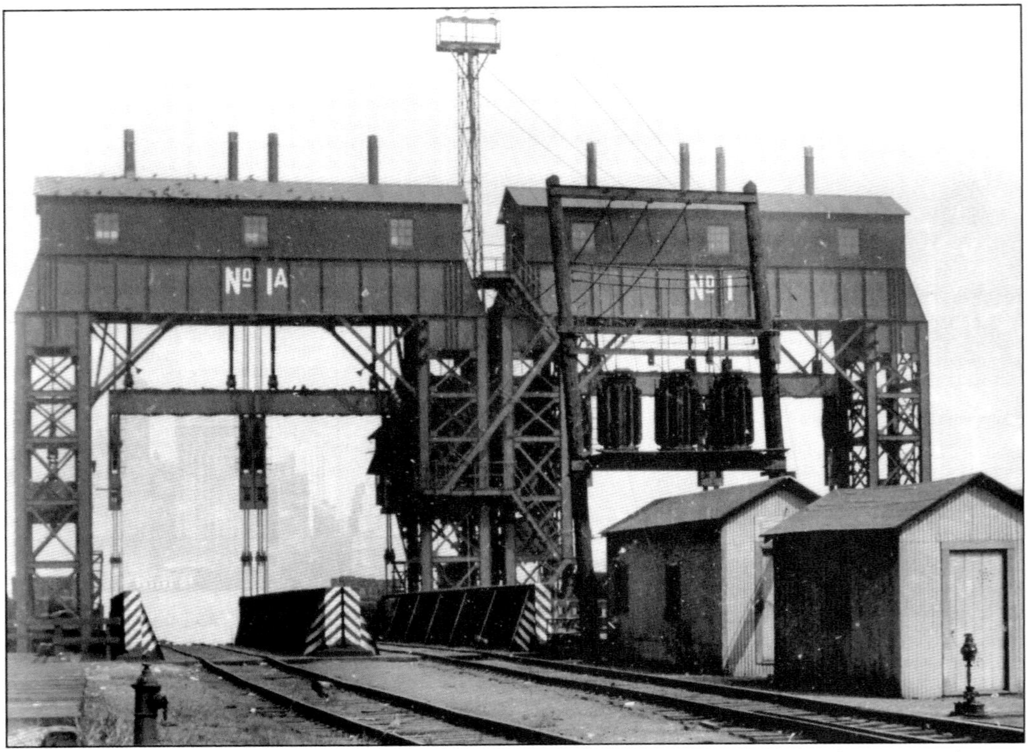

Looking east, the LVRR's two most modern float bridges, Nos. 1 and 1A, frame Manhattan Island. Built to expedite the transfer of railroad cars on and off car floats, the design used a cable and pulley system to electrically raise and lower two sets of suspended bridges contained within the structure to compensate for load weight differentials while loading and unloading. (Courtesy of H. G. MacDonald.)

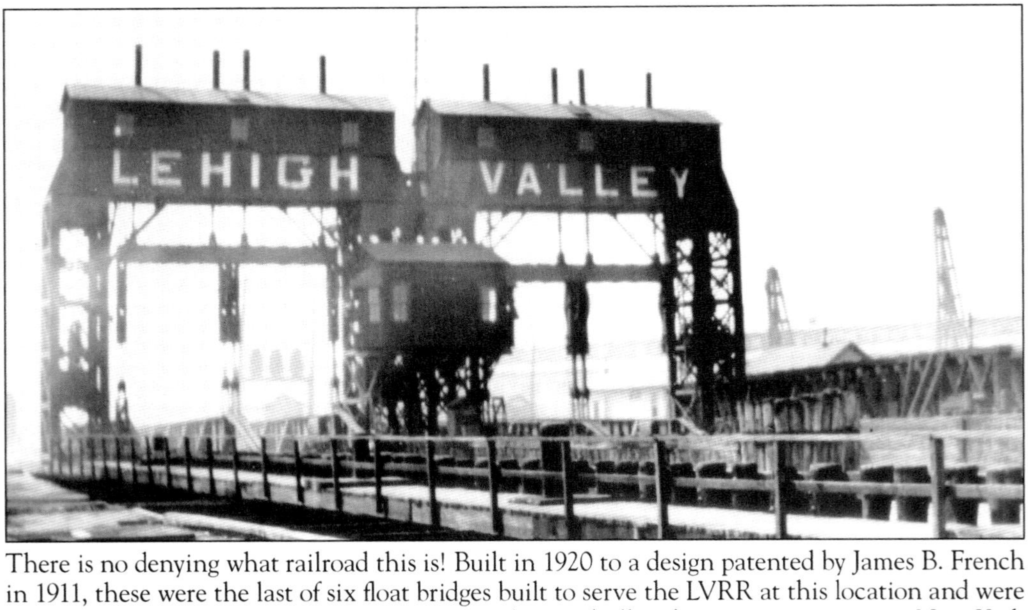

There is no denying what railroad this is! Built in 1920 to a design patented by James B. French in 1911, these were the last of six float bridges built to serve the LVRR at this location and were removed shortly after LVRR successor Conrail ceased all rail-marine operation in New York Harbor in 1976. (Courtesy of H. G. MacDonald.)

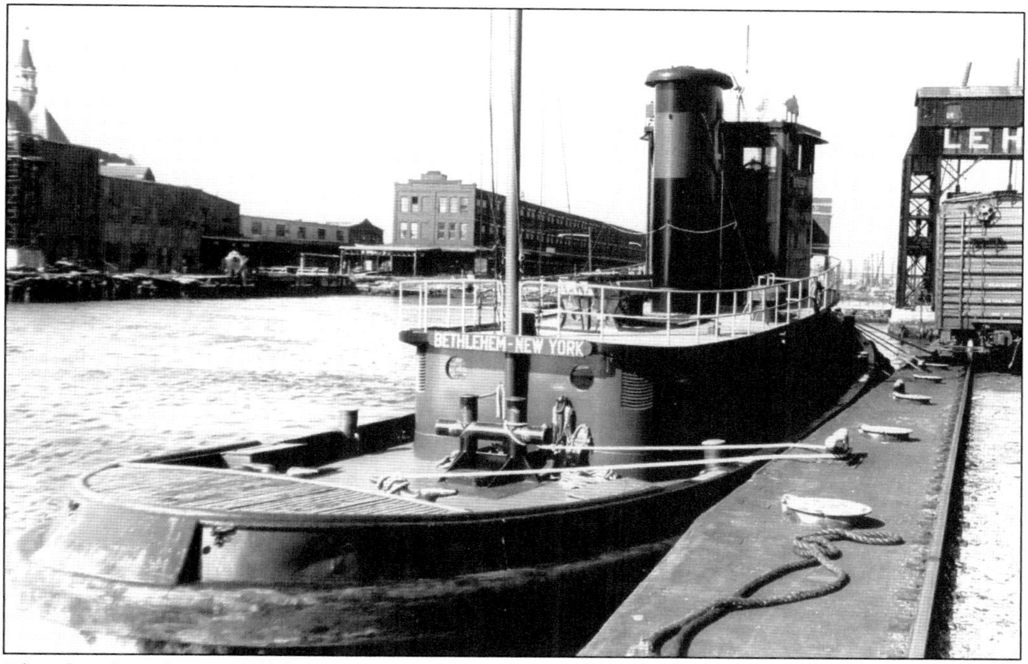

The diesel tugboat *Bethlehem* snugs a car float lightly up against float bridge No. 1 in this photograph taken sometime in the early 1970s. The *Bethlehem* was the second tugboat to bear the name and was built in Oyster Bay, New York, in 1953 by Jackobsen Shipbuilding. It was the last operating tugboat to be used by the LVRR after the 1970 sales of sister tugs *Lehigh* and *Cornell*. (Courtesy of Ralph A. Heiss.)

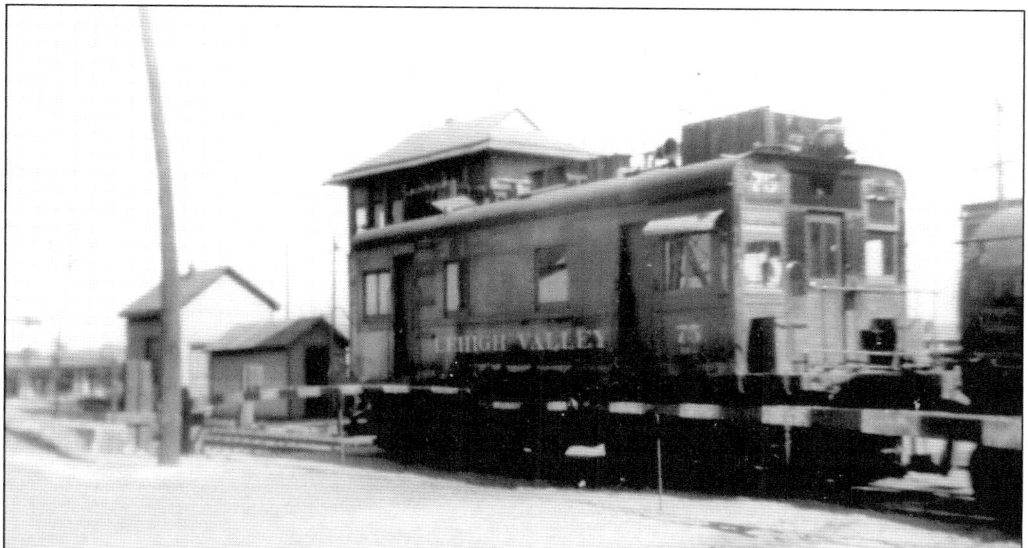

As one leaves the Jersey City terminal and moves north on the National Docks branch to the end of the LVRR's New Jersey trackage at National Junction, one encounters box cab No. 75, previously numbered as No. 115 after the 1940 renumbering to make room in the roster for other diesels, as it crosses Communipaw Avenue past CF Tower in April 1949. (Courtesy of Tom Callan.)

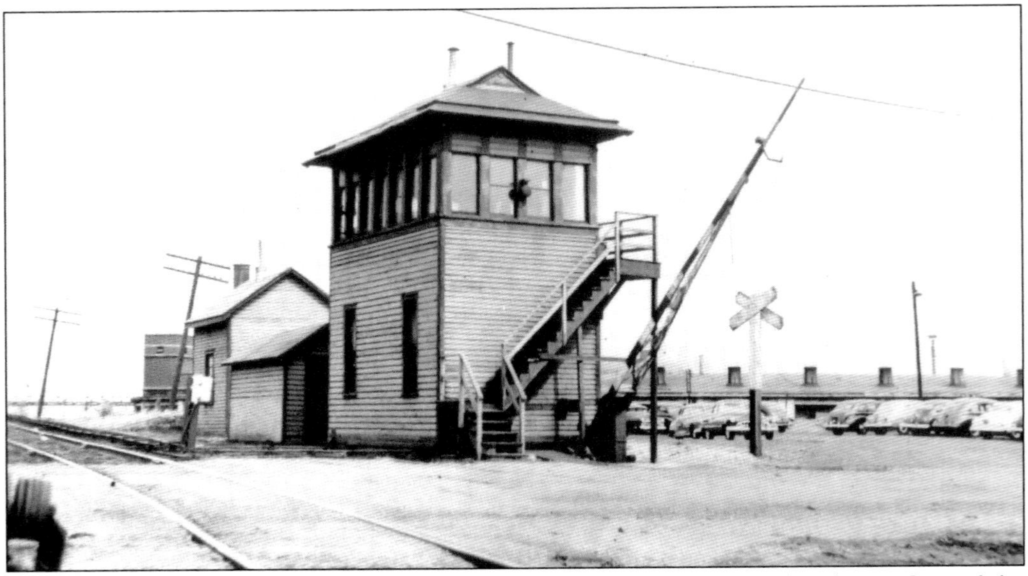

All is quiet at CF Tower on this April 11, 1952, day. In the background is the roofline of the CNJ's Communipaw engine terminal and the powerhouse that supplied its needs. Today the New Jersey Turnpike cuts across this view, and Liberty State Science Center sits on the land once occupied by the CNJ roundhouse. Trains still roll past here, but the grade crossing has long since been eliminated. (Courtesy of H. G. MacDonald.)

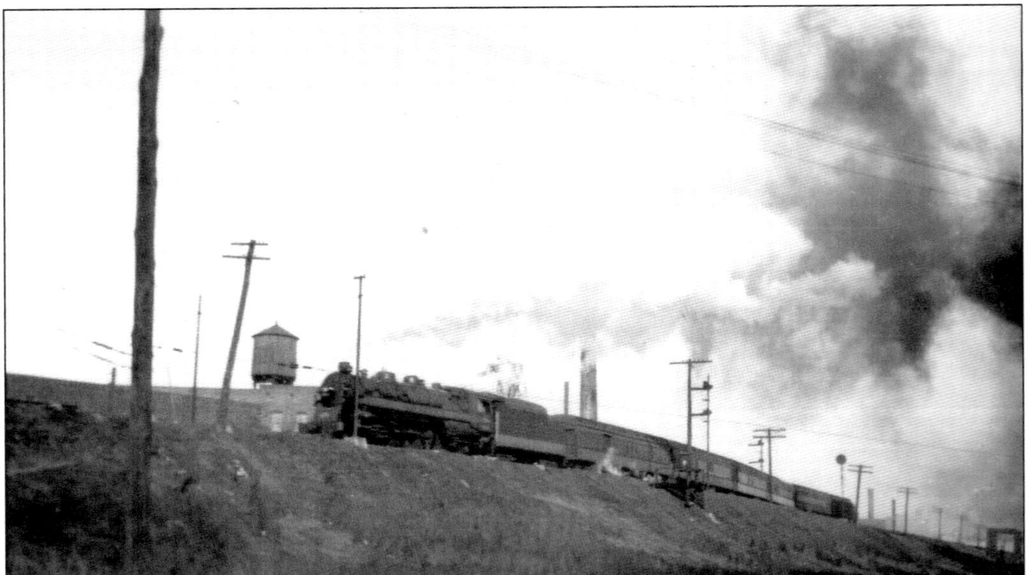

Looking north up at the National Docks branch, one catches a glimpse of the *Asa Packer* that was seen earlier sitting in the yards at Jersey City. The convoluted route the train took once it left the PRR main line at PRR Junction had it running south by compass direction, by railroad direction west, but by timetable direction east. The train is seen here approaching Edgewater Junction on February 7, 1940. (Courtesy of Theodore F. Gleichmann Jr.)

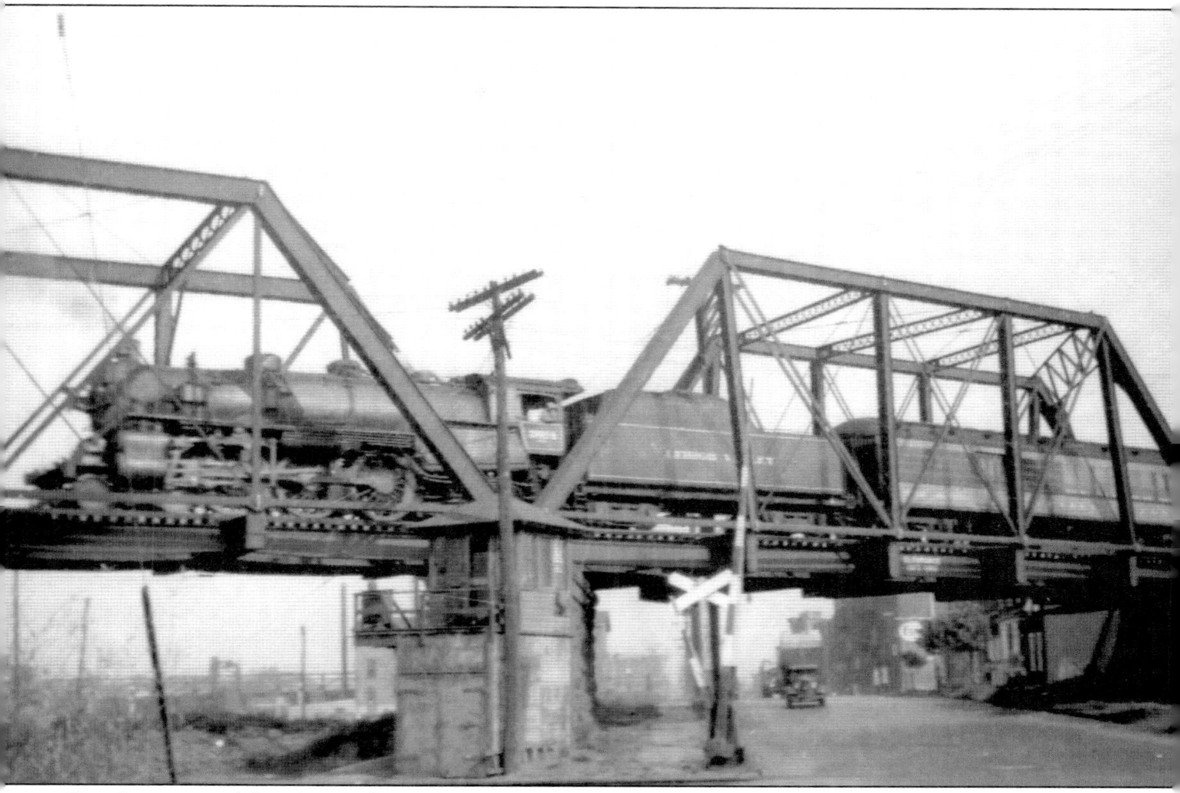

One last view of the *Asa Packer* at Jersey City is seen here as the photographer stands alongside Johnston Avenue facing west and up at the elevated National Docks branch just as the passenger train begins its backing movement down the connecting ramp at Edgewater Junction and into the west yard. The train required two separate backing moves through less-than-perfect yard trackage in order to reach its final destination alongside the float bridges in the Jersey City yards. The tracks in the foreground crossing over Johnston Avenue lead to the wye tracks going into the west yard that the *Asa Packer* will soon be traversing over to allow it to be positioned in the right direction upon its arrival. (Photograph by O. H. Borsum, courtesy of M. D. McCarter.)

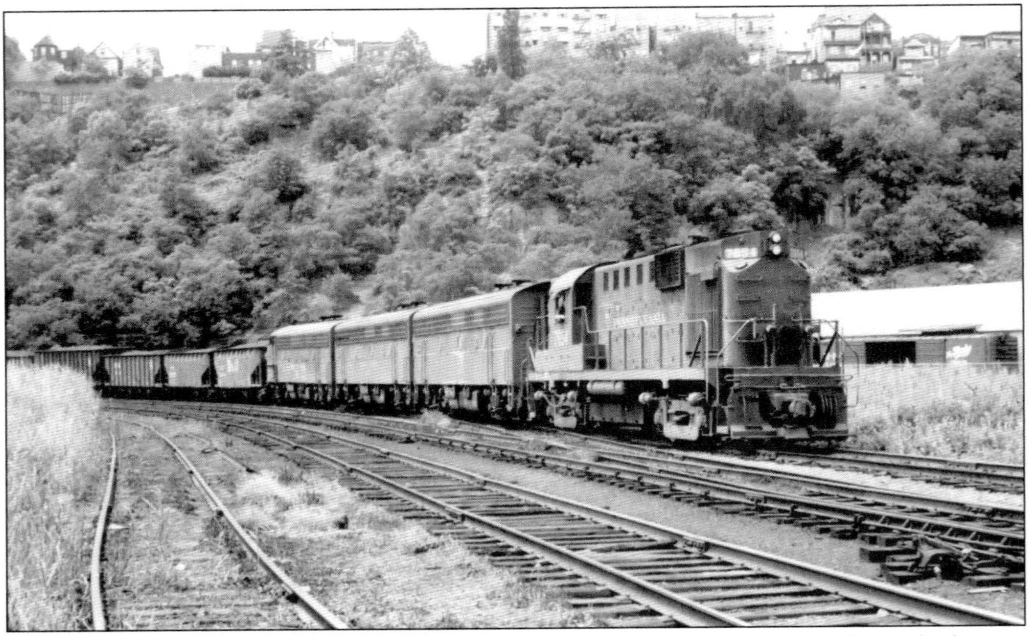

LVRR property ended at National Junction where it connected directly to the NYC. Also known as beltline No. 13, this track was built and operated by both the NYC and the Erie Railroad between Weehawken and Jersey City. Often considered the northern extension of the National Docks branch, the LVRR, CNJ, NYC, and PRR used this track to interchange with one another. (Photograph by Richard Taylor.)

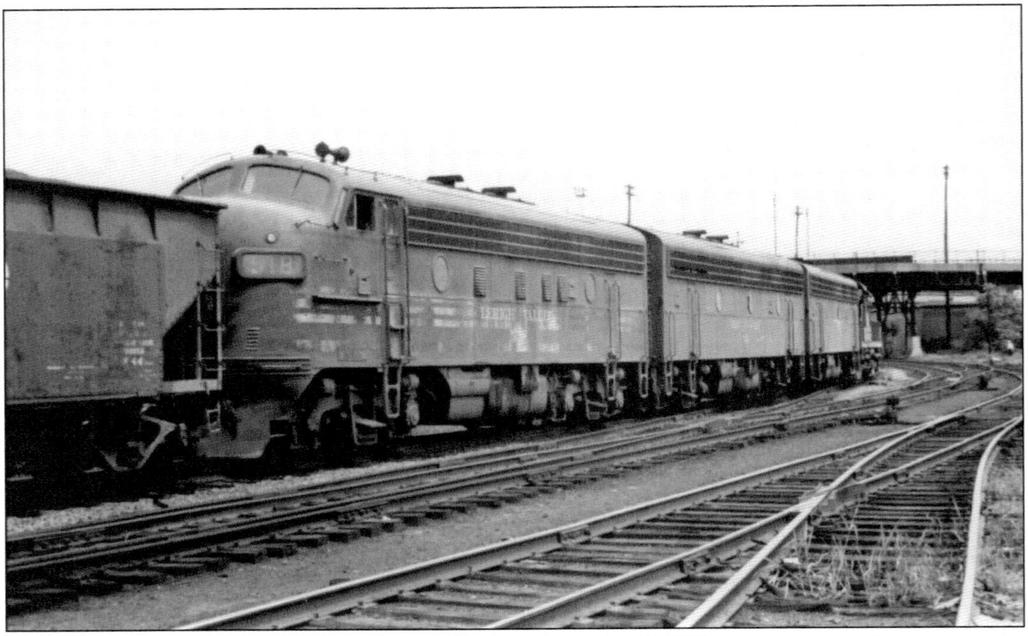

As the author ends this book with one final look at the LVRR, one can see the same train heading north on the NYC and under the Willow Avenue bridge on the border of Hoboken and Weehawken. The train is destined with a load of bituminous coal for public service's Bergen power-generating station on the NYC's tracks in Ridgefield. The date is June 26, 1967. (Photograph by Richard Taylor.)

BIBLIOGRAPHY

Archer, Robert F. *A History of the Lehigh Valley Railroad: The Route of the Black Diamond*. Forrest Park, IL: Heimburger House, 1977.

Bednar, Mike. *Lehigh Valley Facilities*. Vol. 1, *New York Division*. Scotch Plains, NJ: Morning Sun Books, 2008.

———. *Lehigh Valley Railroad: The New York Division*. Laurys Station, PA: Garrigues House, 1993.

Greenberg, William T., Jr., and Frederick A. Kramer with Theodore F. Gleichmann Jr. *The Handsomest Trains in the World: Passenger Service on the Lehigh Valley Railroad*. Westfield, NJ: Bells and Whistles, 1978.

Greenberg, William T., Jr., and Robert F. Fischer. *The Lehigh Valley Railroad: East of Mauch Chunk*. Martinsville, NJ: Gingerbread Stop, 1997.

Jahn, Richard W. "Lehigh Valley Railroad Gas-Electrics." *Flags, Diamonds and Statues* 6, no. 1, issue 21 (1985): 4–37.

Lehigh Valley Railroad: Its Lines to, and Its Terminal at New York Harbor, A Narrative. Philadelphia: Lehigh Valley Railroad, 1915.

Plant, Jeremy F., and Richard T. Steinbrenner. *Lehigh Valley 3, In Color*. Scotch Plains, NJ: Morning Sun Books, 1999.

Trice, Herbert V. *The Gangly Country Cousin: The Lehigh Valley's Auburn Division*. Ithaca, NY: DeWitt Historical Society of Tompkins County, 2004.

Yungkurth, Chuck. *The Steam Era of the Lehigh Valley Railroad*. Andover, NJ: Andover Publications, 1991.